DON'T CRY FOR ME ARGEN'

Is this how you remember it?

Happy Father's Day!

love
Douglas x

The Main Characters

Jim Blyth, goalkeeper, Coventry City
Martin Buchan, central defender, Manchester United
Kenny Burns, central defender, Nottingham Forest
Bobby Clark, goalkeeper, Aberdeen
Kenny Dalglish, forward, Liverpool
Willie Donachie, full-back, Manchester City
Tom Forsyth, central defender, Rangers
Archie Gemmill, midfielder, Nottingham Forest
Willie Harkness, president of the Scottish Football Association
Joe Harper, forward, Aberdeen
Asa Hartford, midfielder, Manchester City
Sandy Jardine, full-back, Rangers
Willie Johnston, winger, West Bromwich Albion
Derek Johnstone, forward, Rangers
Joe Jordan, forward, Manchester United
Stuart Kennedy, full-back, Aberdeen
Lou Macari, midfielder, Manchester United
Ally MacLeod, manager
Gordon McQueen, central defender, Manchester United
Don Masson, midfielder, Derby County
Bruce Rioch, midfielder, Derby County
John Robertson, winger, Nottingham Forest
Alan Rough, goalkeeper, Partick Thistle
Graeme Souness, midfielder, Liverpool
Ernie Walker, secretary of the Scottish Football Association

DON'T CRY FOR ME ARGENTINA

Scotland's 1978 World Cup Adventure

MIKE WILSON

MAINSTREAM
PUBLISHING

EDINBURGH AND LONDON

For Inga, Freya and Grete

First published in 1998 by
MAINSTREAM PUBLISHING COMPANY (EDINBURGH) LTD
7 Albany Street
Edinburgh EH1 3UG

ISBN 1 85158 895 7

Photographs courtesy of the *Daily Record*
A catalogue record for this book is available from the British Library

Typeset in Van Dijck MT and Bodoni Classic
Printed and bound in Finland by WSOY

Contents

Acknowledgements

Grateful thanks to the Scottish Football Association for permission to reproduce extracts from their Minutes. Ditto to Alan Bold, for reproducing gilded lines from his poetry collection, *Scotland, Yes!* (his poem on Kenny Dalglish received the highest literary honour when it was reproduced in the match programme for Kenny's Testimonial). And ditto again, to Adam McNaughtan, British Lion Music Limited, EMI Music Publishing Ltd and Windswept Pacific for reproducing the lyrics to a selection of songs.

Thanks also to Sir Tim Rice for okaying the use of the song title, *Don't Cry for Me Argentina*. The song is from the musical, *Evita*, which had its London première around the time of the World Cup. Nice one.

I am particularly indebted to Russell Galbraith for unearthing a 50-minute television documentary on Scotland's 1978 World Cup campaign, *That Time in Argentina* (transmitted on 18 September 1978 – three months after the final), which he produced for Scottish Television. Great to have pictures to rekindle memories.

Leigh Edwards was invaluable when compiling the player fact files. Robert McElroy was also helpful. The computer genius of Kevin Miller prevented a few disasters.

Big thanks to Alan McKinlay and Rikki Raginia for their support and proof-reading. And thanks particularly to Simon Pia. I got interested in writing through a friend, Sharon Taaffe. Simon cut some of my pretentiousness. He helped proof the book too.

To Bill Campbell, Judy Diamond and the staff of Mainstream, thanks for your assistance.

There isn't a lot to be said for working a book around the demands of a young family. Inga, Freya, Grete – life gets easier. Love you.

Finally, what can I say about the thrill of speaking to the players and other interviewees who gave their time freely and with good grace? Without you, none of this would have been possible.

Preface

Every Scot has at least one memory of the 1978 World Cup. Such was the spell cast by Ally MacLeod, the team manager, and the preceding hype, it was unavoidable. Football fan or not. For Scots, the defeat by Peru in the first game of the finals ranks alongside the assassination of President Kennedy as one of those I-remember-where-I-was-when-I-heard moments.

I was a teenager living in England when World Cup fever swept Scotland in 1978. Not just living in England, but in South Devon, about as far removed from the football heartlands as it is possible to get in the UK. I was studying for A-levels, had a vague notion of Scottish devolution and was infatuated with a woman ten years older than me.

It couldn't have been a pretty sight. But, back then, 20 years ago, it came with the territory of being an exiled Scot, young and naïve.

Ally's Tartan Army and Argentina '78 flitted in and out of the memory as the years passed by.

But, a couple of years ago, I saw Bruce Rioch, then the manager of Arsenal, being interviewed on the television. It was unspectacular until a question was casually thrown in about 1978. Rioch answered with characteristic politeness but there was something in his slight grimace which suggested more. I was curious. If it was a psychological scar, how many other players felt the same? With the twentieth anniversary looming, it seemed as good a time as any to ask each and every one of them.

Twenty-year-old memories were never going to produce a complete picture of what happened in Argentina. Some players have merely forgotten, others have simply got it wrong. Most have developed a selective memory. Some have preferred to let sleeping dogs lie. A couple refused to speak. Kenny Dalglish was tried time and again. Rioch talked at length but refused access to a diary he kept which, in the future, may form the basis for his own literary journey. Joe Jordan indulged my attempts to convince him to talk but, in the end, wouldn't budge. Jordan's interview became an inconclusive discussion about the value of history: he saw no point in looking back. In the end, he answered a couple of the most important questions, but a blether would have yielded more. I ended the conversation by saying he was both a hero and a bastard. Twenty years ago, that was certainly the case, if for different reasons.

Mike Wilson
January 1998

I. On the March

1978. 25 May. Thursday. 7 p.m. There is the murmur of summer in the air, with the promise of a heatwave and history about to be made. It's an evening for languid promenading along yon bonnie banks. Except that on this one particular evening, almost all roads lead to Hampden Park, the somewhat dilapidated home of Scottish football. Well over 20,000 fans have made the journey, paying 30 pence to get into the ground, 50 pence to sit in the stand. Ten pipe bands are there. Television crews, too, as the BBC and Scottish Television get in on the act. There too is Ally MacLeod, the manager of the national football team. He is about to be joined on an open-top bus by arguably one of the greatest squads ever assembled in the name of Scottish international football. As the players are individually welcomed to the centre circle of the pitch, they look self-conscious. They ought also to be a little nervous. In a few hours' time, they are flying to Argentina. Their plane, *The Robert Burns – the Scottish Bard*, stands ready on the tarmac of Prestwick airport, down the coast in Ayrshire. A nation expects.

Scotland have qualified for the 1978 World Cup, which is being held, despite protests about the human rights' record of its government, in Argentina. It hasn't been an easy qualification. Against Wales, in their final game, the Scots are helped through by a controversial penalty decision. At home against Czechoslovakia, the Scots are fortunate to be playing a side still travel-weary and missing some key players. Luck has carried Scotland a long way. If it's a sign, the fans are interpreting it only one way. The appetite for celebration is boundless. A few preach caution but are lost in the cacophony.

The mood is captured by the adverts in the press and on television. 'We're Right Behind You,' declare the brewers of Younger's Tartan Special. 'Scotland can beat anybody but I reckon nobody can beat D.E.R. colour,' says injured star Danny McGrain on behalf of a television manufacturer. 'Watch the World Cup in Colour – and have a dram on us,' promise the Co-op. On telly, an advert for Chrysler has half a dozen players smiling out of car windows and, especially in the case of goalkeeper Alan Rough's bubble-perm haircut, looking generally silly. A couple appear to be nursing hangovers from the night before. The advertising spotlight even falls on Mrs MacLeod.

The Hampden send-off swaggers on to both BBC1 and Scottish Television, the latter going for a live show starting at 7 p.m. At the BBC, the 7 p.m. slot remains the sacrosanct property of *Tomorrow's World* followed by *Top of the Pops*. Boney M's 'Rivers of Babylon' is halfway through a five-week stint at number one. Rod Stewart's song with the World Cup squad, 'Olé Ola', reaches number four. On Scottish, it's *Argentina Here We Come!*; on BBC1, a little later, it's *Good Luck Scotland*. Even later, at 9.25 p.m., it's *Des O'Connor Tonight*. It always is.

Scottish Television finish their Hampden broadcast at 7.40 p.m. But the skirl of the bagpipes continues to echo. Until 8.35 p.m. and *The Streets of San Francisco*, it's *Thingummyjig*, a bit of musical shortbread featuring Jack McLaughlin with the Alexander Brothers, Joe Gordon and Sally Logan, plus Company Policy, Morag McKay, Johnny Grand, Thrush, and Bert Shorthouse and his Band. Twenty years on, some of the names are still recognisable.

In Scotland, the domestic football season has just ended. Rangers have won the Treble – the League, the Scottish Cup and the League Cup. The international side has been on duty as recently as the previous Saturday, playing – and, ominously, losing – the last of their three end-of-season games against the other home countries. Over the walls of Hampden, beyond the potholes and fast-food caravans, the football talk straddles the domestic and the international. Both Rangers and Celtic are preparing for new managerial eras. By the time Scotland play their first game in the World Cup, John Greig and Billy McNeill will be the new bosses at Ibrox and Celtic Park, with McNeill's departure from Aberdeen paving the way for a certain Alex Ferguson to build his own managerial dynasty.

Across Scotland, the football is laced with nationalism. *The Scotsman* newspaper that day has, splashed across its front page, fears of oil-rich Arabs becoming the new lairds of the north, by buying up Scottish castles. And there's also the no small matter of Scottish Home Rule. Westminster is grappling with the Scotland Bill. A referendum on devolution is to be put to the Scottish people, but not before the conclusion of numerous political games.

But there is no doubt that, for a few precious minutes on Thursday, 25 May 1978, Scotland has eyes only for Hampden. As Ally smiles a chirpy, slightly bashful grin, his shoulders – though he shrugs them a lot during conversation – seem broad enough not just for the football aspirations of a nation, but for the political ones too. The open-top bus does its lap of honour. Children cheer and grannies weep. And grown men believe Scotland are about to win the World Cup. As reported in the next day's press, the Scottish Secretary of State, Bruce Millan, not only attended, but used the opportunity to announce redevelopment plans for Hampden. All those 30 and 50 pences taken at the turnstiles will be added to the budget.

In retrospect, the send-off seems like high farce. Pipe bands, majorettes and 'We're on the march wi' Ally's army'. But the sea of Lions Rampant that is Hampden in hysteria reveals a nation that jettisoned its natural scepticism eight months earlier when midfielder Don Masson scored against Wales from the penalty spot to send Scotland on their way. The nation has already gone way beyond critical mass. MacLeod mirrors the mood of a people and the people passionately hang on to his every word. Scotland *can* win. Scotland *will* win. It is a heady, liberating feeling. Like Hogmanay without the need to wait for one night a year to shed the inhibitions.

Tacky? Premature? Twenty years on, the send-off has people squirming with embarrassment. But it only looks that way in light of the subsequent results. The send-off is high-risk and MacLeod later pays heavily for failing to deliver.

It is also, however, an exercise in crowd safety. The hype has to be managed. The same hype that excites advertisers and brings in the commercial baubles. The same hype that, despite 20,000-plus at Hampden, still turns Prestwick airport into The Beatles at JFK.

Tom Forsyth: You would think we had won the World Cup with the send-off we got. On the drive down to the airport, after the parade at Hampden, people were gathered at every junction, beeping their horns. We hadn't done anything. All we had done was qualify for the World Cup! That will never happen again; no Scotland side will have that again. It was so Americanised. You must blame Ally for that. It wasn't just the supporters that were being hyped up. We, the players, were hyped up.

We thought that all we needed to do was go out on the park and that would be it. And it didn't happen. We were hyped up and we never did anything. That was what sickened. It was all built up and we got caught in it. We went on to the park and, all of a sudden, we had a battle on our hands and we weren't prepared for it. Mentally, we weren't prepared for it. I learned an awful lot from it. I learned never to expect anything from football, because it kicks you in the teeth when you least expect it, especially when things are all rosy. I can't get away from that send-off.

Ian Archer, journalist: The media travelled down to Prestwick in a bus behind the team coach, across the Fenwick Moor. And there were buses from wee Ayrshire villages, driven up to the side of the road, with all these people cheering us, with all their banners. The airport was mobbed, there were thousands, on roofs, with flags. It was extraordinary. There were five million people who believed we would win the thing.

You see, we had done so well in the 1974 World Cup in West Germany. We played and should have beaten the world champions, Brazil, and we came away undefeated. 1974 was our first finals for 16 years [since the 1958 World Cup in Sweden] and we had done awfully well. So, it was thought that, with the experience of West Germany under our belts, and with the good players we had, we should do pretty well in Argentina.

Everybody got caught up in it. I was working at *The Express* and we had Ally MacLeod under contract, along with [players] Alan Rough and Gordon McQueen. And I was also working with Scottish Television and was doing a weekly piece with MacLeod every Sunday when we were on for about 15 minutes. There was a bandwagon going on. And it was very, very difficult to get off it – virtually impossible.

Just before we left for Argentina, *The Express* did about six pages on the World Cup, on MacLeod, on how we would win the World Cup and such things. And I managed to convince the editor that, as well as all the other stuff I had written, I should do a little sidebar piece, saying, 'Good luck to you, Ally, but there are a lot of other teams who might win this damn thing in front of us.' A few days later, I got a shoebox through the post with this giant turd inside it, a toilet roll and the message, 'You traitor, I hope you die of cancer.' It was very weird, it was a wild time. I mean, everybody had their reservations, but nobody came out and said, 'What a load of nonsense all this hype is.' Nobody can hold their hand up and say, 'I told them what it was really like.'

It was just a massive bandwagon that ran out of control until we started to play football.

The wild scenes at Prestwick airport are an extension of similar, raw emotions when Don Masson does his bit from the penalty spot and Scotland qualify for the World Cup with a 2–0 win over Wales at Anfield Stadium, home of Liverpool FC and officially a home tie for the Welsh despite the ground being commandeered by Scots.

The passion has become endemic. The crowds at the time are massive: 63,000 for the Scots' first qualifying game at Hampden; 85,000 for their second. As World Cup fever begins to take hold of the nation at the turn of 1978, the figures become locked in the stratosphere: 65,000 for a friendly against Bulgaria on 22 February and 64,000, 70,000 and 88,000 for the summer's Home Internationals, all at Hampden and against, respectively, Northern Ireland, Wales and England.

Against England, the game ends in a 1–0 defeat, courtesy of a goal by Steve Coppell, and yet the fans still insist on a lap of honour. That the Scots are unlucky to lose is barely relevant. Scotland are going to Argentina; England are not. They have failed to qualify. MacLeod is quoted afterwards jauntily dismissing the set-back as 'a goal laid on by the second-worst player on the park scored by the worst player'. In an era when Scotland v England matches are a sometimes depressing low point of the season – because of attendant violence – the Scots have discovered a world perspective. For a little while at least, they can afford to shrug off defeat by the English.

Including the hosts, there will be 16 sides playing in Argentina, among them Holland, Brazil, Italy and West Germany, the defending champions. Despite the long-established pattern of the winner emerging from the continent hosting the finals, the Scots are high on anticipation. Remember, after Scotland finally deigned to grace the World Cup finals with their presence in 1954, a squad of only 13 players was sent and each had to wear their own club training kit. Scotland have come a long way in just over 20 years.

As Gordon McQueen now says, it is a 'fantastic time in Scottish football', a point echoed in the minutes of the Scottish Football Association, which, nearly a year after Scotland slunk home from Argentina in disgrace, has at least the decency to remark: 'Regardless of the depressing aspects of Mr MacLeod's latter days in the Association's employ, it would be quite unfair not to comment that he was largely responsible for kindling an enthusiasm for the Scottish team that far exceeded anything which had gone before, even in this land which has never been slow to revere its football heroes. The Association benefited considerably from that enthusiasm and should not forget it.'

Passage to the finals means having to overcome the challenges of Wales and Czechoslovakia, newly crowned European champions. The group has an uncomfortable ring of familiarity – Wales for obvious reasons, Czechoslovakia because Scotland had been pitted against them on their way to qualifying for the '74 finals.

There are only four games, Scotland's campaign beginning on 13 October 1976 with an awkward away tie in Prague, the Czech capital. At this stage, Willie Ormond is the national team manager. MacLeod is still in club football – ten years at Ayr United, one with Aberdeen, during which time he wins the League Cup. There is no room for laxity. Scotland lose 2–0 to goals by Panenka and Petras. Ormond praises the performance of goalkeeper Alan Rough: 'More than any other, we have Alan to thank for keeping that second-half down to a beating and not a drubbing.'

In the next game, a month later, at home to Wales, and still under the stewardship of Ormond, Kenny Burns has an outstanding game, Kenny Dalglish works tirelessly, Scotland hit the woodwork twice and – ironically, given what was to happen 11 months hence – Scotland are denied what seems to be a clear penalty when Ian Evans up-ends Joe Jordan. By the close of play, it requires an own-goal by Evans to get the Scots back on the rails. Don't mention the goal to Kenny Dalglish. He feels he should have been awarded it; kind of important when you are sharing the Scotland goals record – as he does – on 30, with Denis Law. In his autobiography, he wrote: 'Danny McGrain cut the ball back and I scored with a back-heel that went in off Ian Evans, who was sliding in. For some reason, the authorities never credited me with the goal. It went down as "Evans' own-goal". If that had been added to my tally, as it should have been, I would eventually have taken Denis Law's record of most goals for Scotland. I don't mind sharing the record with Denis. He wasn't a bad player!'

It's not until September 1977 – all of ten months away – that Scotland play their next qualifying match, against Czechoslovakia, this time at home. From a Scottish perspective, the interim translates to eight games, four wins and that summer's Home Internationals title (the second, successive series win). Plus a highly satisfactory tour of South America. It also marks the departure of Ormond, who returns to club football disheartened that the SFA appear to be secretly sounding out Jock Stein as his successor. When Stein stays at Celtic, it is Hail, MacLeod! taking over in time for the first Home International match of 1977 against Wales.

The 0–0 draw in Wrexham is not the most auspicious of débuts but the relative disappointment is soon wiped away with wins over Northern Ireland (3–0) and England (2–1). The latter prompts an invasion of the Wembley pitch. The crossbar snaps and po-faced commentators predict the collapse of civilisation.

A win against Chile, a draw against Argentina and a defeat by Brazil add up to the useful exercise in South America. But, just as importantly, while the Scots are coming to the boil, the Czechs are losing form. Come the autumn of 1977, the qualifying group is wide open. Thanks to a 3–0 home win for Wales over the Czechs, the three teams have one win and one defeat apiece.

MacLeod looks back on the game against Czechoslovakia as being near perfect. The win helps: 3–1. Joe Jordan, Asa Hartford and Dalglish are the scorers. But the performance has him writing, in his 1979 autobiography: 'I didn't dare hope that we would have the kind of night when things would go just right. It had happened to me, at that stage, just three times in my career – Ayr United's first match after promotion in 1969 when we beat Hibs; Aberdeen's League Cup semi-final against Rangers in 1976; and that friendly international match against Chile.

'But when we opened the dressing-room door at Hampden and felt the wave of noise from 85,000 singing and super-confident fans, I suddenly knew this was going to be another of those memorable, magical matches.'

Four players – Dalglish, Sandy Jardine, Jordan and McGrain – are veterans of a dramatic win over the Czechs in 1973 at Hampden to guarantee a place for Scotland in the 1974 finals. The Czechs arrive laboured by bad omens as well as declining form. Besides having lost out to Scotland for a place in the 1974 World Cup, they have never won at Hampden. And, despite their European Championship win conferring upon them the title 'Princes of Europe', they are clearly a team in trouble, accentuated by the 3–0 defeat in Wrexham by Wales. There are only six survivors from the side that defeated Scotland in Prague. And since losing to Wales, they have failed to score in three out of four games. They sorely miss defender Anton Ondrus, sent off (with Scotland and Aston Villa's Andy Gray) in Prague. Ondrus, the backbone of the Czech defence, is suspended for the remainder of the group matches.

If loss of form isn't bad enough, the Czechs arrive in Glasgow the victims of an air strike, forced to complete the last leg of their journey by travelling overnight by rail from London. World governing body FIFA refuse their request to postpone the fixture for 24 hours.

Joe Jordan and Don Masson are superb. Jordan, the focus of constant aerial bombardment, scores his first goal for Scotland in three years. It is a moment which reawakens memories of the pandemonium-inducing performance of 1973. He scored in that game too. Masson, meanwhile, has MacLeod writing, '[He] set the tone with one of the most complete games I've ever seen from any player, reading the game like a dream and organising the set-pieces brilliantly.'

The press are equally lavish in their praise. An injury to full-back Danny McGrain and a goalkeeping error by Alan Rough, gifting the Czechs a consolation goal ten minutes from time, fail to take the shine off the performance. Scotland are 3–0 up before Gajdusek sends his 30-yard trundler beyond Rough. Scotland's third, from Dalglish (not long transferred from Celtic to Liverpool), is dispatched as early as the 54th minute.

Don Masson: Football is a simple game made complicated by people doing silly, hard things. It is the easiest game in the world. The easiest football I ever played was with Scotland because I played with people on the same wavelength. The further down the divisions you go, the harder it becomes because all you see are people's backs running away from you. With Scotland I had five or six options every time I got the ball. I used to say my game was getting the ball off the back four and being the link, being a general, though at that time this concept was unheard of in Scotland.

I would say to Martin Buchan and Gordon McQueen that as soon as they got the ball I would come and get it off them and, by the same token, I assumed Archie Gemmill and Bruce Rioch would be the next step up from me. And the next step from them would be the forwards.

So all you were doing was playing five-yard balls. In my mind, I would be at least two moves ahead, already picturing what would be unfolding once I had the ball passed to me. Playing with Scotland, the pictures were easy because there were so many options. I remember a piece of advice I was given when I was 15, that the ball never gets tired when it is beating the opposition the right way. But you see so many players today receiving the ball and not knowing what to do with it, so the ball becomes laboured and is asked to do too much.

There's too much eye-of-the-needle stuff when it would have been better to have taken the simple option in the first place. What's the point in trying to ping the hard pass when it comes off once in ten attempts? I can't understand players not having an urgency about the ball – not urgency as in 100mph stuff, but urgency to do the right thing at the right time.

It was easy when I was at QPR because we had the same system there as we did with Scotland. Dave Sexton, the QPR manager, believed in having a defensive midfield player, who was Johnny Hollins; a general, who was myself; and an attacking midfielder who was Gerry Francis. With Scotland, Bruce was the holding player in defence, I was the general and Archie was the forward player who was allowed to play off the front two. It was unheard of, our 4-3-3 system, but it was easy, easy. When you look at some of the names in that Scotland squad, it's frightening. Buchan, McQueen, Danny McGrain – they were world-class players. As were others in that side. Look at the midfield: Asa, me and Bruce along with Archie, Graeme Souness and Lou Macari. It was unbelievable. It took me towards the end of my career to achieve what I did, but I thought I was very lucky.

A vital victory over Czechoslovakia, then. But the situation is far from conclusive; the group remains wide open and, to clinch it, Scotland still have to get a result against Wales, away from home. It's win or bust. Wales are in just as good a position as Scotland to go through.

The match looms just three weeks away, but the Welsh FA, no doubt mindful of the tie's drawing power, decide to host it at Liverpool's Anfield Stadium instead of a smaller home venue such as Wrexham (capacity 16,000) or Cardiff (capacity 19,000). In doing so, whatever they gain in monetary terms is blown out of the water by what they concede in vocal support. By being staged in Liverpool, the game effectively becomes a home match for the Scots. A crowd of 51,000 attend and, of those, perhaps a few thousand are Welsh supporters. Only a third of the tickets were meant to go to the Scots, but hundreds of fans travel to north Wales and buy tickets direct.

The Scottish invasion is raucous and driven by a sense of destiny. The game coincides with the publication of a report by the Working Group on Football Crowd Behaviour (also known as the McElhone Report) which, among other things, seeks to stamp out alcohol on buses to matches and within stadiums. Meanwhile, broadcaster Archie Macpherson believes he is witnessing a new, worrying type of behaviour among the Scottish support. He writes in his autobiography: 'The area around Anfield resembled a kind of medieval fair, with pickpockets plundering the great and the mighty just outside the main entrance, people shouting and bartering for tickets, and others making arrangements about how they were going to travel to Argentina. Everywhere there was singing, drinking and waving of banners. The final congestion just inside the main gates was claustrophobic. It was the carousal of confidence. It was the kind I have never enjoyed hearing from Scottish people. It was blatant and aggressive and intimidatory.' Only a victory for the Scots, he feels, can save the city from destruction.

The noise is no less deafening once the game gets under way, prompting Jock Stein, sharing a television gantry with Macpherson, to worry that it is making the Scottish players too nervous. At the Kop end there are sporadic outbursts of fighting among the fans.

On the field, much maligned though he is during most of his international career, goalkeeper Rough, eventually the winner of 53 Scottish caps, has one of his best-ever games, with one save in particular proving to be a turning point. On the hour and with the game hanging in the balance at 0–0, he acrobatically manages to push clear an intelligently chipped shot by Liverpool's John Toshack, facing his beloved Kop and with just the keeper to beat after evading the Scottish offside trap.

It was, said MacLeod, a result determined by two raised fists: one belonging to Rough, to deny Toshack, the other of a more indeterminate ownership when a high ball into the Welsh goalmouth is contested in the air by Wales's David Jones and Scotland's Joe Jordan. Earlier in the match, French referee Wurtz had dismissed Scottish claims for a penalty when goalkeeper Dai Davies appeared to bring down Kenny Dalglish. This time, in the tangle of Jones and Jordan battling for the ball, the referee believes he sees a hand making contact with the ball and adjudges that it belongs to Jones. Penalty to Scotland. The Welsh protest. Jordan clasps his clenched fist with his other hand in a gesture of timeless ambiguity. MacLeod says he spoke to Jordan only once about it and, when given the assurance the hand belonged to Jones, never raised the subject again.

From the penalty spot and with just 11 minutes remaining, Don Masson does the needful. And though Scotland win the game 2–0 – their second a stunning, flying header by Dalglish – the game will always be remembered for the referee's controversial decision. The penalty cannot be taken out of the equation to leave Dalglish's header, three minutes from time, as the deciding factor. The second goal flowed from the confidence that came from the first.

'Hypothetical arguments, particularly in football, are pointless,' writes MacLeod, 'and just to put the result beyond argument, Kenny Dalglish scored a magnificent second goal from Martin Buchan's cross to clinch it. Having stayed firmly in my seat at the first goal, I admit I leapt out of the dug-out so high at the second that I almost landed in the centre circle.' The police decline a lap of honour by the players. But the fans keep singing, 'Que sera sera, Whatever will be will be, We're off to the Argentine, Que sera sera'.

> *Joe Jordan*: [on the penalty award] Wisnae me. It is the same now as it was 20 years ago – wisnae me. *So you'll take to your grave that it wasn't you?* Certainly will. I live too near Wales. It is now what it was then. It was a goal from the penalty spot.

Martin Buchan: I've never played in such an electric atmosphere. It was unbelievable. It was like a home game for Scotland. I've played in front of a lot of famous terraces, like the Stretford End at Old Trafford, the Holte End at Aston Villa. And of course, it was the Kop at Anfield. And on that night, it was heaving.

I was a substitute, I came on for only the last 12 minutes to replace Sandy Jardine, and although I'd never played the position before, I knew exactly what to do because of the teaching of Eddie Turnbull when he was my manager at Aberdeen. I knew where I should have been at any given time. And there was a move in midfield and I was there in the space to take the ball on the right wing. I was in the space because my brain told me I should be there, not because I was a raiding right-back. And I crossed the ball for Kenny. I teased him afterwards: 'I made you a star.' The goal reduced the controversy of the first goal.

Afterwards, in the dressing-room, Ally comes across and says, 'Great cross. When you got the ball, I was shouting to you to take it into the corner to waste time. But, no, you looked up, you saw Kenny and now we're going to the World Cup,' and I said, tongue in cheek, 'Aye, that'll teach you to leave me out of the team.'

Ally's Tartan Army

Chorus: We're on the march wi' Ally's Army
We're going to the Argentine
And we'll really shake 'em up when we win the World Cup
'Cos Scotland are the greatest football team.

I've heard it said that Beckenbauer's the best there's ever been
Some people think that Pele is the greatest ever seen
There's Bobby Moore and Charlton, they're England's famous two
But Ally's Tartan Army love the boys in Scotland blue.

Repeat chorus

When it comes to managers we've surely got the chap
When Docherty and Ormond left to join some other camp
We had to get the man who could make all Scotland proud
He's our Muhammad Ally, he's Alistair MacLeod.

Don't Cry For Me Argentina

Repeat chorus

When we reach the Argentine we're really going to show
The world a brand of football that they could never know
We're representing Britain and we've got to do or die
For England cannae dae it 'cos they didnae qualify.

Repeat chorus

(Words and music by Billy King © 1978; reproduced by permission of
EMI Music Publishing Ltd, London WC2 0EA; reached number six in the
Charts)

2. Preparation

Today, despite nearing his 50th birthday, Martin Buchan still works in football, which will surprise some of his team-mates during the late 1970s. At the height of his powers as a player – he captained Manchester United for six years, having previously played with distinction for Aberdeen – he appeared to have a love-hate relationship with the game. The squad that travelled to Argentina in 1978 had its tensions – most football squads do – and he was certainly an oddity as far as some of his colleagues were concerned.

He was bookish, for a start. He enjoyed word games and verbal one-up-manship. He didn't play cards travelling to away games. He didn't fraternise with the press. He was not afraid to voice his opinions. To put it bluntly, in the closeted, cosseted world of football, he was considered in some quarters as something of a smart arse. 'Velocity' was his now-famous reply to a journalist who asked – impolitely, Buchan thought – for 'a quick word'. No sooner had the squad arrived at its base in Argentina, The Sierras Hotel in a village called Alta Gracia, he was complaining about the standard of the rooms, immediately dubbing the accommodation 'Alta Dis-Gracia'. When he briefly went in to management – at Burnley – at the end of his playing career, he quickly bailed out, saying, 'Management is about making decisions and after three months I decided it wasn't for me.'

Still, he was a leader of men, an intelligent reader of the game and he could be engaging company. He played the guitar, he could speak Spanish. Even if some team-mates will have been inclined towards the shut-that-fucking-guitar school of thought, he was only 20 when he was made captain at Aberdeen.

In the summer of 1977, he is heading for South America on a three-match tour of Chile, Argentina and Brazil. He is with Scotland, and the national team is not short of club captains. As well as Buchan, there is also Archie Gemmill and Bruce Rioch. Gemmill is the current incumbent when Ally MacLeod is appointed Scotland manager in May 1977. Gemmill is relieved of his post, as the new manager insists a new régime requires a new captain. In his autobiography, MacLeod says he introduced himself to the squad thus: 'My name is Ally MacLeod and I am a winner.' The captaincy issue was an early test that he mishandles.

'I remain convinced that this was the right decision,' writes MacLeod, 'though I now feel, with the benefit of hindsight, that I did not appreciate Archie's qualities as much as I should have done at the time.'

He is even more apologetic when it comes to deciding which player will replace Gemmill as captain. Buchan and Rioch are equally compelling candidates, though MacLeod feels that Rioch is the slightly more outgoing of the two. He hedges his bets, inviting Rioch to captain the side during the Home Internationals which are due to begin in a matter of days, and asking Buchan to take over during the tour of South America.

'That piece of indecision was later to land me in a bit of trouble of my own making,' admits MacLeod, 'for which I had to apologise to Buchan. For our opening tour game, in Santiago, Buchan was not quite fit and I asked Rioch to continue as captain. But after Gordon McQueen had injured himself in training and called off from the match, Buchan typically volunteered to play. Somehow, I completely forgot to sort out the situation of having two captains in the side.

'Martin said nothing at the time as Bruce skippered us to victory over Chile, but raised the matter when I asked him to take the team out in the following game against Argentina, when Rioch was missing. We had several long chats on the subject after that, and I came to accept that while he was very keen to play for his country and for me, he felt the captaincy put him under extra pressure.'

Archie Gemmill: If you had been captain of your country and a new manager comes in and bombs you out, you can hardly say you liked him that much. But I was, at that time, a professional and, as in life, you don't always get what you want. If Ally MacLeod thought Martin Buchan or Bruce Rioch were better than me, it was his choice, he was the team manager. As it happened, the captaincy came back to me anyway [against Iran, during the World Cup finals]. A manager's job is a particularly hard one, especially if he has 22 good players and can only pick 11. If you don't get picked, you have to accept the decision – there's nothing else you can do. If you go away and sulk about it, you will never get picked again. So what you have to do is stand up, brush yourself down and start all over again.

Martin Buchan: At Aberdeen, when we travelled a lot by train, you would have half the lads in a card school and the other half the Brains Trust. We used to do word games and whatever. It wasn't because there was a split in the camp, but the compartments in the train naturally split the team into two. We had a super time. That's what I miss in football. I don't miss playing. I had a good, long career, I finished when I was 35 and had as long a career as could be reasonably expected. But I miss training and the banter. It was cut and thrust all the time. We were always scoring points off each other.

I had a reputation as a loner at Manchester United – you know how the media like to stick labels on people. I wasn't a gambler, I wasn't a card player. So when the card schools were going at Manchester United, I would be sitting on my own reading a book. So, immediately, I was dubbed a loner. To be honest, I didn't discourage it. I didn't give my telephone number out to the press boys. There is no harm being different. I wasn't ashamed. I could go to the toilet on my own. There were times I could be the life and soul of the party, could play a bit of guitar for a sing-song.

The last thing I did before leaving for Argentina was go to a book shop. I could speak Spanish, but I didn't want to make a song and dance about it because I would have been running around for everyone. And I could have happily watched the local TV because I would have understood it. But I was there to play football. I was like Tom the Cabin Boy in *Captain Pugwash*: smiled and said nothing.

The flight across was, of course, a bit of a marathon. But when we got off the plane at Córdoba and on to the bus for our hotel, one of the players said, 'I'm bored.' I clearly remember him saying it – I'd rather not say who it was – but it just showed that when it comes to picking players for a long trip it's vital to think about their personalities as well as their football abilities. I did an interview after the World Cup and was asked how I felt. I said I was ashamed but felt some of the players didn't have the brains to be ashamed.

The captaincy was not an issue in 1978, but it *was* the year before. Ally's first meeting with the squad was at the start of the Home Internationals in 1977. I had played in the FA Cup final that year, but with a bad knee. So when I reported to the Scotland squad a few days after the final, my knee was a little sore. We went to the Mercury Hotel in Chester, because we were to play Wales at Wrexham, and Ally MacLeod introduced himself by saying, 'Hello, my name is Ally MacLeod, the new manager. And you will find that I'm a man of my word.'

And he pulled me aside after addressing the squad as a whole, and said, 'I want you to be my captain.' I replied, 'I'll not be fit for the Home Internationals.' And he said, 'Never mind, you can be my captain when we go on a tour of South America,' which we were doing in about a fortnight's time.

So, I didn't play in the Home Internationals but travelled to South America. We had beaten England at Wembley and Bruce Rioch had been captain. At no time did Ally say, 'Look, I know what I promised but Bruce has done well and I would like to leave him as captain.' Anybody is entitled to change their mind. But he played Bruce and me in the first game in South America, against Chile, and Bruce was captain. It wasn't a big deal to me because my father had brought me up to believe there should be 11 captains in a side. But as fate would have it, Bruce got injured against Chile and before our next game, against Argentina, we needed a new captain because Bruce was out. But I learned that I had been made captain before Ally told me in the dressing-room because he had announced the decision at a press conference. So, in the dressing-room, when Ally said he would like me to lead the team out, I told him, 'I'll do it, because I don't want to embarrass anyone, like my parents, but don't you ever ask me to do it again. You broke your word.'

The South American tour that summer of '77 is an inspired idea, a fact-finding mission that provides MacLeod and the players with a taster of the culture and climate that awaits in '78, plus the opportunity to measure themselves against some of the best football nations in the world. There is a question mark about the strength of the Chilean side that succumbs 4–2 in the opening fixture, but there are no such doubts voiced about Argentina and Brazil. The Argentinians, who will go on to win the World Cup on their own patch the following year, are fortunate to snatch a draw at 1–1. The Brazilians, as expected, are too powerful but not by nearly as much as is feared. Scotland, not playing too well, lose 2–0. It is MacLeod's first defeat in six games as manager.

Rioch is captain against Chile and Brazil. Striker Lou Macari scores twice against Chile. Against Argentina, the result is decided by two converted penalties, the first by Don Masson – deadly from the penalty spot – to give the Scots the lead. When Argentina score their late equaliser, Alan Rough angers them by running up to their penalty taker to find out the number on his back. A dossier on the Argentinians – provided by Don Revie who had led England on a similar tour a few weeks previously – predicts that since it is No. 6 taking the penalty, the kick will go left. As it is, the shot is miscued down the middle.

The side palpably oozes confidence. And since it contains the bones of the team which is brought together for the World Cup, it is easy to understand why they inspire a sense of destiny.

There is a seductive stability. Against Chile, the team line-up reads: Alan Rough (substituted by Jim Stewart); Danny McGrain, Willie Donachie, Martin Buchan, Tom Forsyth, Bruce Rioch (Archie Gemmill), Don Masson, Kenny Dalglish, Lou Macari, Asa Hartford (Sandy Jardine), Willie Johnston. Against Argentina, it is: Rough; McGrain, Donachie, Gemmill, Forsyth, Buchan, Masson, Dalglish, Macari, Hartford, Johnston. And against Brazil: Rough; McGrain, Donachie, Rioch, Forsyth, Buchan, Masson, Gemmill, Dalglish, Hartford, Johnston (Jardine). In other words, ten players – Rough, McGrain, Donachie, Buchan, Forsyth, Gemmill (one game as substitute), Masson, Dalglish, Hartford and Johnston – feature in all three games.

Absentees? There is no Kenny Burns, unable to travel after suffering a back injury after falling off a horse. And no Gordon McQueen or Joe Jordan, both of whom are injured. Since MacLeod has made attendance in South America a pre-condition of playing in the remaining two World Cup qualifying games, Burns is prevented from featuring in the subsequent qualifying victories over Czechoslovakia and Wales.

Only externally does the tour of South America excite controversy. The team plays in the same Santiago stadium used to detain political prisoners during the Pinochet coup, the same one featured in the harrowing film, *Missing*, about a straight-laced American patriot played by Jack Lemmon searching for his missing son (though the film, made in 1982 by Costa-Gavras, never actually mentions Chile). Subsequently, the team is subjected to protests from human rights organisations. Chile in 1977 appears more of a political hot potato than Argentina the following year. The protest is symbolised by a song, 'Blood Upon the Grass', written by Adam McNaughtan, on Ed Miller's album, *Home and Away – Songs of the Scottish Folk Revival*.

Blood Upon the Grass

On September the eleventh in 1973
Scores of people died in a vile machine-gun spree
And a Santiago sports ground became a place to kill
Now your Scottish football team's gonna grace it with their skill.

But there's blood upon the grass
Aye, there's blood upon the grass.

Oh, did you go there Archie Gemmill? Did you play there Tam Forsyth?
Where so many folk met early the grim reaper and his scythe
Those people weren't terrorists not even party hacks
And maybe some were goalkeepers and some were centre-backs.

But now the blood's upon the grass
Aye, the blood's upon the grass.

And Victor Jara he played guitar when they took him to the ground
So they broke all of his fingers so the strings no more would sound
But he just went right on singing songs of freedom, songs of peace
And even when they shot him down his message didn't cease.

But now his blood's upon the grass
Aye, his blood's upon the grass.

So did you go there Alan Rough? Did you play there Andy Gray?
Did it worry you to hear the ghost of Victor Jara say
"Somos cinco mil", we are 5,000 in this place
And now your Scottish football team has helped the Junta's dark disgrace.

There's blood upon the grass
Aye, there's blood upon the grass.

So do you stand upon the terracing at Ibrox or Parkhead?
Do you cheer for the Hibs in green and white or the Dons in flaming red?
Those Santiago victims, they were people of your kind
Too bad our football bosses couldn't change their narrow minds.

For now there's blood upon their hands
Aye, there's blood upon their hands.

Argentina was chosen to host the 1978 World Cup at a meeting held in London as far back as 6 July 1966, a meeting which also decided that Spain should host the 1982 competition and Columbia the 1986 one (in the end, it was Mexico in 1986). On 19 November 1975 in Guatemala the qualifying sections were drawn up at random. Some 106 countries had signed up to take part – a record – and although a number withdrew before qualifying began in earnest, 97 countries were eventually involved. FIFA's João Havelange had already begun his campaign to increase the number of finalists to 24, but it was decided to set the number for Argentina at 16. Of course, Argentina (as hosts) and West Germany (as holders) had already qualified. Once the other 14 nations had qualified, the finals groups were selected on 16 January 1978 at the Cultural Centre of San Martín, in Buenos Aires. Scotland will be joined in Argentina by Italy, France, Hungary, Poland, Tunisia, Mexico, Austria, Brazil, Spain, Sweden, Holland, Peru and Iran.

Given the devolution debate, Scotland in 1978 is, arguably, in turmoil; but Argentina in 1978 is a country at war with itself. This is the era of death squads and the mothers of an estimated 12,500 'disappeared'. The era of the military Junta, headed by Lieutenant-General Jorge Rafaél Videla. Adolfo Perez-Esquivel, one of the country's leading human-rights campaigners and a Nobel Peace Prize-winner, claims shanty towns are being bulldozed indiscriminately, and that in Rosario a façade has been built – the 'Misery Wall' – to disguise the few slums left standing.

And only a few weeks before the start of the tournament, a policeman is killed and another is injured as they try to remove a bomb planted in the Buenos Aires press centre. Worrying, because Montoneros, one of the two principal terrorist groups, has announced a termination to their activities for the duration of the tournament. In the 16 May edition of the *Daily Record* there is a story of three local fans being killed by police after trouble flares up in a queue for match tickets. Early on in the competition, there are newspaper reports that pop star Rod Stewart had to dive for cover during a shooting incident at a restaurant.

In the run-up to the opening match – between Poland and champions West Germany on 1 June – Amnesty International keeps the pressure on, publicising abuses of human rights and atrocities (including imprisonment without trial). In Britain, the National Union of Journalists urges football writers attending the World Cup not to gloss over atrocities. Two years before the tournament, General Carlos Omar Actis, newly installed as World Cup organiser, is gunned down on his way to his first World Cup conference. Immediately, two possible perpetrators are mooted: left-wing subversives and jealous enemies within the Junta itself.

A New York public relations company is hired to present a polished image at a fee of $1 million. It is small beer compared to the cost of staging of the tournament, which is estimated at between $340 million and $700 million, thanks partly to the building of three brand new stadiums – Mendoza, Córdoba and Mar del Plata – and the substantial refurbishment of those at River Plate, Velez Sarsfield and Rosario. And to satisfy world television audiences, a modern, satellite-based colour television system is needed, as are better road links.

Such hefty investment within so short a timescale leads to massive inflation (900 per cent per annum in the lead up to the finals and 165 per cent by the time they get under way) and internal rows within the government prompt Treasury Secretary Juan Alemann to describe the staging of the finals as 'the most visible and indefensible case of non-priority spending in Argentina today'.

The World Cup is an opiate for the people. Argentina will win and that makes the people deliriously happy, at least for a while.

Internally, besides Buchan's stance on the captaincy, the 1977 tour is rated as pretty much trouble-free. Willie Johnston is sent off; but since Johnston is always being sent off, there is no great surprise in that. It seems, however, that he is, on this occasion, a completely innocent party. His dismissal is against Argentina. Johnston is on song, giving defender Vincente Pernia the runaround. In the end, Pernia cracks, but both are sent packing, Johnston being applauded by the Argentinian fans as he heads for the dressing-room, Pernia being bombarded by cushions. The incident almost has Buchan leading his players from the field in protest. The foul count in the game is Scotland 14, Argentina 41. For Johnston, minor headlines now, major ones 12 months on, during the World Cup itself. Johnston had a hunch he should never have gone to the World Cup in 1978. His hunch would prove correct.

Willie Johnston: The year before the World Cup, we played in Argentina and drew 1–1. Who was one of the best players in the world? Me. Who was sent off? Me. And who went back to Argentina who shouldn't have done? Me. Who was the only team that was going to win the World Cup? Are you telling me I wasn't set up? I wasn't welcome in Argentina. I was a threat. The moment I stepped off the plane in 1978, you could tell from the vibes that I was not welcome.

I wasn't supposed to be going to Argentina. I had told my brothers, I told my mother, I said I wasn't going. After I got sent off in 1977 against Argentina, I went for a drink with one of their players and he starts telling me, 'We win World Cup,' and I says, 'We also a very good side.' Remember, this is in 1977. And he tells me they have one very good player, and that's when I found out about Maradona, though he didn't actually play in the finals. [Maradona was on the fringes of the squad, but team manager Cesar Menotti decided he was physically and emotionally too young.] This guy was pretty insistent that Argentina would win and I thought there was something very sinister about it. I just thought, 'Why do I want to go back there? They are animals.'

What no one realises from the South American tour is that it represents a high-water mark rather than a platform for greater things to come. With hindsight, it is easy to see that the 1977 side possessed an edge, most notably in midfield, that was not nearly as incisive 12 months later.

Archie Gemmill: The only thing I remember was playing against Brazil in the Maracana stadium and I played up front on my own and I loved it. It was most enjoyable. I caused havoc.

Bruce Rioch: We didn't go to the World Cup with the best results behind us; we hadn't done so well in the Home Internationals. Whereas in 1977, before our tour of South America, our results were very good. And we went out there full of optimism and did well. We had a 4–2 win in Chile, a 1–1 draw in Argentina with Argentina equalising from a late penalty and a 2–0 defeat in Rio with Brazil playing extremely well against us. From 1977, the expectations were higher than ever before. We had the nucleus of an outstanding squad. I look upon the World Cup with a mixed view: very disappointing, in such a major event in your life; yet a great learning experience for the future.

Graeme Souness: I wouldn't criticise MacLeod. If there was any criticism, it was that he allowed the press to wind the situation up to a state where the whole nation believed we would go and win the World Cup. But that is the only criticism I would make of him. I thought he was a genuine man, passionate about his football. But he should have tried to temper it somewhat. Psychological scars? None whatsoever. At the time, I was a young fella, along for the ride. I think the experience did me good in the long term, I think it was an experience that I could look back on and learn from.

Joe Jordan: I don't see the point of going over events of 20 years ago, on something that is finished with. When I finished as a player, I used my experiences, good and bad, to put into practice when I was a manager. But I don't see the point in looking back at that chapter. All I would say is that I have no criticisms to make about anyone. When I came back I made no criticism and 20 years on I make no criticism. Life goes on.

The only scars I carry are on my legs. Football is an easy game and when it is played simply it looks good. I don't think it is a complicated sport. I think people try to read too much into it. I think it is a great game.

Kenny Dalglish is even more circumspect. He's notorious for it. Through various secretaries over the course of a few months, he declines to be interviewed. There wasn't even an 'um', 'eh' or 'maybe' about it. He is, of course, involved in his own book projects.

Ally MacLeod: In all the time I was Scotland manager, the entire conversation I had with Kenny could be written on five lines of paper. He just sat and listened, and did what you told him. I doubt if I had more than ten minutes' conversation with him but I knew he would do what I asked of him. And he was without a doubt one of the outstanding players in that squad.

The 22. The 'lucky' 22. Not exactly a happy band of brothers charged with the task of bringing the World Cup back to Scotland. A squad that initially numbered 40 in March 1978 and needed to be whittled down three months later as per the requirements of FIFA. 'I'll be wearing my bullet-proof jacket from now on,' MacLeod is reported to have said after choosing his final squad on 3 May. How prescient. What he meant, however, was that not everyone would be happy with his choice, not that he would need protection on his return from Argentina with nothing to show but eccentric elimination.

One issue is already beyond debate. There is no question that, had he been fit, left-back Danny McGrain would have made the 22. Probably the starting 11. He is, after all, a player of international stature. As it is, he doesn't even make the 40, ruled out of the reckoning by injury, a loss MacLeod believes hits Scotland harder than Johan Cruyff's withdrawal from the World Cup does Holland.

Having already been diagnosed a diabetic, McGrain's ambition to play in the 1978 World Cup is shattered when he is injured in a tackle in a match against Hibernian in October. In the magazine *Action Replay*, he explains: 'It was a tackle on my old pal John Blackley, and both of us, as you do with pals, went in with real ferocity. I got up and limped away, not wanting to show John I was in any pain, thinking, "I've got him", but my foot was so sore and I should never have tried to run off the pain. It gradually got worse over the next few weeks and when normal physiotherapy didn't help – I spent six weeks with Freddie Griffiths down at Manchester City – I turned to anything. Our masseur Jimmy Steel [at Celtic and with the 1978 squad] was into herbal remedies and he put me onto a guy who did acupuncture. I went for the first session and remember how strange it was to see all these needles sticking out of my foot. Afterwards, the foot still didn't feel any better and I thought acupuncture was a lot of crap. But I stuck with it for three months and it got me back quicker than the hospital and surgeons who couldn't pinpoint the trouble. It might have taken me a year and a half going the normal route.'

Those caught in the cull include Leeds United goalkeeper, Dave Stewart, mainly because he is no longer commanding a first team place with his club. There then follows a raft of players whom MacLeod feels can wait their turn until another day. These include Neil McNab of Spurs, Dundee United's Dave Narey, Paul Hegarty and Graeme Payne, the St Mirren duo of Frank McGarvey and Tony Fitzpatrick, Ipswich player John Wark and Roy Aitken of Celtic. Another Celtic player, Roddie MacDonald, falls by the wayside simply because there are more than enough experienced players competing for the central defensive berths.

Although MacLeod knows that Manchester City's Willie Donachie will be suspended (because he had picked up two bookings during the build-up) for the opening match in Argentina, against Peru, he opts for Donachie, Sandy Jardine of Rangers and Stuart Kennedy of Aberdeen to compete for the full-back positions, meaning no place for John Brownlie of Hibernian.

At the expense of Arthur Graham of Leeds United, he opts for Nottingham Forest's John Robertson on the opposite wing to Willie Johnston of West Bromwich Albion. Robertson is new to the manager and Scotland, but he strikes MacLeod as being the sort of player who knows his limitations and will therefore put in a good shift whenever he plays.

Joe Jordan is MacLeod's main striker, despite having scored just two international goals since the previous World Cup (he was not, in fairness, a Scotland regular throughout that period). But who to choose as his understudy? At the time, the obvious candidate is Derek Johnstone of Rangers – scorer of 41 goals for his club that season – ahead of Andy Gray of Aston Villa who is famed for his bravery in the box. Johnstone offers to play centre-half if needed but MacLeod persists in naming him as one of his centre-forwards and, instead of adding the popular Gray to complete the roster, elects Aberdeen's Joe Harper to deputise for Kenny Dalglish. The belief is that Dalglish and Harper are a similar type of player – good at feeding off scraps.

The process is agonising and MacLeod likes to think he has no time for sentiment while making his choices. The final 22 are: goalkeepers Alan

Rough, Jim Blyth and Bobby Clark; full-backs Sandy Jardine, Stuart Kennedy and Willie Donachie; central defenders Martin Buchan, Gordon McQueen, Tom Forsyth and Kenny Burns; midfielders Bruce Rioch (captain), Don Masson, Archie Gemmill, Graeme Souness, Asa Hartford and Lou Macari; and forwards Kenny Dalglish, Joe Jordan, Derek Johnstone, Joe Harper, Willie Johnston and John Robertson. The reserves are Leeds United winger Arthur Graham, Aston Villa striker Andy Gray, Coventry City striker Ian Wallace, Aberdeen defender Willie Miller, Newcastle United defender John Blackley and Middlesbrough goalkeeper Jim Stewart. In the event, none of the reserves is called up.

Later, much later, on 31 May, four days before the side's opening match against Peru, the TV stations unveil their 'squads'. On the BBC side are Alan Weeks, Barry Davies, Jimmy Hill, John Motson, David Coleman, Frank Bough, Archie Macpherson and Tony Gubba. And turning out for ITV are Brian Moore, Johan Cruyff, Brian Clough, Pat Crerand, Kevin Keegan, Ian St John, Jack Charlton, Arthur Montford, Hugh Johns, Gerald Sinstadt, Martin Tyler and Gerry Harrison.

> *Lou Macari*: I remember when I was picked for the squad of 40 thinking, probably like a lot of players, 'That's the first hurdle done.' Such was the competition for places you weren't even sure you would get into the 40, never mind the 22. The biggest relief came when you were in the 22.

Contracted to the *Scottish Daily Express*, MacLeod gives his opinions on each of his squad in the edition of 4 May. Some of his comments are revealing in light of subsequent events: 'Don Masson – I've built the side round him. Most of our attacks start and revolve around this man. If he plays as well as he can, then the whole team plays as well as it can; Graeme Souness – I've been a fan from his youth days. He tackles, he opens up play more even than Don Masson. Obviously you wouldn't play the pair of them; Martin Buchan – has proved with Manchester United and Scotland he is a world-class player. He's intelligent, he reads the game superbly, and, to be quite honest, I just cannot see a flaw in him; Joe Jordan – I think too many managers have got into Joe Jordan's head that he can't score enough goals. He can and he must believe in himself; Kenny Dalglish – what can you say? He is quite simply the best player in his position in Europe; Derek Johnstone – he's Player of the Year. You can't have better credentials than that. He might be even better if he really believed that centre-forward was his best position. Willie Johnston – now Willie could turn out to be one of the great players of the World Cup. He is an absolute key man for us because he gives us width.'

Of course, come the end of the World Cup, with so many players having failed to rise to the occasion, one of the many accusations levelled at MacLeod is that he has been inspired too much by sentiment when choosing his final squad. Lou Macari is a case in point. He travels to Argentina shortly after his mother's death, missing the Home Internationals that summer as a result of his bereavement.

The debate over Andy Gray is particularly gruelling. While McGrain is ruled out well in advance, his defensive colleague Gordon McQueen is touch and go. MacLeod has the option of taking Gray instead of McQueen. The defender is injured before the deadline. MacLeod persists with McQueen. The hope is that he will be fit in time for at least one match. Of course, at the time, the presumption is that Scotland will make the latter stages of the competition. They never do and McQueen never plays. At least McGrain will make it to the 1982 finals, held in Spain. McQueen, who travelled as an understudy to Jim Holton in West Germany in 1974, won't. His chance came and went in 1978. Typically, the injury that rules him out is daft, sustained against Wales in the Home International match played just over a week before departure for Argentina. He goes to kick away a ball that was going clear anyway, smacks his leg against a post and damages his knee ligament. Bang.

Gordon McQueen: In all seriousness, it nearly broke my heart not playing in the World Cup. You hear players saying how devastated they are over something; well I was absolutely devastated, without a doubt, when I heard how serious my knee injury really was. When I went to bed the night of the Wales game, all I had was a bit of sticking plaster on the knee because I had grazed it. I knew I had done a bit of damage, but I didn't think anything of it. Then, during the night, it became absolute agony and I woke up the next morning with this huge, ballooned-up knee. I went to see a specialist and I knew then that I was really struggling, that it was highly unlikely I would be playing in Argentina.

Against Wales in the Home Internationals, Kenny Burns made a defensive mistake and it looked as if the ball was going to trickle over the line. It didn't, but I had dived in to stop it and, in those days, the goalposts were square. Had they been round, like they are now, I might have played in the World Cup finals because my knee would have slipped off. It certainly would not have made the same impact.

The diagnosis was that I had damaged my medial ligament. At the time, Manchester United were away on tour, so in the week or so between the Home Internationals and our departure for Argentina, I went to the physiotherapist at Manchester City, Freddie Griffiths, and he just dedicated himself to getting me fit in time. I am talking eight in the morning to six at night. Working, working, working. It was the hardest I had ever worked. As it happened, I wouldn't have made the second phase had we got through. I was fit only by the time pre-season training came along with Manchester United. Once the medial ligament gets even slightly better, you can do all the running you like – you just cannot kick a ball or tackle anyone, because the impact can do all sorts of damage.

I had gone to the 1974 World Cup in West Germany, but it was under different circumstances. I was Jim Holton's understudy. I made my Scotland début in a warm-up game against Belgium because, as it happened, Jim was also struggling with a knee injury. But he recovered in time for the last warm-up and played in the World Cup itself. But the disappointment was easier to take then because I knew I was his understudy.

But 1978 was different. There were only five players who played in all the qualifying games – me, Kenny Dalglish, Asa Hartford, Joe Jordan and Alan Rough. I had just moved that season for a British transfer record, from Leeds United to Manchester United. So there was plenty of hype around the likes of myself. Foreign journalists would ask to speak to me. I was being flown to places like Germany for photo-shoots. I was probably playing the best football of my life, I was scoring goals from set-pieces and I felt that, by going to Argentina, I was going to make an impact. You can have 20 good years in English football, but it is at the World Cup that players really make their name.

I felt that Argentina was going to be it for me. Scotland were being hyped up. I thought we were a decent side and I felt I was going to go there and be a success. And then one stupid little injury, when I was probably feeling as sharp and as quick and as fit and as confident as I had ever done in my life . . . well, it's hard to explain, really hard to explain. It's not as if occasions like that crop up every year. That was it. My chance had gone. I wasn't involved in the 1982 World Cup. I was inconsolable. I was, as I have said before, absolutely devastated and I still think about it now. Of what might have been. Most footballers like to think they can make a difference in a tournament even if they probably can't. I would wake up in the morning hoping it wasn't there, because I had worked so hard on getting treatment. Ally MacLeod must have thought it was worth taking the gamble. I was playing well at the time. But there was a clamour for Andy Gray to be included in the squad.

I was so desperate. I never went for monetary reasons – I couldn't give a toss about anything like that at the time. I just wanted to give myself even a small chance. It was maybe a bit selfish. But you just live in hope, especially when you are that little bit younger.

I always, always put Scotland before anything else when it came to football. I was never one of these people who would bail out at the slightest wee knock. Never. If I was anything like fit, I was there. I had a million injuries, I missed umpteen caps because of serious injury. I had two Achilles tendon operations, for example. I loved playing for Scotland, so to miss the World Cup finals was indescribable. I was given the captaincy for a game against Romania in June 1975 and it was a phenomenal feeling, even though the game itself was fairly meaningless.

I get the impression that players now are a bit more blasé about international football than a lot of us were in the past. A club manager wouldn't dare suggest to me that I should pull out of a Scotland squad because there was an important club game coming up. He would just know. I would not be told. When I was at Leeds, Don Revie, the manager, would try all the time to keep players off international duty if there was a big club game looming, but he didn't dare try that with me.

Anyone who was sitting by me must have felt so bloody miserable listening to me moaning and complaining. I don't think I made very good company. Sitting in the stands, not even on the bench, I was on an unbelievable downer. When I got off the plane on our arrival in Argentina, and my knee had got more and more painful during the journey, I wished I hadn't gone.

Hoat pies for us, Argentina

Chorus: Yes it's true the boys in blue are in the World Cup
And we're gonnae win it wi' a wee bit Scottish luck.

They took him offae Aberdeen, Al MacLeod's the name
And now we're off to the Argentine and fitba' is the game

Repeat chorus

The fans, they will be travelling by air and plane and sea
And some are goin' by Concorde so they'll get hame for their tea.

Repeat chorus

Ted Heath is sailing some of the boys and he's feeling really proud
He's painted and re-named his yacht, 'Morning McCloud'.

Repeat chorus

They can seed all the Brazilians, the Italians and the rest
Before the end they'll all concede that Scotland is the best.

Repeat chorus

The English call me 'Scottish' with a smile that's near a sneer
How come they call me 'British' at least once every fourth year?

Repeat chorus

Well, we've no' got a Johan Cruyff and we've no' got a Pele
But I'll see Bruce huddin' up the Cup on ma wee Scottish telly.

Repeat chorus

I'll no' be goin' myself for I'm playing it really cool
I'm still saving up the train fare to get back from Liverpool.

(Sung by Bill Barclay to the tune of 'Johnny Lad'; reproduced by kind permission of British Lion Music Ltd)

3. Optimism

By the time the DC-10 carrying the Scotland team to Argentina arrives at Córdoba airport, in the middle of the country, the players have spent the best part of 21 hours on an aeroplane. There were five stops between Prestwick and Córdoba, including one at Buenos Aires, the capital of Argentina, a 70-minute flight away. But at least they travel first class, feasting, according to *The Scotsman*, on a menu that features smoked Scotch salmon and Chateaubriand steak with mushrooms and barbecue sauce. There is a four-course breakfast on offer between the Brazilian stops of Recife and Rio. The cabin crew devise a cocktail in honour of the party, called 'Ally's Tartan Cannonball': Soak a cube of sugar in angostura bitters in a glass 'frosted' by dipping the rim in sugar. In a jug, put ice cubes, one measure of Drambuie whisky liqueur and a measure of orange juice (about a third of a wine-glass). Stir vigorously and strain into the glass. Top up with champagne and garnish with an orange slice and a cherry. Mmm.

The squad arrives to a tumultuous welcome at Córdoba – where the team are to play their first two matches of the World Cup, against Peru and Iran – from, amongst others, the Buenos Aires-based St Andrew's Society pipers. If Córdoba is excited, Alta Gracia, chosen as the team's base for the first two games, is off the scale. The Scots are embraced like heroes. Alta Gracia is a 40-minute bus ride from Córdoba. On the way, in a two-bus convoy, one of the vehicles – the one carrying the players – breaks down. The stopping and starting through the cheering crowds has taken its toll. It is hilarious at the time, only becoming symbolic later on as the results against Peru and Iran amount to a comedy of errors.

Back home, on the day of their departure, the Scottish National Party has just started its annual conference amid much soul-searching after two by-election setbacks and a disappointing performance in local government elections. At Westminster, Member of Parliament Denis Canavan is attacking the Argentinian Government's record on human rights. In *The Scotsman* James Naughtie writes of bedlam in Argentina over tickets for the media. According to his report, there are 5,000 press people to be accommodated and less than 2,000 tickets available for the first-round games. The Austrian and Hungarian delegations have yet to receive any tickets. The Argentinians, however, seem to be more than well off.

There is also a rumour that 'new philosopher' Bernard Henri Levy has been turned back at Buenos Aires airport because his suitcase is full of Amnesty International literature. In total, little more than 20,000 visitors arrive in Argentina for the tournament.

Kenny Burns: The second bus had to push the other one up the hill. But we kept waving like the Queen. What plonkers we must have looked. The swimming-pool? Bikes and prams in the swimming-pool. Martin Buchan, whom I regard as a very tidy player but who was a funny lad, was piping up, 'I'm not staying here.'

There are no bikes and prams in the swimming-pool. But there is no water either. Buchan complains about his room but can't remember now whether he was transferred to another one. Buchan's recollection is that the room he and Lou Macari were first allotted had plaster peeling off the walls. The hotel, The Sierras, is a sprawling white building (dubbed 'Château d'Espair' by some), set in massive grounds with an ornamental garden. The Mexican and Tunisian squads are also based here, but in the wings. Scotland gets the main entrance. There are placards dotted about inscribed with lines of Robert Burns' poetry. The dining-room is decorated with Scottish insignia. The training pitch is bare and rutted.

In *The Scotsman*, Mike Aitken describes the hotel as, 'Grand but friendly, opulent if slightly run-down. A good place for Scotland to stay. The facilities are first rate. There are places to train and places to relax – a golf course, heated swimming pool, tennis courts and so on.'

The 50,000 capacity Córdoba stadium is also written up by Aitken in glowing terms: 'It looms up at the end of the newly built stretch of highway as impressively as the mother ship at the grand finale of [the sci-fi film] *Close Encounters*. This ground is rather sensational.' In the centre stand, there are seats for 700 journalists. In the *Glasgow Herald*, Jim Reynolds is equally optimistic.

Tom Forsyth: I remember walking across the floor of the room in my socks and getting a skelf [splinter] in my foot. The accommodation was terrible. What was I used to? A carpet for a start.

Ally MacLeod: I do believe if the World Cup had not been held on the other side of the world, we would possibly have performed far better. People are apt to forget that when you go to Argentina, you are sleeping when your body clock says you should be awake, and you are awake when you are meant to be sleeping. When we went on the tour of South America the year before, we just flew in, played the games and flew out.

The body clock thing was a major factor, plus the fact the hotel and the food were terrible. Maybe we should have been out there longer, to acclimatise [they were there for nine days before the first game]. It was steak, after steak, after steak. And it wasn't cooked the way it is over here. And not everyone likes steak. If you asked for an omelette, you couldn't get one.

Ernie [Walker, secretary of the Scottish Football Association] and I had chosen another hotel after going out there when the draw was made. And when we arrived for real, we were told it was fully booked and we had to take second best.

The food was absolutely terrible. It was not the hotel we had booked. We didn't intend to base ourselves in Alta Gracia, but in the general vicinity. We should have known that is typical of these countries.

We went on the tour [in 1977] to get used to the place, and find out about the hotels.

Ernie Walker: We inspected hotels all over Argentina and made provisional bookings depending on where we were drawn to play. And when we were assigned to Córdoba, the hotel we were more than happy with was The Sierras.

We did a very intensive piece of work on the whole thing. Host nations normally assist competing nations by providing lists of hotels and relevant details. And for this reason or that, many are not suitable.

I remember flying all over Argentina to check on hotels. On one occasion, in Rosario, we were involved in an earthquake. I remember waking up with the headboard of my bed slapping against the wall and the lights swinging in the room. Ally was quite ill with the shock of it.

We had done our work before the draw because after the draw there is a scramble and you don't want to be left with what no one else wants. After the draw, quite unbelievably, the Iranians asked me, 'Where is Córdoba? Where should we stay?' So, I told them we were staying at The Sierras but there was a hotel near by, which had been a close second, which I advised they might try. Anyway, the next day, I arrive in Córdoba to confirm our booking with The Sierras, and the manager – whom I knew well by this time – tells me he had just turned away the Iranians who had offered him money to turf the Scots out and take them instead.

At the time, Ernie Walker disagrees with criticisms of the hotel, claiming it to be 'first rate', a point he reiterates in a report to his committee. In it, he argues the hotel was 'perfectly adequate' for the camp's purposes and better than the majority of hotels available to other countries' squads. As far as he was concerned, the food was good, the setting was peaceful and attractive and the rooms were adequate (although certainly not as modern and luxurious as would normally be found in Europe). In short, he says it had nothing to do with the team's lack of success, it seemed to be satisfactory as far as the Dutch were concerned (who moved in when the Scots left) and would have been used by the Brazilians had their draw required them to base themselves in the area.

> *Ernie Walker*: All the stories of it being a horrible concentration camp are quite simply not true. Frequently in football, hotels are blamed for results. I had learned that lesson before Argentina, which was why I developed the practice of taking the coach with me so that the coach knew in advance what the accommodation would be like. Had we won the matches, you would never have heard a word about the hotel.

The squad has arrived in some style, though the shine is slightly removed by reports that Joe Harper and Bruce Rioch have both been laid low by a bug. There are tales, mostly (but not entirely) apocryphal, of rogue entrepreneurs back home in Scotland offering cut-price travel for fans on clapped-out German U-boats, fishing trawlers and such like. Almost all the 700 or so fans who travel to Argentina to follow Scotland do so by conventional means, at about £2,000 a throw, through their local travel agent. Flying in, flying out (in the case of a few disgruntled supporters, departing before Scotland's final game against Holland).

A few fans, however, decide to make a life experience out of the World Cup, flying cheap to New York and taking a few months getting to Argentina as inexpensively as possible. The 'hard route' mostly involves hitch-hiking. But there is the odd bus journey and, out of necessity, a flight across the Darien Gap, a Godforsaken finger of land on the northern coast of Panama, not yet bridged by the Pan-American highway and which, portentously, had brought Scotland's economy to its knees in the 17th century (and precipitated the Union of Parliaments in 1707) when, in 1698, there was an expensive and failed attempt to carve a trade route across it, like an early version of the Panama Canal. Once in Argentina, the Scottish fans are besieged by local people wanting to meet them and have them sign autographs.

John Duffy, fan: I was 22 at the time. I flew to New York on one of those £59 single tickets with Freddie Laker's planes. I made the mistake of heading north to have a look at Canada. I shouldn't have bothered – I froze my ass off and had all sorts of problems getting back into the US because this wee woman at the border crossing, at Niagara Falls, wouldn't accept my papers.

I hitched down to Argentina. It was brilliant, mostly. You would get lifts lasting for a couple of days at a time with truck drivers who would tell you, 'I'm from the south, man, they're all Yankees up here. I am a Johnny Red. Can you give me a wee badge? Do you want to come to this wee club to meet my mates?'

I had earned a few bob to see me through. Between us qualifying in Liverpool and the World Cup, it became an obsession. It was the chance of a lifetime and I said, 'Fuck it, I've got to go for it,' so I worked on building sites in Germany over the winter. It was real *Auf Wiedersehen, Pet* stuff. The deutschmark was strong.

I did initially fancy travelling to Argentina from Germany, through Europe, on to Africa and then across from there. But the £59 carrot was dangled. Flying to New York would at least get me to the Americas. Getting across from Sierra Leone to Brazil might have been dodgy, plus there was a war going on in Spanish Sahara. Mind you, there were wars going on in Central America. It was well dodgy. I could have got whacked there. My passport saved my life on at least one occasion. There was a civil war just kicking off in El Salvador. Once, I was looking to have a nap – a wee siesta – in a field and, two minutes later, there were six guns pointing at my head. It was the El Salvador army looking for guerrillas. I showed them the passport and they went, 'Inglés?' and I said, 'No, Escocés. Football el mundo, el mundo.' And they twigged and then took me to the barracks for a fucking drink. One minute, I was about to be blasted, the next they wanted to buy me a drink.

I couldn't get out of Central America quick enough. I had a problem once I got to Panama City at the Darien Gap. The Pan-American Highway didn't go across the Gap, so I had to take a wee internal flight into Colombia. I knew that, once there, I would be into South America and on my way.

I arrived in Córdoba four days before the team, but that was after spending a couple of weeks with some good people in the Andes, the only time in my life I smoked dope, straight from Colombia. The stop in the Andes was needed to unwind. You would pick up wee stomach upsets and bouts of diarrhoea. I needed time to relax and get over the side effects of all that travel. They had this home brew, like whisky, which was nectar.

Alex Smith, then manager of Stirling Albion: I was there through the Scottish Football League which sent out an invitation to all clubs to make the trip at a cut price. And, as far as I am aware, only Alex Stuart, Ayr United's manager, and myself went. It was a fabulous experience, though of course there were times when it was very disappointing and heart-breaking. Nonetheless, it was worth the effort. No Premier Division managers went, though three clubs – Aberdeen, Celtic and Rangers – were each in the throes of changing their manager at the time.

The trip was organised by Campbell Ogilvie, who was then assistant secretary at the League [now secretary of Rangers]. We stayed in the Hotel California, which could well have been the inspiration for the album by The Eagles; it was horrendous. There was this wee reception and wee spiral staircase that took us to some rooms where it was two or three beds per room and the beds were these army metal things with army blankets. It was probably average or above average by local standards.

But there was this great wee restaurant near by. The food was excellent. Fantastic steak. You could never get one 'well done'. They were just touched and over, very rare.

The people were so friendly. I actually went back the following two years. I watched Boca Juniors – then world club champions – train, along with other teams. I was still at Stirling Albion. Though I watched Scotland train in 1978, you were prevented by security from watching other countries train.

Brian Fleming, fan: I flew to New York from Prestwick with a pal, Dave Ednie, and we bought a Chevvie Impala in Connecticut which we planned to drive down to Argentina.

We got as far as Mexico, and then got talked out of taking it any further. We were told we wouldn't find a decent road to traverse the Darien Gap and we were also advised there might be a problem finding petrol stations. So we drove back up to San Antonio, in Texas, and parked the car outside the flat of a friend.

In general, it was very easy to get lifts, particularly in Argentina. The kilt was brilliant. I was 31 at the time, I was single and drove taxis in Edinburgh. I was away for about six months. I stayed for the final between Argentina and Holland, but I couldn't face the return journey overland. I sent for some money so I could fly to Miami. The thought of travelling thousands of miles back was too much.

It was a good laugh on the way down – don't get me wrong. We didn't hitch all the time. We would get buses sometimes. There were some places you just couldn't hitch, such as Bolivia where, if you hitch-hiked, you'd still be charged. A lot of the buses were cheap. Some of the journeys lasted days.

In Argentina, there were a lot of roadblocks. You would get stopped by the army quite a few times. Only once did I have a problem when a soldier got very cocky with us when we were hitching out of Mendoza on our way to Córdoba before the start of the competition. We had just come across the Andes from Chile. He wanted to look at our papers and was going on about our kilts. Next thing, he had his hand in my pocket, saying he wanted a cigarette. I said, 'Nah, nah,' and before I knew it he was pushing me into the back of a jeep and driving me across a bit of desert. He swung a punch at me, just the one, and then let me go.

By that time, there were three of us hitching together. But I was slung into the jeep on my own. There was nothing the other two could do. Though only one soldier was being cocky with us, he had a couple of mates and they all had guns. I didn't honestly know what was going to happen next, but I wasn't that frightened. My pride was hurt because I couldn't retaliate after being punched.

Otherwise, the people could not have been friendlier. Once the World Cup was over, in Buenos Aires, with only a few of us Scots left, there was a wee bit more aggression. An Argentinian, a military guy, was just chatting to us about the football in a café, and he was suddenly frog-marched out by these other guys in uniform.

Fleming vividly recollects arriving in Córdoba before the Scottish squad and coming across a gun-placement on the streets which then disappeared overnight. He also remembers being taken to Córdoba airport as the squad flew in from Prestwick and being allowed to get closer to the players than the media.

By that stage, the media presence from the UK is substantial. Gordon Airs of the *Daily Record* is among the first there and he is quickly joined by Alex Cameron and Ken Gallacher (now at *The Herald*) from the same newspaper. Mike Aitken is there for *The Scotsman*, working with James Naughtie (who now anchors *The World at One* on Radio Four). Trevor McDonald (who now anchors *News at Ten* on ITV) is another journalist on the case. Ian Archer is there for the *Express* and Scottish Television. Broadcaster and avid World Cup fan Ruth Wishart 'fortuitously' decides not to go. Jim Reynolds is the main football correspondent for the *Glasgow Herald* while Brian Scott is likewise for the *Daily Mail*. There are dozens, maybe even a hundred or so, sports and news journalists from the UK, including about 30 from Scotland.

But the access afforded to the fans at Córdoba airport has a sinister edge to it. For Fleming, Duffy and others, everything is just too good to be true. As one, they think, 'Secret Police'. It doesn't, however, prevent them taking advantage of the doors being mysteriously opened for them.

Brian Fleming, fan: We were on this bus, organised by this Argentinian person. We actually went to the airport. And then the bus driver disappeared and this Scots guy got up from his seat near us and started driving the bus. One of the officials wanted the bus away. I don't know if it was in gear, but the bus started jumping forward. Some of the [welcoming] band started looking at the bus because it was jumping forward towards them. But, in the end, the driver got the bus under control. Turns out he was a proper bus driver from Glasgow. We were on the third of three buses headed for the airport. The other two were to pick up the team. We stayed on the bus and ended up going to Alta Gracia. So, three buses went to Alta Gracia. I decided to stay on the bus and return to Córdoba but some stayed the night in Alta Gracia.

Adrian Haren, fan: A few of us were befriended by an Argentinian with impeccable English who said he was a wine importer. He got us to the players at Córdoba airport and, later, into the team hotel for a beer and a blether with the players.

When the bevvy is flowing so freely and there is someone else organising things for you, you tend to let them get on with it without asking too many questions. Only later did I wake up to the possibility the guy was from the secret police or intelligence and it was in Argentina's best interests to organise us rather than leave us to our own devices.

I was 29 at the time. At the 1974 World Cup, I promised that, come hell or high water, I would be in Argentina if Scotland qualified. It took me three months of hitch-hiking from New York to get to Argentina and five months to get back. I hitched down with a friend, but he had to get back sooner than me because he was getting married. So I returned on my own. It took longer because I was just so emotionally shattered by the way Scotland played. I needed that length of time to recover. And the Argentinians were so nice to be with. Their generosity was nothing like I had ever encountered before. At times, they would make you feel genuinely humble. They were my convalescence from the whole thing.

At the Scottish base in Alta Gracia, the security is a mix of the unbelievably lax and the frighteningly strict. Armed guards, some crudely disguised as gardeners and waiters, roam the hotel complex. Trees appear to move of their own accord. On one occasion, a trio of players are stopped at gunpoint. Yet, all a fan needs to do to gain access into the compound, it seems, is wear a Scotland shirt, call himself 'Willie Donachie' or 'Derek Johnstone' and breeze through the main entrance.

For the players, there is a strict routine. A pass has to be issued by the Scotland management. It isn't that MacLeod is reluctant to grant players the freedom to wander – quite the reverse, in fact. He begins the campaign believing that if he treats the players as adults, they will reciprocate in kind. Curfews will be set, but not during the first days at Alta Gracia. With a week still to go before the first match against Peru, there is little need for such heavy-handed supervision.

Joe Harper: The place we were in was like a Mexican hacienda, like a big ranch with a white wall around it. And for me to get out, if I wanted to get a postcard, I had to go to Ally MacLeod, get a note from him, go down to the gate and the guard would take the note and ask how long I was going to take. If I said half an hour and wasn't back after 45 minutes, you can be sure there would have been a full-scale alert. And these two guys at the gate had machine guns. I probably exaggerate, but I think they had about 16 gardeners, guys sitting at a wee bush, turning the soil over and over, with sub-machine-guns tucked under their jackets.

Trevor McDonald, journalist and broadcaster: There is a general view that when big sporting events occur, especially abroad, then two groups of journalists go: the sports reporters and the others who try to pick up peripheral scandal surrounding the sportsmen. We [at ITN] went to do news events surrounding the sporting event and not at all to touch the scandal.

Scotland had gone to the World Cup and, to all intents and purposes, they were the representatives of the United Kingdom. We thought there would be lots of interesting stories about the Scots, whether they were doing well or whether they were doing badly; we sincerely hoped they were going to do well.

I got to know Ally MacLeod very well before we left. The general feeling was that they were going to do well; he certainly talked a really good game. I remember having lunch at his house once and he was describing how impossible it was to walk down the street in Glasgow or Edinburgh because so many people were anxious to rush up to him and wish him well. And we were caught up in that euphoria and wanted to go along with it.

I was in Córdoba on the evening the Scots arrived. And they turned up late one afternoon, a wonderful moment, to the dying rays of a golden sun. And all the people from Alta Gracia came out to meet the Scottish bus. And they were hammering on the doors, shouting, 'Welcome, welcome.' And I said to Ally MacLeod, 'My goodness, isn't this wonderful. Why do you think they have come out to greet you, why are they giving you such an enthusiastic welcome?' And he replied, 'Because they know we are the winners.'

This kind of euphoric view spread to us from him. We were imbued by that; we felt we were on to a good story. You might think a story of catastrophic failure makes good news. But there would have been nothing like a story of Scotland going to Argentina and conquering the world. That would have been a great story and we wanted to be part of it, which was why, beforehand, I spent a lot of time in Scotland getting to know Ally MacLeod. Not to do the dirty on him – we went with the best will in the world – but to report Scottish glory.

What he failed to understand when he turned up at Alta Gracia was that Argentinian people were encouraged to welcome with open arms everyone they saw. I spoke to one Scottish fan who had hitch-hiked to Argentina and he was telling me how he arrived in Córdoba and a family just took him in, gave him breakfast, then had him round that evening for a drink and so on. Before the World Cup began, the authorities ran TV commercials to get the public to look after visiting fans. MacLeod thought the Argentinians were more than usually interested in the Scots. In fact, they weren't; they were giving a great welcome to everyone because they had been told to do so by the government.

MacLeod's arrival in Argentina for the World Cup finals constitutes his third visit to the country in a year. Twelve months earlier he had led the Scotland party on a tour of South America. At the start of 1978, he was over in Argentina for the draw to determine the Round One action. In the cultural centre of the San Martín theatre in Buenos Aires, Scotland are to find out who they will have to sweep aside to progress to the later stages of the finals. They are fortunate. Iran are considered makeweights, Peru are believed to be over the hill. Only Holland pose a threat, but since the top two out of each section make it through, MacLeod and Scotland think they can rest easy.

The trip for the draw is interrupted by earth tremors and a bit of bungling on Ally's part. The tremors are, in some places, the worst experienced for over half a century, and are strong enough to destroy houses and cast doubt (even if the authorities seek to assure otherwise) over the tournament going ahead at all.

MacLeod didn't feel the first tremor, knocked out as he was by a sleeping pill, only to wake up in the morning to find, bleary-eyed, that all the other guests had fled. He is in his bed again, the following night in another hotel in another town, when there is another tremor. And this time, unable to sleep, he feels its full force, with his bed thrown across the room and the floor suddenly at a petrifying angle to the walls. 'I found myself fighting to keep my balance as I struggled across the steeply sloping floor towards the door,' he recalled. 'I tugged at the handle in my panic, the door flew open, and I found myself face to face with a lady dressed in black from head to toe. I was convinced she was some kind of angel of death, though I remember wondering what on earth she was doing with a tray of fruit. It was only when she laughed at the expression on my face that I realised she was one of the hotel maids.'

Charmed and charming. MacLeod, however, lands himself in trouble over what flag to allocate Scotland – the Saltire or the Union Jack. To most Scots there ought to be no debate. Not for Ally. No sooner have he and Ernie Walker touched down in Buenos Aires than he is suggesting to FIFA that, in the circumstances, Scotland might better be identified as Great Britain.

The reasons for MacLeod making such a suggestion go back to a stint as a guest disc-jockey, when his mellifluous tones serenaded the listeners of Radio Clyde. Asked on one occasion if he hated the English, he replied, attempting to be funny, 'Hate them? I detest them.' The incident immediately rebounded on him, and no one was more upset than MacLeod himself, especially since he was already receiving good luck messages and offers of support from every part of the British Isles, including from Brian

Clough, whose time was then being taken up masterminding Nottingham Forest's league championship win.

So, to cut a long story short, when an official from FIFA asks which flag should be shown against Scotland's name during the televising of the final draw, MacLeod feels compelled to say something along the lines of: 'I would love it to be the Saltire, but I suppose, in the circumstances, it had better be the Union Jack'.

Now, the Scots boast a lot of Anglos in their squad at the time. Indeed, of the 22 players who travel to Argentina, all but seven — Alan Rough at Partick Thistle, Bobby Clark, Stuart Kennedy and Joe Harper at Aberdeen and Sandy Jardine, Tom Forsyth and Derek Johnstone at Rangers — are based in England. But it doesn't stop Walker 'exploding' when he sees the Union Jack unfurled in the cavernous theatre where the draw is to take place. One way or another, a Saltire is found before the cameras begin to roll.

When the draw is finally concluded, MacLeod is careful to caution against over-confidence. At the same time, though, he can't believe his relative good fortune. The tide is with Scotland. Their luck is in. It had run with them when playing Czechoslovakia and Wales during qualifying. 'The conditions in Argentina, I was convinced, favoured a World Cup win for a European side,' he considered. 'And why, I considered with Great British optimism, shouldn't that be us?' In the immediate wake of the draw, he is quoted as saying, 'In the past we have blown our chances with silly mistakes, like those against Zaire in 1974. This time, I promise, we won't throw away the golden opportunity.'

After losing against Scotland in the last qualifier, Wales's Terry Yorath is quoted in similar upbeat fashion: 'The Scots are a fine side. I'm backing them to win the World Cup.'

Few disagree, least of all the players and the press.

Olé Ola

When the blue shirts run out in Argentina
Our hearts will be beating like a drum
And your nerves are so shattered you can't take it
Oh, no matter when you reach out for the rum.

But there really isn't any cause for panic
Ally's army have it all under control
It is not merely speculation, it's not just imagination
To bring the World Cup home is Scotland's goal.

Chorus: Olé Olé, Olé Ola
We are gonna bring that World Cup back from over there.
(twice)

We've got Dalglish, Buchan and Macari
We've got Archie Gemmill, Johnston and McQueen
We've got big Joe Jordan waiting at the middle
And the best support this world has ever seen.

We've got Donachie, Rioch and Don Masson
We've got Andy Gray and Asa Hartford too
And with this lethal combination, it's a fair affirmation
That the World Cup will be ours at the end of June.

Repeat chorus

Oh, Brazil, this time, I don't think so
Holland without Cruyff just ain't the same
Germany we feel may be a challenge
The Italians can still play the game.

But there's really only one team in it
We'll be singing as we get off from the plane
We are bound for Buenos Aires, we don't care just what the fare is
Only wish we had Danny McGrain.

Repeat chorus

They'll be singing up in Aberdeen and Dundee
Glasgow will be reaching fever pitch
'Cos for a nation of five million, we're gonna really turn the heat on
'Cos we invented football anyway.

Repeat chorus to fade

4. Internal Affairs

Since MacLeod, Scotland has been led by men who have preached pragmatism, planned meticulously and studiously avoided over-exciting the public with promises they might not be able to fulfil. No matter the quality of the squad. Good, bad or indifferent. Against the experience of 1978, there is the World Cup of four years later, held in Spain. Scotland qualify and are led by MacLeod's successor, Jock Stein. It is flat. Deliberately so. Dave Narey's toe-poke puts Scotland ahead against Brazil and the Scots proceed to let Brazil back into the match, almost by way of apology, for having ideas above their station.

MacLeod's squad is impressive, even without the injured Danny McGrain. It remains impressive even without the fully fit central defender Gordon McQueen. It is still a pretty impressive squad despite the knowledge that Willie Donachie is going to be suspended for the opening match of the finals, against Peru in Córdoba.

Curiously, though, while he has a decent-enough squad of players to draw on, MacLeod has precious little to fall back on when it comes to his own back-room staff. He has an assistant, John Hagart, an ex-manager of Heart of Midlothian; a couple of trainers, Donny McKinnon from Partick Thistle and Hugh Allan from (and still at) Kilmarnock; and the bubbly character of masseur Jim Steel of Celtic. Technical director Andy Roxburgh (who, years later, is to become Scotland manager himself) is there but has more to do with the Scottish Football Association than with Ally's back-room team.

These days, it would be considered little more than a skeleton staff. Though a sizeable contingent of officials from the SFA and Scottish League travels with the squad, for the most part they are anonymous figures, save for their blazers, certainly as far as the players are concerned.

Alex Smith, then manager of Stirling Albion: Scotland have come a long way since 1978. When you think how few technical staff Ally had – basically John Hagart, his assistant, with a few medical people. I think we quickly learned how important it was to have a bigger back-room staff. We didn't anticipate the demands of the world's media. Ally was waylaid a lot, having to speak to the media so often

– he was such a big media attraction. But it meant we were even more short-handed working with the players and checking up on the opposition.

Only when things start to go awry do onlookers realise the paucity of MacLeod's own support network. MacLeod visibly loses weight in Argentina. The famous television pictures of him holding his head in his hands during the match against Iran reveal a man in despair. As the days wear on, the jaunty personality with a ready quip for the media – he enjoys the nickname 'Muhammad Ally' – becomes a withdrawn figure, increasingly defensive. At one press conference, as he surveys a mongrel dog sidling up towards him, he remarks, 'I think he is the only friend I have got left.' Twenty years on, he adds that the dog then went to bite him.

It is simultaneously funny and heart-rending. The timing is significant too, uttered with Scotland's second match, against Iran, still to come. On the day of the match itself, sympathetic journalists are reporting a man looking ill, almost having to rise from his sick bed to hit back at 'distortions, lies and innuendo'.

The players would say so, wouldn't they? Namely, that the squad was, for the most part, well-behaved. But there is so little evidence to suggest the contrary. Journalist and author William McIlvanney, following the team, writes of one player – identity a mystery – boasting to a group of women in an Alta Gracia café-bar the very night after arriving in the village that instead of chatting to supporters they might be better off speaking to the players. And of the same player later crudely asking McIlvanney if he has shagged the woman sitting nearest him. A hanging offence? Hardly.

Willie Donachie: There was drinking. I have never, ever had a drink within two nights before a game. I think there was probably too much drunk given it was a World Cup. But the players never went over the borderline, for example, two nights before a game. It was accepted then that drinking could go on when not preparing directly for a game. Now, players are expected to stop drinking completely during a tournament. The modern player is drinking less than his counterpart of 20 years ago. We didn't drink outrageous amounts – certainly not as much as the England team before Euro '96.

There is the odd womanising story, but it was very low key. I think a little bit went on but we were out in the wilderness, so it wasn't much. In any football squad there will be players on the look-out, but there wasn't much at all.

Obviously, as in any squad, there will be some players more dedicated than others, but the behaviour was, in general, very reasonable. Certainly, better behaved than many squads I've been involved in. I've seen lots worse on other occasions, lots worse.

Gordon McQueen: The behaviour in 1974 [the West Germany World Cup] was not much better. There was beer and schnapps being drunk there. But, there, the results were okay.

Boredom rather than deliberate misbehaviour is, however, a real problem. It doesn't help that the swimming-pool is out of action (no water) and the catering lacks variety (steak, chicken and soup pretty much morning, noon and night). Tom Forsyth is struggling with the time on his hands. But then he struggles with two-day trips for club matches in Europe. Don Masson likes the occasional autobiography but says he can hardly be expected to spend all day reading. Jim Blyth, ironically, has chosen George Orwell's *Animal Farm* for the trip. Gordon McQueen is one of the few who doesn't complain about boredom, but that's because he's wrapped up in himself, hoping to recover from injury in time to play and therefore constantly shuttling back and forth between the kitchen and the treatment room with bags of ice for his damaged knee. Bobby Clark also manages to avoid the worst of it by having to write a daily newspaper column. Bruce Rioch is keeping a private diary. It is often assumed that Macari was doing likewise. He says he isn't the type to keep a diary. Graeme Souness has a couple of Harold Robbins best-sellers and, according to his autobiography, the odd copy of *Playboy*. Martin Buchan suspects there might be a problem as soon as he steps off the plane at Córdoba and overhears a team-mate utter a disconsolate 'I'm bored' within minutes of arriving in Argentina. The media, too, has started picking up similar signals, admittedly well after Buchan's observation, but, still, well before Scotland line up against Iran. Scotland are clearly cracking up with one game played and two still to play; in other words, with qualification to the latter stages still a possibility.

Gordon McQueen: I liked Ally, got on fine with him. He stuck by me when he probably shouldn't have done. He always praised me highly in the newspapers. More often than not he would single me out. I would be loyal to Ally. There was a whole succession of things that made his job impossible but he wasn't entirely blameless.

He was cracking a bit under pressure, there was no question about that. I felt very sorry for him. He was in tears when he was there. I think when the stories got through about his house being attacked, it got too much. He broke down when a few of the lads were there. But the same fella made the Scottish Football Association a fortune and he might have got more backing. I mean, did everyone want Ally to say we had no chance? I think he just went for it and he got everyone, players as well, believing. The whole nation. It was a fantastic time in Scottish football – fantastic until the game started.

Joe Harper: We had a tennis court with no net or rackets. Eventually, we put a bit of string across it and found some rackets. Alan Rough and I played two of the guards and were beating them when they started to take the huff. We quickly scrapped the game because we didn't fancy arguing with a couple of guns. We had a swimming-pool with no water. I really think the 1978 World Cup was the competition which made it better for every Scotland World Cup team afterwards. We were bored, we had about 20 videos with us which, after about four days, everybody had seen. We had our wee bar where people had their coffee or coke and would play cards. The television stations were local ones and, in general, there was no entertainment. We had one game of golf about halfway through on a nine-hole course, which was pretty good. But, basically, we would get up for breakfast and then get on the bus for the journey to Córdoba where we did our training.

Bobby Clark: I wrote a weekly article for the Aberdeen Journals for eight or nine years. When I went out there, they asked if I would do a daily piece. I think that was one of the things that saved me. I had to find 600 words every day. I always wrote the articles myself – they were never ghosted. That gave me something to do. It was good because I think one of the problems the players had was finding something to do with their time. Not every player wants to read books; the television was in Spanish and there weren't many channels. It is always easy to be wise after the event, but I don't think the guys' time was well organised.

I was fine. I played golf, I played tennis, but not everyone likes those sports. Then again, you can't play golf or tennis close to game time. When you start off by losing your first match, doubts set in and that is when it is very important to have people's spare time occupied so they don't get homesick. It is easy to get homesick and I think that was one of the problems, especially when the media started concocting – in my opinion – a lot of nonsense.

I think a lot of rumours occurred because fans were mistaken for players. I thought it was one of the quietest trips I had ever been on with a Scottish team. I have nothing against having the odd Guinness, but on that trip, for some reason I don't know why, I never really took a beer. The only alcohol I actually had the whole time was celebrating Kenny Dalglish equalling Denis Law's international appearance record [of 55 caps, against Peru]. There was a whole group of players who just didn't drink. I think it was just orange juice for Stuart Kennedy's 25th birthday [on 31 May].

Ally was successful at Ayr United and again he was successful when he was at Aberdeen. He was a great motivator, but I don't think he had the experience of having boys together the length of time that he did. Remember, we had the Home Internationals first and then we were at home for a week and then we were away again. That's about five weeks together with one week's break. You have to work hard at keeping them active, how they are going to amuse themselves. If there's a golf course, then have little golf tournaments, play a 'Texas Scramble', where everybody has to play. Same if there is a tennis court. Make everyone participate.

The rooms were shared pretty much on a club-by-club basis. Myself and Stuart Kennedy from Aberdeen, Kenny Dalglish and Graeme Souness at Liverpool, and so on. It is the way things naturally go that the Anglos will congregate, same for the Rangers-Celtic players and also the same for the rest. I think nowadays there is more awareness about team-building and team-bonding. Having said that, there was very little discord.

The hotel in Alta Gracia was superb, the food was superb. The first time I experienced something like that was in 1967 when Aberdeen went on tour to Washington DC. We had ten weeks at the Hilton in Washington, went off in May and came back in July. The first week, we couldn't believe it. There we were, staying in the Hilton! By the third week, everyone was fed up with it, you were desperate for your ma's mince 'n' tatties.

So, at Alta Gracia, it was the same. If you went out for a meal with your wife and were served the food we got at Alta Gracia, you would say, 'Great meal'. But it got too much when it was every day. You could say we acted like spoiled boys, and maybe we did. But nowadays, what you would try and do is vary things, go to different restaurants, go on little bus rides around the place, try to keep things as fresh as possible.

Don Masson: It was just a joke. We would go 20 miles to the training camp, then back to the hotel, with nothing to do. We were promised tennis or a swimming-pool, anything just to pass the time, and there was literally nothing to do. The rooms were a shambles, dirty. It was a complete débâcle from start to finish. At the best of times, football is about wasting your life for 90 minutes every few days. In Argentina, we were bored mindless. I'm an active person, I need to be doing something. We would train for a couple of hours and then there was nothing for us to do. There was nothing to do at night. I used to love a game of backgammon, but you can't play that all the time.

There wasn't a sense of mutiny, but there *was* unrest. The good thing about the squad was that it had been together for about three years and the camaraderie was brilliant. There were no divisions among the players but there was unrest towards the committee. Not Ally – he had the sympathy of the players. But the SFA. I can't remember the players receiving – not for one minute – the kind of preferential treatment the members of the committee got. You might see them in the hotel corridors, but you wouldn't know any of them. For one thing, there were so many of them to know. They were faceless people. The only SFA person I knew was Ernie Walker [the secretary]. But all he would do was exchange pleasantries after a match.

The boredom is exacerbated by poor training facilities at The Sierras hotel. It is quickly decided to use facilities in Córdoba instead, meaning the squad has to endure a 40-minute bus journey before they can do any serious preparation. Television pictures of the training area at Alta Gracia show a pitch that is rough and worn. The sprinkling of a few grass seeds has failed to do its job. And there are those who are none too impressed by MacLeod's training methods.

Jim Blyth: I remember feeling his training methods left a lot to be desired when I attended my first training session with Scotland, prior to a friendly I played against Bulgaria at the start of 1978. We would have a full-scale practice match and every time he blew the whistle we would have to shoot in the other direction which meant, as a goalkeeper, sprinting 120 yards to play in the other goal, to be invariably met with the whistle being blown again. Maybe putting a forward immediately into defence had its value, but it didn't appeal to my thinking and did so even less as I got older and reflected on it.

Blyth has little to thank MacLeod for. He and John Robertson are the new boys in the squad, and he is anxious about being too pushy. That said, on one occasion, he is brave enough to warn John Hagart not to lay a finger on him as the assistant manager starts slapping other players on the back. He is also daft enough to go chasing a newspaper photographer out of an Alta Gracia café. Quiet and serious, you might say. But he has plenty to dwell on. He genuinely feels he should have been the first-choice goalkeeper, ahead of Alan Rough, and was wrongly blamed for an own-goal scored by Willie Donachie during the Home International match against Wales a couple of weeks previously.

Jim Blyth: Given the same circumstances against Wales, I would do exactly the same again. There were only a few minutes to go and I was running the clock down. I had given the ball to Stuart Kennedy, he gave it back to me, and I threw the ball from the far side of the box to Willie Donachie. But instead of controlling the ball and wasting a wee bit more time, he sent it to me with his wrong foot, first time, and screwed it straight into the bottom corner. I think that left a mark in Ally's mind – maybe put a doubt.

Willie Donachie: The ball came to me and I controlled it badly and ankled it in. It was nothing to do with Jim. I would dearly love to blame him, but I can't. It wasn't a matter of feeling silly. It was a cross between embarrassment, self-disgust and other things. All the players and the manager were brilliant about it. I got a lot of mail encouraging me. The last couple of minutes of the game I got the crowd on my back, but I can understand that. But then the reaction of the crowd during the next game against England was brilliant and made up for everything. I wanted to do well, obviously. But when I was in the dressing-room, I could hear them shouting my name, which takes some doing because, at Hampden, the dressing-rooms were right underneath the main stand and you don't normally hear the crowd. I was on a real high, a big adrenaline rush. Steve Coppell – he must have known there was no way he was going to have the beating of me. Because of this adrenaline rush, I could out-jump him, out-everything him.

It gets worse rather than better for Blyth. He breaks a curfew a couple of days before the game against Holland and appears to pay for it big-time. Blyth had felt he was in the running for a call-up. It doesn't happen. It appears to be linked to breaking the curfew. And when he returns to the UK, his career is blighted by injury – particularly to his back – which scuppers a transfer to Manchester United, keeps him out the game for months at a time and eventually forces him to retire from football at the relatively early age of 30.

Jim Blyth: When it got as far as the Holland game I felt in all honesty I should have been playing.

There was supposedly a curfew – which I was totally unaware of – and I was sitting on my own watching a video in the television room. And Ally walks in and tells me I should be in bed. He said, 'There is a curfew, you should be in your bed,' and I said, 'Okay,' and didn't think any more of it. It must have been half past ten at the latest. I didn't know about the curfew but I don't think there was proper organisation, from top to bottom.

So, after the Holland game, which I was on the bench for, we had a couple of drinks and our dinner and Ally happened to come across to me and Gordon McQueen and one or two others and he just says, 'You would have been playing today if you had not sat up and broken the curfew.' At that time, I was 23 and very new to the whole scene and it just broke me up straightaway. On reflection, I think he was covering his own back because he knew he should have played me in the first place and my staying up was just an excuse. If it hadn't been for the own-goal against Wales, he might have had enough confidence to put me in.

He looked across the table and just said it. And I just got up and walked away towards an exit with two glass doors. Accidentally, one of the doors smashed as I was shutting it behind me. I went up to my room and was just choked up. I'm thinking that was why I was dropped, because I had watched a *Morecambe and Wise* video. It was only later that I thought he was covering himself.

Throughout the World Cup, I felt I was better and I've said I was better ever since. Alan Rough was a part-time goalkeeper [this is not strictly true – for 13 years he was a full-time keeper with a part-time club, Partick Thistle] and it showed in his performances even though he did have some outstanding games. More often than not the goals he conceded were poor goals to let in. Had he been that good, why did one of the top teams in Scotland not go for him? I think, technically, he was very poor. His positional sense left a lot to be desired. On occasion, he could pull off a great save, but his overall knowledge let him down. We never spoke to each other about goalkeeping. I was a 23-year-old first-timer and I didn't think it was my job to start a discussion on goalkeeping.

Kenny Burns: [Regarding Jim Blyth and his supposedly ignoring a curfew] I think it is worse if you're tossing and turning in bed. We would go away with the gaffer, Cloughie [Brian Clough, manager at Nottingham Forest], and he would *make* us have a drink. Every time we went away, we would have a drink. You sleep better with a drink in you, whether it is one pint, two pints or whatever. We would be drinking till half past twelve before League Cup finals. We drank beer on the coach on the way to the European Cup game against Liverpool at Anfield.

Alan Rough: Other people thought it was a problem [not playing for a big club], moving from playing in front of a crowd of 2,000 at Partick Thistle to a crowd of 80,000 at an international. It wasn't a big problem for me because I could shut it out. It never, ever bothered me. People used to say I was really laid-back. That wasn't quite the case. I got nervous like everyone else, but could put on a front. But I didn't get too nervous. My first Scotland v England game was at Hampden in season 1975–76 and I remember being in the tunnel just before going on to the field, standing alongside Mick Channon, Trevor Brooking, Kevin Keegan and all those other England guys. And you know how much I was earning? £35 a week. And I was standing with these guys in that tunnel and thinking, 'What am I doing here?' And that's where I learned to shut out the distractions, to concentrate on being your own guy, there because you had been picked on merit.

Blyth's strength was his agility; he was light on his feet. If he had a weakness, it was dealing with players running in at him at close range. Rough was a great shot-stopper. He was not one for coming out to gather crosses – though with defenders such as Gordon McQueen operating just in front of him, that was barely necessary. Bobby Clark, the third goalkeeper in Argentina, feels there was little disharmony, that the three keepers worked well together, with him, patently Ally's third choice, cheerfully taking up a coaching role.

Bobby Clark: I think Ally knew I worked very well with the goal-keepers. Alan Rough, Jim Blyth and I were a really close group and I would like to think I supported them throughout the tournament. Everyone wanted to play, to be the number one guy, but I definitely found myself as the third goalkeeper. I trained hard, worked hard, and I didn't go there thinking it was a holiday. You always dream you'll get a chance. I think Ally had made up his mind that Roughie was his goalkeeper, so there was no point in me being picked for a Home International game, for example, and playing well and then confusing things.

I had been a regular with Tommy Docherty [manager until December 1972], who was replaced by Willie Ormond and whose first game was the SFA Centenary game in 1973, against England, where we got beaten 5–0. Willie dropped me after that but brought me back into the squad in 1975 against Spain although David Harvey actually played in goal. And that was me involved again.

But then Ally came in and I think he felt a bit duty-bound to keep selecting me. We didn't always see exactly eye to eye, though I must say I quite like Ally – he's not a bad lad. I had always been spoiled for coaches at Aberdeen. Eddie Turnbull was a tactical genius and then Jimmy Bonthrone had a really good knowledge of soccer. But Ally was very much a motivator through the media, which wasn't really my way. We never fell out but he was just different from the person who had been my mentor, Eddie Turnbull.

After that 1973 Centenary game, the whole of the back division was dropped. I remember Eddie Colquhoun, who never played for Scotland again, coming up to me after the game and saying, 'It was fun while it lasted. I got nine caps, nine more than I thought I would get.' A wee while afterwards, I got a card from Martin Buchan, who also played. It was signed 'Yours in jest, Martyr Buchan'. It read, 'Come in, Number One, your time is up.' It took a bit of time for Martin to be recalled. The whole lot of us were nailed to the cross. It was an awful night. It was played on a field that should never have been passed fit. I actually tried three different pairs of boots – I even retried them on through the game. The match would never have been played had it not been a friendly. I had lost two goals during the previous six or seven games. I hadn't touched the ball until we were 2–0 down. I think Martin got recalled because three central defenders had called off for a game against West Germany the following year and they had no choice but to take him.

Ally was my club manager at Aberdeen before he became the national manager. Willie Ormond had chosen the squad for the 1977 tour of South America. He called me up about it and asked if I would be interested, and I said I would love to — you don't get chances like that very often. And then, the next thing, Willie is out of the job and Ally, my club coach, is in it. He never put me out of the squad, but I always felt I was the third-choice goalkeeper, which was always disappointing because I felt I was playing better then than when I got the bulk of my caps.

5. Money, Money, Money

Team spirit is very much in the eye of the beholder, and while the Scotland squad has its tensions, how corrosive they are is impossible to tell. The evidence of the three games is far from conclusive, given the widely contrasting effort put in. The squad does well to avoid complete disintegration, given the barrage of abuse they come under; by the same token, however, they are too prone to internal division when they should have had one, and only one, goal in mind.

There is, of course, no telling how the atmosphere would have been lifted had the results been better at the start of the campaign; just as there is no telling how the morale of the squad was damaged by an increasing tendency by the media – mainly news journalists as opposed to sports writers – to report on alleged, often unsubstantiated, bad behaviour by the players.

What disharmony there is boils down to, mainly, two factors: bonuses and cliques.

Money being the 'root of all evil', it takes no time at all before the first wisps of controversy over the bonuses being offered by the SFA quickly escalate into a full-scale storm. When the players arrive in Argentina, there is confusion as to what exactly is on offer. Instead of the matter being fully resolved before departure for Argentina, it remains a running sore during the first days of the squad's stay at its HQ in Alta Gracia.

With some players pulling in one direction and others pulling in the opposite direction, a few feel the confusion is a sign of poor organisation. And when bonus details are finally revealed, they are doubly aggrieved, believing their status as professional footballers is being insulted. Equally, many couldn't care less about the bonuses; simply playing for Scotland is reward enough.

Lou Macari: At the time, the financial rewards in England were greater than they were in Scotland. And in England they were laid out on paper, in black and white, before you took part in any competition. At this World Cup, it was a case of 'You'll be well and truly looked after. You don't need to worry and if you do the business, you will be rewarded.' Everyone marched off to the World

Cup believing that, unlike the previous World Cup where there had been trouble over the size of the bonuses, this time around there would be no problem. But there was nothing on paper.

I think the figures started to come to light after Ally was put under a wee bit of pressure by one or two members of the players' committee to come up with more details. It was a terrible disappointment. They were poor. There was, obviously, a wonderful bonus if you won the World Cup; well, actually, even that wasn't that fantastic.

I wasn't an agitator. Someone told me what the bonuses were and I said they were crap. I've got my opinions on most things. I don't need to be led by anyone else. I didn't think it was any big deal voicing my opinions. I wasn't one of the players' committee, which included, obviously, the captain Bruce Rioch. I don't remember many meetings about bonuses. I wouldn't say it was an issue that divided the squad. It was an issue that the majority of the squad found quite unbelievable. That we were playing in the biggest competition in the world and all we were being told was, 'Don't worry lads, you will be well and truly looked after,' instead of having the details down in black and white.

I think Bruce having to approach Ernie Walker about bonuses at all was the fault of the SFA because they hadn't actually told the players what the bonuses were. Bruce's representations were perfectly normal under the circumstances. He was being told by the players, 'You'd better find out what the bonuses are.'

It was a niggle. The method of going to a major competition, the method of the players' rewards, which is normal for any competition, the methods of doing it were slightly abnormal in this competition.

Don't forget that, at the end of the day, you were there at a World Cup, you were delighted you were there.

You would be clutching at excuses if you said a dispute over bonuses was the reason for the way we performed. We went there as a team that supposedly had a real chance of doing something when we should have gone as a nation just delighted to be taking part.

I think a bigger problem than the bonuses was the way the players' pool was being divided [before the finals started]. I don't think there was an equal split. You had some players making more personal appearances than others – especially if they were based near Glasgow where a lot of the build-up functions were taking place – and making a bit extra because of it. I think that caused a few resentments. But I don't think anyone resented at all what Ally MacLeod might have made out of the competition – I certainly didn't. I think it was a case of him deserving whatever he got. I liked the fella. I thought he was a genuine man who was trying to do a good job but sometimes didn't say the right things, like we all do. We all sometimes say the wrong things.

Martin Buchan: Lou and I were room-mates and got on well. For ten years we stripped next to each other at Old Trafford. It doesn't take much to move to the other side of a dressing-room if you don't like somebody. Was our room a ferment of rebellion? I wouldn't say we didn't discuss things, but I can't remember it being much. I was there to play for my country, I wasn't there to worry about bonuses. In the '74 World Cup, we had a wrangle over a kit endorsement deal. But I can't remember discussing bonuses in '78. When I was at Manchester United, I lived on the basis of the basic wage. So if I got a win bonus, that is how I treated it. I didn't build my lifestyle around the expectation of bonuses. Maybe that was my Aberdonian upbringing. Any bonuses I did get would go into the pension scheme, into savings. Maybe I said to Lou, 'Aye, you're right,' but then the SFA in these days were not renowned for throwing money about.

Ally MacLeod: I can't remember anyone, at any time before we left, asking what the bonuses were. They had nothing to do with me – they were an SFA matter. I could only fight for bonuses. They were outwith my control. Not until we got there was the matter raised. I said, 'Are you not better to win the section first and then you will have a strong hand to negotiate with?' But a few of the players – not them all – argued the opposite and thought it was better to know in advance what they were playing for.

Sandy Jardine: I was on the players' committee to look after the players' pool and make representations on behalf of the players. MacLeod thought the bonuses situation was sorted out before we left, but it wasn't. It should have been sorted out long before we left for Argentina; we should have had everything out in the open when we were in Scotland, had our debate there. We were dealing with Willie Harkness, the SFA president, over a situation that was, to be honest, very poor. People say, 'You should be happy playing for Scotland for free,' but the bonus system is part and parcel of the game. But Willie Harkness was from Queen of the South. I don't suppose Queen of the South paid much in the way of bonuses. The players made their point but it should never have got to that. Though Lou Macari might have been louder than most about it, he had exactly the same sentiments as most of the squad. The bonus being offered showed disrespect; it was a slight.

Ernie Walker: I have to concede we were probably a bit naïve about the bonuses; we were naïve about a lot of things, I suppose. It was the first time many of us had been involved in a World Cup. We lived and we learned.

In subsequent World Cups, we issued written details of the money on offer. We did ask MacLeod before we left to convey to the players our thinking on bonuses. And to the best of our knowledge that had been done – until we arrived in Argentina and players started complaining.

In subsequent World Cups, we drew up the bonuses package – in consultation with the coach – and explained it to the players well in advance of departure. And if anyone didn't like what was on offer, they were entitled to stay at home; we weren't going to start bartering. And, to be fair to players, I never ever heard another word about money in all the time I was at the SFA thereafter, and that was until 1990. There was never ever another meeting of players talking about money.

Graeme Souness: Obviously, there is blame in both camps, both the SFA and the players. I think there was a feeling that the SFA could be held to ransom a wee bit, and I felt that money should not have been the most important thing at that time. But in certain people's eyes, that was a reason to complain a great deal.

It is two players per room and most pairings are on a club-by-club basis: Macari and Buchan; Kenny Dalglish and Graeme Souness; Joe Jordan and Gordon McQueen; Stuart Kennedy and Bobby Clark. By necessity, there is some mixing. Coventry City's Jim Blyth shares with fellow goalkeeper Alan Rough from Partick Thistle. Willie Johnston from West Bromwich Albion and Don Masson from Derby County are billeted together. So too are Derek Johnstone from Rangers and Joe Harper from Aberdeen. Some of the mixes work well. Johnstone and Harper are still close. Ditto for Johnston and Masson although – for no particular reason, nothing sinister – they have not spoken to each other for 20 years; indeed, not since

Johnston was dramatically whisked away from the team camp before Scotland had played their second game.

If the dispute over the bonuses illustrates anything, it is that the squad is criss-crossed by tiny fault lines: Anglo-Scots versus home-based players; the glamour club versus the less glamorous. On such occasions, team spirit is only as strong as the weakest link.

Kenny Burns: I roomed with Robbo [John Robertson], who was unbelievable. He was one of those people who, if it was sunny in the morning, would close the curtains and go back to bed. And when he got up in the morning, he would lift his legs over the bed, put his feet down and he'd go straight into his socks, shoes, trousers, shirt, tie, everything, and pull everything up, like a big zip. That's Robbo. He would get up in the morning and go, 'Urgh, oh sunshine, I'm away to my bed.' He kept everyone amused with his [love of] Clint Eastwood and Roxy Music.

I remember trying to light this thing in the bloody room to keep insects away but I think Robbo got bitten all over his arse. Right enough, it was some size of an arse.

I enjoyed the World Cup. It was an experience. If you were a kid and somebody told you, 'You will play in the World Cup but you'll have to sleep in a rough room,' what would you do? Would you care a shit about it? People get above themselves: 'I'm so and so, I can't be having this.' You should be grateful, playing on the world stage. I loved playing for Scotland. My brothers would always be there. I only wish my mum could have seen me play, but she died when I was very young. I don't think there was anyone prouder than me when it came to playing for Scotland. I don't think I ever called off. I would have walked to a Scotland squad session with a broken leg. Scottish players play from the heart. You go down the street and there would be wee women in their peenies [aprons] saying, 'Gie 'em one, get stuck intae them,' and you would feel ten feet tall. You don't get bad teams playing in the World Cup. Everybody is laughing about Peru and Iran, saying, 'How can you get beat or draw against them?' They were good teams. We were a good team, but we didn't play to our potential. It happens.

Ian Archer, journalist: The *Express* deal involved these roadshows and muggins was the MC when we went to Springburn [in Glasgow] one night. There are hard men up there. We had bits and pieces of film and Ally was also talking and this squad came in at the back, half a dozen hard cases. I clocked them but Ally hadn't. And one of them said, 'I have a question to ask Mr MacLeod. Are you going to take Kenny Burns to the World Cup?' and Ally begins: 'Um, eh, we're quite well off for central defenders,' and I quickly write down on a piece of paper, 'These are Kenny's pals,' and Ally, quick as flash, continued, 'But on the other hand . . .'

Kenny Burns: At Birmingham City I got a lot of bookings for dissent. I played up front and if they put the ball in the box I could score. I'm a great believer in my own ability. Nobody could out-jump me, I could strike the ball with either peg, I was comfortable on both feet. So put the ball in the box. If it isn't coming into the box I get frustrated and I get bookings for dissent.

So, suddenly, I'm a wild boy. I liked to go dog-racing. My brothers kept greyhounds when I was growing up. I got married when I was too young. I like wedding cake – I've been married three times. Peter Taylor [with Brian Clough at Nottingham Forest] followed me round the dog tracks and saw I was only betting two quid, three quid, maybe a fiver. So I was signed by Nottingham Forest. The gaffer never, ever said to me, 'This is your last chance.'

I came back from a holiday on the Saturday afternoon, met him at night. Next morning, he took me to a sweet-pea flower show – me, a Glasgow boy at a sweet-pea show! – had a meal, then went to the ground in the afternoon, signed, was told to get my hair cut, and got a bottle of champagne out.

Photographs next morning. And then I never saw him for ten days after that. Ten days training and I had no idea which position I was playing, because I had been playing striker at Birmingham, alongside Trevor Francis. Though we had a few arguments, Trevor and me – because I thought he was too greedy at times – we certainly banged them in there. Nobody really told me I would be playing at the back at Forest. Played a couple of training games at the back. Then we flew out to Germany for a pre-season tour.

We arrived at the hotel and there was Cloughie giving the room keys out. I played a game at the back and, after a couple of matches, I was dropped. I got drunk that night, spewed my guts up in front of him and Mrs Clough. Got carried out by John McGovern and Larry Lloyd. Next day, I went and apologised. I said to the boss, 'Can I see you?' His wife was there and she was about to leave and I said, 'It's you as well, Mrs Clough.' I apologised and Cloughie said to me, 'Just as well. Because if you hadn't come to see me you were on the first plane home.' And we got on well thereafter.

Stuart Kennedy: During the Home Internationals, we stayed at Dunblane Hydro [hotel] and there we mapped out what we were going to be doing in Argentina. And we had a meeting about the bonuses the players would be getting if we qualified for the second phase. And it was all sorted out. Everybody knew what was going on – it was all explained what we would get. And nothing was said by any of the players. Twenty-two players sitting there, listening to the manager explaining things at Dunblane.

But when we go to Argentina, people start coming out of the woodwork, muttering that they are not happy about the bonuses. They never said anything when we were on Scottish soil. They wait until the manager is over in Argentina, obviously more vulnerable, and they start to mutter they are not happy about the bonuses, they are not happy about this, they are not happy about that, trying to put the manager under pressure, undermining the whole situation. There we were, supposedly to play football for our country – some of us would happily have played for nothing – and there was all this upheaval.

I am a team-spirit person and I thought ours was very poor. We were there to play football and we were getting dragged down by a dispute over money. It was disgusting. They were acting like toe-rags. I hoped the situation would go away, but it never did. I would have liked to have said something, but it wasn't that easy. I was not a big-name player, so it wasn't as if I could pipe up and say, 'Excuse me chaps, I'm not awfully sure . . .'

I didn't have too many conversations with too many people there. I roomed with Bobby Clark and had many a long conversation with him. I got on well with Jim Blyth. I had a few good conversations with Graeme Souness. He gave me useful advice about starting a pension. But the rest? Nothing. Even Joe Harper, a team-mate at Aberdeen. Lucky if we exchanged two sentences. For a couple of days I was ill, confined to my bed with some sort of 'Montezuma's Revenge'. Only the doc, Bobby and Jim visited and Bobby could hardly avoid it because he was my room-mate. It was a squad of cliques. I was happy to sit beside anybody in the bus, it didn't bother me who I was with. But, at the same time, you are not going to go cap in hand hoping you might be admitted into somebody's clique. One snub and that's enough for me.

We should have been pulling in the one direction. I didn't play for a fashionable club but nobody put more commitment into their club football than I did. They might have been *as* committed but nobody was *more* committed. But there were a lot of egos and a lot of 'Which team does he play for?' kind of thing. I think if you're with the Old Firm or with a big English side, there is an assumption that, by definition, you must be a better player than if you play for Aberdeen or Partick Thistle.

We had a training match and somebody hit the ball out for about 20 yards. Now I'm the sort of player who will fetch the ball without thinking twice about it. So there's me running after the ball and Archie Gemmill, who has stood watching me do it, then insists he, not I, begins our build-up from the back. But the bottom line on that one is that the reason the ball ended up so far out of the park was because it was Bruce Rioch who had hit the ball and he has some shot. He runs in on goal, Archie makes no effort to make the tackle and from six yards out Bruce blasts the ball past Bobby Clark in goal. Bobby says, 'Archie, can you no' make a tackle?' And Archie says – I quote verbatim – 'If that had been Shilts [Peter Shilton of England], he would have saved it.' Helpful I don't think.

Gordon McQueen: Unrest? There were certainly people not playing who thought they should have been. But there were no serious personality clashes insofar as one player couldn't suffer another. I don't think it was a squad that sniped at each other. But, equally, I don't think it was the happiest squad ever. For example, there were some players who were money-mad. And then you had other players who couldn't give a shit about money, about the bonuses involved. There were all these meetings about money, money, money, which should have been sorted out before we left. Some players were seriously into that and others weren't. Even that causes unrest.

Certainly, there were some players not playing who felt they should. The problem for a manager of an international team is that he can't say to players, 'Your chance will come, maybe next week', as you can at club level. You're talking about a World Cup. It's a once-in-a-lifetime thing, and there aren't that many players – Jordan, Dalglish, but not many – who get the chance to play in two or even three World Cups.

So, once the chance is gone, it's gone. And players know that; they're desperate to get involved. Therefore, it is very difficult for a manager. If you're not in the 16 it is a nightmare. If you are in the stand, you just want to go home. Because you're not part of it, not part of the press coming to interview you, the photographers and the fans. You feel like an outsider looking in. Those six players, they just want to go home. No question about it.

Unless the team is basically picking itself then players will think they have a wee chance of getting a place. In Argentina there were places up for grabs. Nobody could say for sure, 'That is the 11 who are going to start a game.' Had we gone to the World Cup with the side that qualified, people might have said, 'Fine, I understand. That's the back four – Donachie, McQueen, Forsyth and McGrain; that's your midfield – Hartford, Masson, Rioch and Johnston; that's your front two – Jordan and Dalglish.'

In that case, the other players in the squad might have said, 'Well, if one of them got injured or a couple of bookings, then perhaps I might get in, but otherwise I'm not going to raise my hopes.' But it wasn't like that when we went to the finals. There were a lot of question-marks, especially with me getting injured and Willie Donachie being suspended for the first game. Was it going to be Kennedy or Jardine to replace Willie? Who was going to come in for me – Buchan or Burns? Was it going to be Jordan playing up front or Derek Johnstone who did well during the Home Internationals? There were a lot of strong personalities and smashing players not playing.

Don Masson: It was only during the World Cup that we didn't have a good time. The rest of the time we used to have a great time. At Dunblane Hydro, it used to be great. We would have the odd game of golf, and the camaraderie was excellent. Rod Stewart would fly up, have a game of snooker, play in a five-a-side. It was superb. When we went to Brazil in 1977, it was fantastic. The Copacabana, Sugar Loaf mountain. Playing tennis through the night. Never went to sleep. Drank all the way through.

Willie Donachie: There were a lot of strong friendships made through Scotland and consolidated in Argentina. For example, Asa [Hartford] and me have had a friendship for years which will continue, I suppose, to the end of our lives. There was a bit of bitching when things started to go wrong, mainly aimed at the manager and the SFA. Going away for a long time together is a big strain and when things started going wrong, it was a double strain. We were hearing a lot of newspaper reports from home, of players criticising things. I think it might even have reached the stage when there was a ban on people talking to the media. We went out there together and we should have stuck together, in good and bad times. The good teams do.

The symptoms of the bonuses dispute are undeniable. Division, de-motivation, distraction, disruption. Periodically, deputations are dis-patched by the players to speak further with MacLeod. The manager periodically speaks to SFA officials. It is rumoured that MacLeod is on the verge of handing in his resignation because of the dispute. He issues a denial at a press conference. The SFA president, Willie Harkness, tries to restore order by addressing the players in person. In total, it is a fiasco. Entirely predictable and completely unnecessary. A credibility gap soon emerges. On television, Ernie Walker says that if the players succeed, they can expect to be as well rewarded as any European team; again on tele-vision, Lou Macari claims that had the English been there, they would have treated their players far better. Clearly, the truth is buried somewhere between claim and counter-claim. It becomes a quadrangular contest. In one corner, the SFA; in another, the players seeking greater recompense; in yet another, the players irritated by the players seeking greater recompense; and, finally, MacLeod shuttling back and forth between the parties, not entirely neutral, clearly not giving the players all the information they require, yet at the same time trying to maintain calm.

Besides the bonuses, the commercial spin-offs from the World Cup also have the potential to split the camp. A tidy sum awaits players and manager alike from adverts, endorsements and personal appearances. The convention is that the so-called 'players' pool' is divided equally, but it doesn't stop MacLeod being accused of profiting ahead of the rest. As the World Cup captures the imagination of a nation, the MacLeod seal of approval is lent to numerous products. He has contracts tied up with both Scottish Television and the *Scottish Daily Express* newspaper.

He rebuts the allegations. In his newspaper column on 10 May, he writes: '£100,000? I don't blame people coming up with such a ridiculous figure, I only wish it were true,' adding that 95 per cent of the items bearing his 'endorsement' are unofficial. He says a lot of his public appearances are for free – because he likes doing them or they're for charity – and he resents the piracy of his name. Legal action, he assures his readers, has already been taken against some parties. Nonetheless, his agent estimates it would cost a prohibitively expensive £20,000 to pursue every pirate through the courts.

Ernie Walker, SFA secretary (in a report submitted to the SFA international committee, 10 July 1978): In the light of past experience, the Association determined, as soon as we qualified to participate in Argentina, that the main area of potential discontent between the Association and the players, money, would be settled long before the party left this country. There are two sources of income available to the players. Firstly, there is the remuneration from the commercial activities of the players' pool, and secondly, the fees and bonuses paid by the Association.

It was made clear to the players, through the team manager, that all of the commercial activities of the pool must cease prior to the departure for Argentina, and to the best of my knowledge there was no difficulty in Argentina insofar as this aspect of things was concerned. The latest information quoted to me by International Image Consultants, who act for the players in these matters, is that the pool has earned £145,000 to date, with further royalty payments to come.

The Association determined some time before our departure that, in addition to the normal match fee of £100 and the normal bonus of £100 per point, certain incentive payments would be made available to the players. These payments were to come directly from Association funds, plus the transfer to the players of sums due to the Association under the terms of the playing strip contract. When put together, they give the following bonus sums which would have become available to the players, depending on results. It is as well that these figures should be quoted here in view of the erroneous accounts which have appeared in various quarters: To reach the second round: a total of £40,000; to finish fourth: £75,000; to finish third: £95,000; to finish second: £120,000; to win the World Cup: £210,000.

The team manager was instructed to make these figures known to his players at the first opportunity, which would, of course, have been when they gathered for the British International Championship [Home Internationals]. It is fair to say, however, that a measure of uncertainty relating to tax matters clouded this aspect of affairs at the time. The outcome was that whilst the committee and the administration were of the opinion that the manager had given the players the necessary details, subsequent events proved that not to be the case, as certain players, after arriving in Argentina, claimed only to have a very sketchy idea of what their rewards might be. It is evident now, with hindsight, that it would have been preferable had the administration approached the players directly and provided each of them with written details of the incentives. In that way, the committee's policy which had been formulated in the light of past experiences – and which was that any player who was not satisfied with the financial terms should stay at home – could have been carried out effectively. Traditionally, over the years since the advent of team managers, there has built up a hesitance on the part of the administration to have much in the way of direct, official contact with players, for fear of being seen to trespass on the manager's preserves, and the practice has been to communicate with the players, once they have come together, only through the manager.

It came as a considerable surprise to the office-bearers and to me when, after only two days in Argentina, the team manager intimated that the players were requesting a meeting with the president and the secretary in order to discuss money. The request was refused, on the grounds that all money matters had been settled and that there was nothing to discuss. A few days later, when the office-bearers and the secretary returned to the camp after attending the FIFA Congress in Buenos Aires, the team captain, Bruce Rioch, approached me to make the same request again. Initially, I told him that I was not prepared to discuss the subject, or for that matter any other official business, with him, as his contact with me should be through the team manager, and that for the two of us to become engaged in business discussions would serve only to undermine the authority of the manager. He agreed that that would certainly be so but went on to say that he was speaking to me with the full consent and approval of Mr MacLeod. On hearing this, I agreed to listen to what he had to say which was, in effect, that the players had only the vaguest notions about what the bonus payments were to be. He indicated that only a few players were voicing discontent, albeit that the opinions of these few were having a disruptive effect upon the others, and that he, personally, did not desire a meeting. I advised him that I would convey his remarks to the office-bearers and expressed the opinion that it was unlikely that they would depart from the position which they had already taken. In the event, when I spoke to the office-bearers, that is what they decided.

The defeat by Peru and the Willie Johnston affair [when the player was sent home in disgrace for testing positive for substance misuse] had such a depressing effect upon everyone that the president [Willie Harkness] came to the conclusion, and the other office-bearers agreed, that the morale in the camp was so low that it was imperative that he depart from normal custom and speak officially to the players, not particularly to discuss money matters but to try to get them into the proper frame of mind for the match with Iran, albeit that he appreciated that once he was face to face with the players, it was inevitable that money would be discussed. The meeting was duly held and after the president had made an impassioned plea to the players to get their heads up and tackle the remaining matches in the spirit expected of Scottish players, the first questions about bonuses were asked. At this point, the president asked the secretary to detail the various figures to the players. Not all of them reacted with enthusiasm. Four or five spoke out in terms of disagreement and their various complaints were answered – whether or not to their satisfaction is hard to say. The majority were silent and presumably, therefore, had no complaint. A few made it quite evident to the writer, by their expressions and muttered comments, that they wanted no part of the complaints and that they had little time for their self-appointed spokesmen. It would be wrong to give the impression that the mood of the meeting was truculent and aggressive. There were certainly strong expressions of opinion from both sides but at the end of the day it probably did more good than harm. If nothing else, it familiarised the players with the financial position – which should have been done, as has been said earlier, before the party left Scotland. There was no further talk about money during the trip.

The media soon latches on to the fact that all is not well within the camp and that, typically, money is at the heart of much of it. On 9 June – midway between the games against Iran and Holland and a couple of days after the Harkness address – the *Daily Record* declares: 'Exclusive: the Big Cash Row Between the SFA, Ally and the Team', claiming that the players will receive less than £5,000 each for winning the World Cup, representing something of a letdown given they were initially under the impression the amount would be closer to £25,000, the figure quoted in the paper's edition of 29 May when it states: 'All along, the SFA and the team boss, Ally MacLeod, insisted they wanted every matter connected with cash settled before the hard work began. It has been done, and it has been done smoothly. In fact, the bonus offered by the Scots' soccer bosses is as high as any in the tournament. It shows that the SFA have grown up in world football terms and demonstrates once again that this Scotland squad is better prepared than the one in 1974.'

Come 9 June, it is the paper's understanding that for the first three opening games, there is a pool of £15,000 to be shared by the 22 players, i.e. £680 a man. And should Scotland reach the last eight, the pool is raised to £30,000, i.e. £1,363 each, and thereafter to £50,000 and £100,000 for appearances in the semi-final and final respectively. It is also the paper's understanding that the players' pool from advertising and commercial activities stands at £200,000, i.e. less than £10,000 each. In the event, they are not that far off the official figures quoted in Ernie Walker's report.

In time, the SFA accounts are published, and they show that, compared to £7,935 accrued from representative matches in the year ending 31 December 1977, the figure for the year ending 31 December 1978 is £280,174. And specifically from the World Cup, £219,255 is further added to the coffers.

Bobby Clark: I was excited to be part of a World Cup. To be part of a World Cup is a dream for most Scottish boys and that was the way I looked at it. It was a great opportunity. When I managed New Zealand and we went on a tour of South America ourselves, we were up front with the boys about the money and told them, 'This is what the association has got.' Nobody was going to refuse to come because they wanted more money. You're travelling around, you're treated like VIPs, you're playing and around the sport you love. I wish I could get the same chance again – I would go as the boot boy. I would pay my own fare. Look at all the fans who spent fortunes getting across to Argentina.

6. The Fourth Estate

Scotland gripped by a dispute over bonuses! It makes good copy for the press. But in the scheme of things, it is a relatively late-breaking story. Already, the Scottish camp and the media – at least certain sections of the media – are at loggerheads and it doesn't make a pretty sight. That's how it is with relationships built on mutual use. It is great at the start but when it turns sour somebody always gets hurt. What did Scotland expect? Love?

It isn't just the friendly sports hack from back home who is interested in the Scotland story. There are also foreign journalists and news reporters, relatively unknown quantities whose behaviour cannot be so easily predicted. The camp feed the press with great stories and hope it will end there. They have an approachable, highly quotable manager but his 24-carat hyperbole has some journalists coming back for more instead of purring obediently. The news presence during the 1974 World Cup was nowhere near as big.

It isn't just MacLeod. He is more of a symbol. The most vocal, perhaps. It is all-embracing. And then it goes pear-shaped. The frenzy takes on a nasty edge. The media do what the media do. Nothing personal, purely business.

It is the nature of these things that it is impossible to identify who started what and when. Scotland could have gone all coy when they qualified and they might still have had massive attention heaped upon them. They are, after all, the UK's sole representatives in the competition. England had lost out on goal difference to Italy in Group Two of the qualifiers, with both sides playing six, winning five and losing one. Wales had finished bottom of the three-team group won by Scotland, while Northern Ireland finished third in their four-team section, lagging behind Holland and Belgium in Group Four.

And they are, after all, a good-looking side, positively dripping with stars. As Lou Macari says to a television camera at the end of the tournament – albeit while criticising the way the trip has been organised – the Scots players have every reason to believe they are better than their English counterparts. Liverpool's Graeme Souness and Kenny Dalglish have just won European Cup winners' medals (the pair linking up to score the winner against Belgian side Bruges). Kenny Burns, Archie Gemmill and John Robertson have helped Brian Clough's Nottingham Forest secure the English League championship. And, in Scotland, Tom Forsyth, Sandy Jardine and Derek Johnstone have assisted Rangers to the Treble. Also, three players – Souness, Gordon McQueen and Joe Jordan – have each been recently transferred for British record fees.

In the run-up to the tournament, there are good vibes about the squad, a glow of good fortune that draws people in. Charisma? Undoubtedly. During the final two qualifying matches – against Czechoslovakia and Wales – the team enjoys considerable slices of good luck to win 3–1 and 2–0. The Midas touch stays with them in the finals draw itself. Peru and Iran – two relatively minor sides – are drawn in their four-team group.

Scotland ride their luck, ride their luck, ride their luck . . . and then it's gone. Suddenly, there are doubts. And suddenly it becomes okay to voice them. For some, it's probably pay-back time, from the moment MacLeod agreed to an exclusive column for *The Express* newspaper. For others, it is just a natural herd instinct at work. It's important in many cases to separate the straight sports story (critical or not) from the rest.

Some doubts pre-date the departure for Argentina. The form of both the captain and vice-captain, Bruce Rioch and Don Masson, is open to question. Both are in dispute with their manager, Tommy Docherty, at Derby County. They are put on the transfer list but MacLeod refuses to reconsider their inclusion. He says it is how they play for Scotland that matters, not what is happening at Derby.

> *Ally MacLeod*: I've never had any regrets sticking with Don and Bruce in the midfield. Don was probably one of the best players in the squad, was a magnificent passer of the ball. And for a leader of men, I looked through them all, and Bruce was a great choice. He was a smashing bloke, very popular with all the players, and if there was ever a problem he would always come and have a chat with me.
>
> You can't always anticipate how things will work out. Take Archie Gemmill. I don't think he felt he would be picked for Scotland to go to the World Cup and it turns out he was probably our best player. It wasn't just the goal he scored against Holland. He was outstanding in his performance all the time. I believe he came home an absolute hero, in the sense that he played far better than anyone could have expected of him. And I would say, honestly, he wouldn't have been my first choice in that position, but I saw him in training and kept my eye on him when he started to look good.

There are rumours of players misbehaving at the squad's base in Dunblane prior to departure for Argentina. There are anxieties about the way the side is playing – and failing to win – during the Home Internationals. There are fears that the hugely significant Gordon McQueen may not be fit in time to play in Argentina.

And no sooner have the players tested the springiness of their mattresses at their Argentinian HQ in Alta Gracia than the first whiff of scandal is presented to the media on a plate. For the local press it is manna from heaven. If they don't begin with a premeditated agenda to perpetuate the stereotype of the radge, drunken Scot, they soon take up the challenge. All that has happened is that three players are caught taking a prohibited short-cut back to base. It seems harmless enough but is nonetheless granted considerable column inches.

The trio have been granted permission to walk into town. They return via the local casino. It sounds grander than it is. It is not Monte Carlo. It is barely a spit 'n' sawdust bar where a few pesos can be gambled on a roulette wheel and a player can feel like a king with the equivalent of a fiver in his back pocket. But apply a tabloid spin to the words 'casino' and 'gun-point' and the minor infringement that is committed by Sandy Jardine, Willie Johnston and Alan Rough turns into James Bond meets the Cuban Missile Crisis.

What they should have done, on leaving the casino, is walk around the perimeter of the hotel grounds to re-enter via the security gate. It seems a simple decision at the time: either a ten-minute walk to the gate or a quick vault over a fence. They take the short-cut. They are confronted by an armed guard. The players have yet to receive their accreditation passes. The guard can hardly speak English. The media – granted, not all – have a field day. There hasn't been too much by way of moderation these last few months.

The players say it was a wee small fence. Maybe even a piece of string. Gordon McQueen says that because he was so preoccupied with recovering from his knee injury, he didn't even know of the incident until he returned home and caught up with the papers.

Depending on which newspaper report you read, the fence is variously eight-foot-high, made of barbed wire and electrified. And Derek Johnstone and Asa Hartford are victims of mistaken identity.

Alan Rough: We were told to go out and mingle. There was no problem doing that. A few of us just got a bit lost coming back. We took a short-cut, over a wee hedge or something. It was to save us walking all the way around the compound to go through the main gate. Of course, a boy stopped us with a machine-gun and asked who we were. We told him who we were and that was it, fine. I don't know how it got picked up by the media. The next I heard about it was that it had supposedly been on ITN. You were getting the newspapers about two or three days delayed. But it got to the stage where you were frightened to open the papers up. If you weren't in the first three pages, you breathed a sigh of relief.

Sandy Jardine: Because of the threat of terrorism, there was a lot of security, but it was patchy. There was a ten-foot-high fence at the front and a check-in. We called it Stalag 13. But then there was a wee wall at the back. Mind you, even the gate at the front didn't stop the odd supporter getting into the hotel by wearing a Scotland top and calling himself 'Lou Macari'. On our first night, a few of us climbed over the wall at the back after having been out for a walk into town. It was just to save a bit of time. An armed guard stopped us, only stopped us. And we thought nothing more after our identities were confirmed.

Next day, Ally makes a joke out of it at the press conference and people interpret it as a sign that the players are going out drinking every night. All Ally was trying to do was point out how good the security was. We could have walked round to the front, but we didn't. We went for a walk and looked into the local casino, if you could call it that. What's the first thing you think when you hear the word 'casino'? Monte Carlo, chandeliers, the in-crowd. We went into this 'casino' in Alta Gracia. I kid you not, it was basic, like a bingo hall. We went for a walk, put our heads round the door of this supposed casino to see what was going on. We were just curious.

We only nipped over a low wall, not pole-vaulted it or dug a tunnel as some papers had you believe. The guards in Argentina were armed, but that wasn't unusual. There were armed guards during the 1974 World Cup with whom we had a good relationship. If ever we went shopping, they would come with us, carrying their little briefcases containing a sub-machine-gun. They showed them to us. Security was very tight in 1974. It wasn't that big a deal about being stopped. The big deal was the media hyping the story afterwards. It sounds funny now, but at the time, we couldn't get out of Argentina quick enough.

Derek Johnstone: As soon as they heard it was Roughie [Alan Rough], there was the automatic assumption he was with Derek Johnstone, when it was actually Willie Johnston. Roughie, Joe Harper and I hung around together. We were nicknamed 'The Three Musketeers'. I very nearly sued over that. It was wrong and you had to think of the implications back home. My girlfriend was asking, 'What are you doing jumping over fences? What are you up to over there?'

Asa Hartford: I didn't vault any wall. But I did go into the casino, like a lot of players, and we got a taxi back because the journey to the front of the hotel seemed so far away.

Joe Harper: We arrive at the press centre to get our accreditation. And there are these lovely, beautiful typists and lovely, beautiful telephonists. And you would work your way along this desk, giving your name and country, virtually giving them your fingerprints, and eventually they would take a picture of you to be used in your pass. And while you were waiting for your official badge being made up, you hung around a cafeteria for about 20 minutes.

So, while we are doing that, Sandy Jardine, Asa Hartford and Willie Johnston are sitting at one of the tables, a small table for three guys, drinking their Cokes. And this guy comes in and says to Ally MacLeod, 'I work for *El Grafico*, the biggest paper in Argentina, can I have picture of your players?' and Ally says, 'Go on.'

So he goes and gets two of the girls over so the photo is player-girl-player-girl-player. And he takes the picture and nothing else is thought about it. This is meant to be the Scotland team meeting the local people of Córdoba. Fine.

Then, well over a week later, after the match against Iran and we were having a disaster, our interpreter comes across with a copy of *El Grafico* which has the photo of the three guys and two girls. So we asked what it was all about and she says the caption said it was a picture of Scottish players, the night before the Iran game, in a local discotheque, with singing, drinking and dancing and lots of Bacardi and Coke.

Ken Gallacher, journalist: Being so far away and with the time difference that involved, you were not always aware of what was being printed, and I remember the day the players came in the press centre in Córdoba for their accreditation. And there were pictures taken, of the players with stewardesses from the press centre. And the following week, these pictures were going around the world; in fact, they were sent to *The Record* and we had to stop them going into the paper, because they purported to be pictures of players enjoying a drink with hostesses in a nightclub, which was totally untrue. Most of us [press] were at the centre when the pictures were being taken. The players were drinking cola and getting their accreditation.

This is not poacher-turned-gamekeeper. If you go back and look through my copy, you will see. I hope you are not suggesting some of us responsible journalists over there would say the players were in a nightclub when we knew, fine well, where they were.

So when we saw the pictures, we said what they were, namely pictures taken in the press centre. It was a question of telling the truth.

In subsequent World Cups, there were separate press conferences given to the Scottish press and non-Scottish press. It helps pinpoint where any stitch-up jobs are coming from. Ally didn't know who he was speaking to.

John Robertson: I remember going to a reception with the Minister of Sport, Denis Howell. We all went in suits and, afterwards, we got changed and tried to get back in after the formalities were finished. But then I read in a newspaper that three of us, including me, had turned up in jeans and T-shirt at the start. That upset me. I phoned them and said, 'Hey, you better sort this out, that is not true.'

You had the press picking up stories that I think came from fans wearing Scotland tops and being mistaken for players. I think the players behaved themselves very well. I think they took the rap for a lot of what the supporters got up to. I honestly don't think anyone stepped out of line, apart from the situation with Bud [Willie Johnston] and the drugs.

There were definitely a lot of exaggerated stories. I behaved myself. Being a new boy, you try to make a good impression. I didn't get up to any high jinks. I like a laugh, I was loud, but it's amazing how you can get a reputation. I liked to wear comfortable desert boots – I was never without them. People would look at me and say, 'You great scruffy git.' But the people who know me, they know what I am really like.

For years, I have had people coming up to me and joking about all the fish suppers I was supposed to be eating before Brian Clough took me under his wing at Nottingham Forest. I admit he made me a bit sharper but I wasn't *that* bad before. I have always looked a bit heavy-legged. When I was playing, if I went out once a week, that was it. On a Saturday night. I was never one of these types – and I am still not – who can go into a pub every night and have a couple of pints.

But it all started with the results and you have the fans shouting 'No Mendoza, No Mendoza' after the Iran game. They weren't going to go to Mendoza where we were next playing. Had we got a result against Peru, the attitude would have been different. The players' attitude and the media's. Had we started off with a win, it would have been a happier troop.

Alan Rough: The main problem was the press. First, the local press, then our own. They caught up quickly enough. On a night off, about six of us went for a meal in one of the local cafés, and the only place we could sit was at this big round table, joining some of the locals. Next minute, the owner comes across and says, 'Excuse me, if you look over there in the corner, there is a newspaper photographer.' And sure enough, behind a screen, there was this photographer snapping away. I think it was Kenny Burns who got him to leave. And, of course, a couple of days later, the pictures appeared, cropped to suggest we were nicking about and bevvying with the locals, especially the local women. It was never the case.

There was no security at the main gate – people could come and go as they liked. So you could imagine that if four or five fans in their Scotland shirts had just come from the vicinity of the Scotland camp and were pissed out of their minds, people would jump to conclusions. We, the players, needed permission to leave the camp, but everyone else wasn't so affected. The SFA, who were staying in our headquarters, were partying every night. They were having hospitality functions for the likes of FIFA and the locals and people were saying how it was us who were at it, and we weren't. It was going about that we were the mad whisky-drinkers. But ask how many Scottish footballers drink whisky for a start.

People were on a downer hearing the stories from back home. You'd get one of the players coming off the phone and saying, 'The wife has been telling me . . .' All of a sudden you are on the phone, trying to get through, trying to reassure your own wife that nothing is going on.

Ernie Walker: Fans wearing the same football tops as the players was a new thing for everyone, especially people in South America. I remember returning to Córdoba from a FIFA Congress in Buenos Aires and being met by my Argentinian guide – an excellent, faithful assistant – and he said, 'Thank God you are back, we're in terrible trouble, the players are out drinking every night.' He was so insistent, I was genuinely alarmed. But of course it turned out that it was fans out drinking, wearing Scotland shirts, and being mistaken as players.

Graeme Souness: I was very much aware of trying to keep the head down, because there were all sorts of stories flying around. And I remember Kenny [Dalglish] and I just going to our room after dinner, trying to stay out of the way as much as possible. Even a walk into town had become dangerous. Stories were going back about boys going into town and all sorts of things happening. So, in the end, it was just a case of keeping the head down.

Joe Harper: The press centre in Córdoba was where there was a decent telephone service, because at Alta Gracia you had to book your call two to three days in advance. It was through Archie Macpherson [the broadcaster] that I managed to get a call through to my wife. It wasn't until a few days into the campaign that I had made my booking to phone my wife and I remember seeing Archie a couple of hours before I was due to phone her and I asked him, 'If you get the chance, could you give my wife a phone and tell her not to worry about the stories appearing in the newspapers back home.' So when I got through to my wife, I told her that I had been trying to get hold of her for two and a half days and she said, 'I know, Archie is just off the phone.' So, in two hours, he got through whereas it took me two and a half days.

Stuart Kennedy: Alta Gracia made Shieldhill [a part of Falkirk] look like Las Vegas. Nothing. What the media described as a casino was a game of pitch 'n' toss. It was my 25th birthday when we were in Argentina. Drink? That'll be right. Cokes and that was it. According to the media, we were supposedly paralytic. Not a drop of alcohol in sight.

Martin Buchan: A story came out that the Scots were drunk and making a noise and upsetting the Mexicans who were also staying in the hotel. The fact is that the Scotland players and officials were housed in separate parts of the complex and nobody ever came out and said, 'Well, actually, the noise was coming from the area occupied by the Scottish officials, not the players.' That rankled a bit. There were certain players who took seriously the fact we were playing in a World Cup. Okay, we had nights off and would have a couple of beers. But when it was time for business, we were all pros with top clubs. We weren't there for fun. If I'm being honest, it still annoys me to this day that nobody stood up and defended the players.

There is criticism during the Home Internationals a couple of weeks before which sees Scotland – playing each game at Hampden – draw against Northern Ireland and Wales, then lose against England. But it is mostly muted, as MacLeod is given the benefit of the doubt as he mixes team line-ups so as to give most of his squad a run-out. He won't be submitting the names of his final squad to FIFA until after the England game. But on 2 May, three weeks before departure for Argentina – indeed, 18 days before the England game – the international committee is already noting the names MacLeod has in mind. It is clear the 22 players he has chosen for the Home Internationals are going to be the ones heading for Argentina. Even Gordon McQueen, whose injury against Wales means he will be condemned to the sidelines until approaching the new domestic season.

Ally's profile invites the odd barb. In a cartoon strip, *The Devolvers* (drawings by Bob Dewar, text by Anthony Troon), running in *The Scotsman*, there are a series of thinly veiled attacks on MacLeod's commercial activities, through the main character, McLoot. One particular cartoon, published on 6 June, the day before the game against Iran, has a sketch of MacLeod selling black armbands at 50p a throw.

There is no doubt that some of the players involved in the Home Internationals play tentatively, trying to avoid injury. It is, however, a moot point why MacLeod chooses to tinker with his team line-up right until the last days before departure.

Don Masson: For the England match, we were saving ourselves for Argentina. We were well in control and Bruce and I knew before the match we were only going to play for about a half and Archie Gemmill and Graeme Souness were going to play the other half.

Ally wasn't really bothered and we weren't really bothered. It's not that we just went through the motions but we were trying to avoid injury. In hindsight, you might say the Home Internationals were a sign of things to come, but it wasn't in the players' minds at all. We were just looking forward to the first game against Peru, saving the best for that.

Against Northern Ireland, the opposition are just that bit hungrier for victory. The game ends 1–1. Against Wales, the game is also levelled at 1–1 when Willie Donachie gifts the Welsh a quite bizarre equaliser; mind you, not that long before, a penalty by Wales's Bryan Flynn rebounds off the post to safety. The Scots could do with a victory. They are looking for their third, successive win against England. But despite being the more attractive side, they are guilty of poor finishing. In summing up the whole Home Internationals series, MacLeod is robust, saying, 'The experiments we made were successful. They told me what I wanted to know and I still think I was right to do it this way. Had I played Saturday's team [the one which faced England] in all three matches we would probably have had better results but wouldn't have been as well prepared for Argentina.'

Derek Johnstone: There was no great nonsense at Dunblane, before we left for Argentina. You are talking about 22 bloody fit men, when the manager says, 'We are here for a couple of days; if you want to enjoy yourselves do it now because once we are in Argentina, we are down to business for three weeks.' So at Dunblane, we got a couple of days off and nights out. A lot of the lads went to the horse-racing at Perth, a few of us played golf and at night we would go out for a few beers, like all young men do. It wasn't as if we were in heavy training, it was still a couple of weeks before our first game in Argentina. It was a way of winding down after the three games in the Home Internationals.

A couple of us went to a disco in Falkirk; there were no problems. You always got the usual shouts from those who didn't like you or your club. The majority of people were wishing you all the best. There were no problems. We came back in a taxi at two in the morning, or whatever, had a few beers in the hotel, got up to a few pranks such as knocking on the doors of the players who were sleeping. It was what all players do.

There was nothing at Dunblane that would have had the manager saying, 'Right, that's you not going to Argentina.' In Falkirk, it was like outside any disco at that time in the morning when it's shutting, there were police outside just in case there is trouble. There were certainly people who were noising us up, I don't know if they were Celtic fans or the boyfriends of the girls who'd been trying to chat us up. You always get that. There was no problem. We got out, spoke to the police, and they asked, 'Do you want us to give you a lift to Dunblane?' and we talked about going to Argentina. It was all friendly. And then we just got a taxi back to the hotel. And that was it.

There were a couple of incidents involving a couple of the players in Argentina, but I assure you nothing that warranted the manager sending them home. You are always going to have one or two out of 22 players who maybe go a wee bit over the score. But what could you do in a place like Alta Gracia? It was a wee village. On the few days you did get out, you just sat outside the café, as you would do on holiday. Of course, people know who you are. But the sad thing was that you'd be sitting down having a Coke or a coffee and, all of a sudden, you would have all these snappers [photographers] around you.

What disappointed the lads were the numbers of the known press boys out there who were there for one reason: to send stories back that were absolute bloody nonsense about the Scotland camp – and we couldn't do anything about it. If we ever had a beer it would be back at the hotel; we would only have coffees and Cokes when we were out. We were getting angry and at first we couldn't find out who these press people were. We eventually did. We had words with a couple of them. One of them tried to tell us, 'I'm here to do a job, same as you.' But we did argue with him. Certainly, strong words were used, though there were no hands raised. But we left him in no doubt what we thought of him and I'm sure he had the wind put up him. That's Scotland for you. It wouldn't have mattered had we won the World Cup, you would still have had these people trying to bring back the bad stories. If things are true, fine. You accept you'll be slaughtered in the press. A lot of what they reported might have been true, but it was exaggerated. We would have liked to have done a diary on some of the press boys and what they got up to – as we suggested to a certain Gordon Airs of the *Daily Record* whom we ran into in a lounge after the Holland game.

There were a lot of sports journalists who were fine. The football people. It wasn't their job to write about the things going on off the field – that was why news reporters were sent there. I work in the media now. I think today's players might appreciate that, because I know what players get up to when they are abroad – the pranks they get up to, the pressures some of them are under – simply because I've been there. There are a lot of youngsters writing for the papers these days, and they are far too young to be doing it.

They don't have the experience. Get a group of footballers and it's the same from one generation to the next. You'll get a couple who are the dressing-room jokers and the rest will just laugh at them. I find it hard to take seriously anyone who is pushing themselves in the media as a match summariser on television or radio who's never played the game at a high level. When you hear on the radio someone like Chick Young [BBC Scotland sports reporter] going on about the 'midfield four doing such and such', I just turn the radio off.

Joe Harper: The two biggest mistakes Ally made were, firstly, not doing enough homework on Peru and Iran, and, secondly, allowing the press into the camp for an hour every day before we went to training. And you know how it is, you would wake up and have a blether over breakfast, 'What a carry-on last night . . .' And before you knew it, the story was being blown out of proportion.

Apart from the Willie Johnston thing, there was nothing out of the ordinary. You couldn't step out of line because you couldn't get out of the place. It was like Alcatraz. You had to go through the boss to get permission to get out, and if you were not back by a certain time, there was a problem. And you knew that, because they told you. You had to be back, otherwise there was a security alert. And, throughout, there were no alerts.

You would go to a café, to have a Coke or an orange juice – you didn't drink the water and the coffee was disgusting – and suddenly a photographer would appear from nowhere and it would look as if you were drinking alcohol with the locals.

I heard of one Scottish journalist going around with photographs of the players and asking the locals if they had any stories to tell. I remember after the Iran game, another journalist asking, 'How are you doing?' and I said, 'It's like a morgue in here.' It becomes a headline and results in me being called to explain myself to the manager. There is one journalist in Scotland, still working, who knows never to phone me and probably every player from Argentina, because of some of the things he wrote.

And of course I had a past – I was one of 'The Copenhagen Five'. [Billy Bremner, Arthur Graham, Pat McCluskey, Willie Young and Joe Harper were accused of causing trouble in a Copenhagen nightclub after Scotland's 1–0 win over Denmark in September 1975. All were initially banned for life, though, after a year, Harper and Graham were found to be innocent parties and acquitted.] So, anything that had me looking like I was in a discotheque or café was like Christmas come early. No matter how hard you protest your innocence, you'll get the 'No smoke without fire' line.

As a country, we love to put people on a pedestal and then knock them down. I'm sure that because Ally had the contract with the *Express* there were a few journalists from other papers just waiting for him to drop his defences so they could stick the knife in.

Ian Archer, journalist: Argentina was the best country – and Cordóba was the greatest place – most of the media had ever been to. Some very happy memories. Parties. Wonderful people. So, of course, when we went to the squad camp, they are interested in what we are doing and they are beginning to brood over us, going, 'Well, you never guess what we did last night.'

Bobby Clark: My wife, Bet, got this anonymous call from somebody ranting on about nightclubs, drinking, gambling and so on. It was the only time she got a harassment call like that. And then, ten minutes later, she got a call from a national newspaper asking what it was like being at home with her husband in Argentina. It seemed too much of a coincidence.

Typical of some of the reporting, Derek Johnstone (though on this occasion he could hardly claim he was being 'framed') appears in a photograph showing a girl tickling his beard, with the accompanying caption: 'It's fun and tickle time for bearded star Derek Johnstone as girl fans crowd round demanding the big striker's autograph. You could say it's one of the perks of the job!'

In one particularly damning article, journalist Fraser Elder claims in the *Sunday Mail* that the Scotland HQ was drunk dry within the first few days, that two players turned up at a formal British Embassy function unshaven and wearing T-shirts and jeans, that players not involved in the match against Peru were drinking in the stadium during the game.

In his post-World Cup report, Ernie Walker, secretary of the Scottish Football Association, asserts the association did more than it had ever done to accommodate the media. He writes: 'Certainly, there were times when the temptation to exclude all representatives of press, radio and television from the camp was considerable, but, probably wisely, this temptation was resisted and the pattern of daily morning conferences on which we had agreed originally was adhered to. It is doubtful if even our most severe critic could say other than that the association provided every reasonable facility for coverage by the media.'

Walker's opinion is echoed at the start. On 1 June, three days before the match against Peru, Mike Aitken of *The Scotsman* writes: 'After the shambles of West Germany in 1974, the Scots have prepared admirably for Argentina in 1978. "Your gimmicks are everywhere," an impressed Argentinian journalist told me. The SFA have lifted themselves out of the dark ages and into the current World Cup with a spring in their step and a cheeky hat on their head. They appointed a public relations officer [Bill Wilson, now the SFA's commercial director] before the tournament began, and, armed with badges, programmes, pennants, stickers, t-shirts, posters and goodness knows what else, have systematically gone about selling the good name of Scotland as any modern business would a successful product.' According to Wilson, notes Aitken, foreign journalists are saying that the first press conference held by the Scots is the best so far of all the countries, with MacLeod a paragon of modesty. It is reported elsewhere that at that first press conference, there are 243 journalists, eight TV stations and 30 radio stations.

Back to Walker. The climate changes as the tournament rolls on. He adds: 'We got caught up in a situation where one newspaper would vie with another in trying to publish the most sensational item of gossip. The most serious offenders were, as might be expected, news journalists – as opposed to sports journalists – who had gone to Argentina for reasons that had little to do with football, and who, when they could not find as much of a sensational nature as they might have hoped for, appeared to embark on a course of invention and distortion. One particularly disturbing aspect of the media coverage was the fact that the BBC which, one would imagine, by its very nature, has a duty to the community to be objective, accurate and responsible in its presentation of news, appeared to show, on a number of occasions, a disregard for those qualities. One was left with the impression that perhaps it was not coincidental that the BBC in Scotland seemed to present a much more balanced view of events than did their counterparts in the south.'

Though Walker rejects the suggestion that the quality of the media coverage is responsible for Scotland's depressing performance in the first two matches, he believes, by the same token, that it will not have encouraged the camp in their task. What to do? he asks. To lock them out would probably make the situation more acute. But something needs to be done.

The SFA notes, in its minutes, that Walker is instructed to consult with the association's legal agents to 'determine if one particularly vicious piece of reporting is actionable'.

There is no doubt there are a number of candidates, though among the more damaging pieces are actually those from two of the players on the trip, Lou Macari and Don Masson. Twenty years on, both stand by their decision to publicly criticise the Scottish organisation.

Masson's piece appears in the *News of the World*; Macari's in *The Sun*. Earlier in the tournament, MacLeod succeeds in dissuading Macari from leaving, believing the player to be 'down in the dumps' and requiring a fatherly arm around his shoulder. He does allow Macari to leave a day earlier than the rest of the squad, ostensibly bound for a family holiday in the USA. He also allows Souness to leave a day early, bound for Rio de Janeiro.

Ally MacLeod: The players knew that if they wanted a pint of beer they could have one in the hotel. So long as they were not daft. These stories about players bevvying were a load of baloney. If you think about it, a lot of the squad were teetotal.

Willie Donachie: Asa Hartford was doing a diary for the media. He was quite embarrassed about it and didn't really know what to say. So I said I would leave him in peace in the room [being shared by the two] and come back later. I told a few of the lads what he was doing and we went up to outside the door and could hear Asa talking into this tape recorder: 'Here we are in Alta Gracia . . .' and the door we were leaning against collapsed open with us laughing our heads off.

Asa Hartford: There were a few players doing diaries. I think some-body had pulled out doing a diary for the BBC at the last minute, and I was asked to step in. I don't think it was ever broadcast.

Ally MacLeod: If England had been there, half the problems would not have materialised. Because we found the English press difficult; the Scottish press were generally okay. So if England had been there, there would not have been 24-hours-a-day pressure put on Scotland, it would have been divided between the two.

Lou Macari was just a squad member. I took him along because he was a good player, but he was not one of my recognised starting line-up. And there is a tendency – at club level too – for players on the fringes to feel the manager is not doing the best job.

Ernie Walker: It was the first World Cup where newspapers started sending two types of journalists: football writers and news reporters. Beware of news reporters. We learned how to handle the media better in the future. We were walking through fire, there is still a mark seared in my heart. It was a very difficult time.

Lou Macari: I didn't keep a diary. I am not the type of fella that keeps a diary. I had a contract with *The Sun* which I'd had for the previous two years. And it carried on for the World Cup. Others called it a diary. I wouldn't have wasted my time writing a diary. On a single deal to spill the beans? No.

I had a contract with *The Sun*, I was being paid my normal fee for my column. I did leave ahead of the squad, but only to go to America. I didn't go home. I left to go to America where my wife and kids were on holiday.

What happened was that I got to the airport and the guy who ghosted my column, Alex Montgomery, tried to convince me to go back to London with him. He had been told to do two or three articles with me. He met me at the airport, after making a long, round-about trip to get there. He asked me to go back to England and I said, 'No, I'm going to America.' But I did agree to fly with him to Madrid because, for some reason, there was no flight out until, I think, two days' time. So as he was going to London, via Madrid, I went to America via Madrid. And we worked on the articles then. Did I feel I was being conspiratorial? No. I was just doing my usual column. It is only to be expected that if there is a columnist out there playing in the World Cup that he should be writing about it.

I did feel down during the World Cup. We were doing badly. There were niggles in the squad about the bonuses and accommodation. I had gone to the World Cup with my mother having just died – and dying not under normal circumstances. She had been lying in her house for ten days, dead. Body unrecognisable. I had gone up to Glasgow to meet up with the rest of the Scotland team for the Home Internationals, at the Excelsior Hotel. Phoned my mother's house in Largs. Got no answer. Tried to make contact throughout the day. I got very worried because she would always have been there at some time, and so I contacted the local police and asked them to go up. Later that night, walking through the doors of the hotel, is my cousin, who is a doctor. When I saw him, I knew there was something up. It was natural causes. She had just lain there. She had lived on her own. I didn't really want to go to a World Cup. My mother had been my only parent left alive. I missed the Home

Internationals. But I eventually made the trip to the World Cup. I was somebody making the trip who had just lost their mother. It wasn't ideal. I didn't need support for my football, but as the competition wore on, there was a reaction, a delayed reaction, over my mother.

Macari's association with *The Sun* means that, on the day before Scotland's match against Holland on Sunday, 11 June, the back-page splash in the paper is 'I Want to Go Home — Exclusive, Lou Macari's Plea to Ally MacLeod'. And then, two days later, on the Monday, it's a front-page exclusive: 'I'm Off! New Sensation as Scots Star Lou Macari Walks Out' (the story actually says he is *about* to leave). In the first piece, he is quoted as saying: 'I honestly was not trying the coward's way out. But the pressure here really got to me last night. I went to see the boss on Thursday evening and said I wanted to go home. He turned down the request flat.'

The *coup de grâce* is, however, delivered later, in the paper's editions of 14 and 15 June. His first piece, under the back-page headline 'Uncensored — Now Lou Macari Tells All and Every Word', begins: 'Ally MacLeod told me he was ready to quit as Scotland manager — four days before we played our first World Cup game against Peru. Archie Gemmill, Bruce Rioch and Asa Hartford were there as well. How's that for a start to a campaign I and every other player wanted to be the most memorable of our career — and which will be, for all the wrong reasons?' He adds that three or four players, including himself, would have wanted to return home had Scotland progressed to the next round. He talks of the 'battle of the bonuses that shattered morale'. He claims he will make £102 (after tax) for his part in the finals and wouldn't have made much more had Scotland done better. He says the Tunisians, also staying at Alta Gracia, were on $4,500 a win per man. He reveals figures, later published by the SFA, that the deal was £100 per appearance and £100 per point.

The second piece — this time tucked inside the paper — runs under the headline, 'We Ran into a Frame-up — Orgies not at Stalag 115'. In it, Macari attacks the stories of players bevvying. He writes: 'I'm not a drinker, but believe me, as an old Scotland player, this was the quietest squad I have travelled with.' He says the players were under a 10.30 p.m. curfew. 'We lived like prisoners to such an extent that Martin Buchan and myself called it room Stalag 115. We never seemed to escape from it.' He says the team played well against Holland, despite having done no training during the previous two days and having had to endure a brass band striking up at 10.30 p.m. the night before and the din of army tanks rumbling outside.

Had it all been, he idly speculated, a massive conspiracy by the Argentinians, trying to knobble a fancied team?

Ally MacLeod: For a start, I would not mention that sort of thing [possible resignation] to a player. I might have said something jokingly. There were times when I thought I should have stayed in club football, because I had done well at club level. When a player feels low, he has other players to speak to. But when you are manager, you are basically on your own. I suppose I could have spoken to Ernie Walker, but I decided to keep things to myself. I think I coped well. The worst moment was when we missed the penalty against Peru. And we almost made it against Holland. I managed to turn things around for the last game. We had done so well in the run-up to the World Cup – we hadn't met major problems. But when we did in Argentina, I managed to turn things around.

You didn't hear people complaining about the manager when we were winning the Home Internationals in 1977 or doing well in qualifying for the finals. At club level you find that too. If you are winning, people think you are the greatest. And if you are losing, you will get four or five players saying, 'If I was the manager I would do this, I would do that.' With the Scotland squad, you occasionally heard, 'Oh, but that's not what we do at club level.' You just have to take things with a pinch of salt. The good as well as the bad times.

I must be honest, I enjoyed my time with Scotland. We won the Home Internationals in 1977. We beat England at Wembley that year, and I got a piece of a goalpost [pulled down by fans after a pitch invasion] mailed to me when I lived in Aberdeen. No idea where it is now, probably in the garden of my old house in Aberdeen.

Archie Gemmill: [On the tanks] I can't remember the exact details, but it went on for a couple of hours. It was a horrendous noise. As to the reason, I couldn't tell you. It was just for the one night. I wouldn't give it even the remotest thought that it was a deliberate ploy to keep the Scots awake. Scotland would have been well down the list of teams to be worried about. The Argentinian team that won the World Cup was absolutely outstanding.

Don Masson: I certainly stand by what I said. And I got [dropped from the Scotland squad] *sine die*. I don't think we even got a letter.

It was announced. I doubt they would have picked me again, anyway. The money I got for the piece was an irrelevance. I needed to tell people how I felt. I wasn't really interested in what the consequences might be. I needed to get things off my chest. I didn't have any other way to tell people but to get in touch with a journalist and tell it how it was. I didn't feel guilty because I was vice-captain.

Sandy Jardine: The 1974 World Cup was my personal high and the 1978 World Cup was my all-time low. In 1978, there were so many things wrong. First of all, the expectations were too high. It was absolutely ridiculous to say a nation like Scotland was going to go and win the World Cup. Realism went out of the window. Success for Scotland would have been getting through their section, which was a hard section. Anything after that would have been a bonus. If you look at the team, it had done really well to qualify but once it qualified it went over the edge. It dipped. The send-off at Hampden was one of the most embarrassing experiences of my life. It was ridiculous, walking on to the pitch in front of all these fans before flying out. And then there was the SFA not being professional enough in sorting out the money side of things before we left. When you go to a tournament like that, you don't want to talk about money. You want to say, 'That's it, let's forget about it now.' But it hadn't been sorted out and ended up causing a wee bit of aggro. We had to have meetings to try and sort it out. And, of course, we under-performed during the games.

I played in the 1974 World Cup and we came back heroes even though we didn't qualify for the next round. We played Brazil in that competition and to think that something like 700 million people watched the game live on television is unbelievable. To be exposed to that sort of thing was incomprehensible, and just shows how the World Cup was developing at the time. There was an excitement and the Scotland team did their usual thing of being glorious failures. But we did well. It lifted the nation, it lifted the players. I came back from West Germany [where the tournament was held] a better player.

During the Holland game I was in the stand, and I remember saying, 'God, I don't want us to go through.' People will find that hard to believe; supporters especially will find that very difficult to comprehend. That you have got the chance to play in the World Cup and you want to go home instead. But it wasn't pleasant. You have basically no contact with the outside world. You are stuck there, you are getting pinged from people left, right and centre. You're phoning your wife and she is asking, 'What's all this about girls and drinking?' You're 10,000 miles away trying to say, 'No, no.' But it's plastered across every newspaper. And then you're asking yourself, 'What am I doing having to defend myself here?' Unless you've been there, it is hard to explain.

The officials and fans were wearing the same Scotland tops as the players and some of the stories we were hearing were absolutely ridiculous. You talk to any supporter – they had the time of their lives. We were in a small town, the locals didn't know a player from a supporter or an official and they were very friendly, having people around to their house. So, obviously, the moment there is any drinking going on, it is assumed it is players rather than officials or fans who are involved and it snowballs from there.

We, the players, were often the last to know about the stories being written or told about us. We had a lounge in the hotel where we phoned from. And you would phone home and the first thing you wanted to know was what was in the papers, because we weren't getting the papers delivered until a couple of days later, if at all. It pretty quickly became a situation of trench warfare, us against the media. We wouldn't leave the hotel just in case. And with the results going against us, it very quickly became a question of, 'Let's get it over with and get out as soon as possible.'

7. The Main Man

Ally MacLeod. The main man. Whose star shone brightly but briefly. In total, he managed Scotland for 17 games, winning seven, losing five and drawing five. His first game in charge was against Wales on 28 May 1977; his last game was against Austria on 20 September a year later. He wasn't immediately sacrificed after he and his bedraggled World Cup foot soldiers limped into the UK to the sound of silence. But, equally, he didn't make it difficult for those who wanted rid of him. He resigned. He was not sacked. A motion – proposer unknown – to sack him at a meeting of the SFA's international committee on 7 July illustrates how quickly the mood of his employers had changed. The motion was defeated but MacLeod didn't leave it long before doing the honourable thing.

He returned to manage Ayr United following his resignation on 26 September. He had also embarked on an autobiography which was published the following year. The style is unmistakably MacLeod, shot through with a happy-go-lucky optimism. Each new development, as well as each new chapter, is usually prefaced with a gauche 'Little was I to know'. As if he was truly hijacked by events he could not have possibly predicted.

Understandably, there is a slant. History is slightly rewritten. But against the 20-year-old memories of the players, MacLeod's recollections – fresh, most still painfully so – provide an invaluable insight. Ally is in his mid-60s now, playing golf most mornings and living in a lovely house with a black-and-white-painted door – the colours of his beloved Ayr United. Fit-looking. But his memory of the World Cup has become a little rusty.

MacLeod, the open book, is laid bare in the first pages of his autobiography. He and wife, Faye, are invited to dine with the Queen and the Duke of Edinburgh at Holyrood Palace in Edinburgh just a couple of weeks after Argentina (indeed the invitation was received during the tournament). And, believing it to be an invitation to a garden party, he almost doesn't go.

'I assumed that there would be a couple of thousand people milling around, and every one of them would be bombarding me with World Cup questions,' he writes. But 'little was he to know' that he, in his brown suit, and Faye would be among only a couple of dozen guests. Her Majesty is quoted as saying, 'Ally, it is nice to see you smiling again,' before, according to MacLeod, displaying an intimate grasp of the game.

Ally's appointment as Scotland's ninth manager on 18 May 1977 on a salary of £14,000 was preceded with playing stints at Third Lanark, St Mirren, Blackburn Rovers (his happiest time as a player) and Hibernian. His managerial career includes ten years at Ayr United, followed by a year with Aberdeen, during which time a League Cup is won. While at Blackburn he campaigns vigorously for the abolition of the maximum wage. At the time, players are being technically paid no more than £20 per week.

When he takes over the Scotland post, succeeding Willie Ormond, Scotland are reigning champions in the annual Home Internationals series. The qualifying stages for Argentina are already well under way and, at that stage, Scotland's place is far from assured, having played two, won one, lost one.

Ally MacLeod: When I was offered the manager's job, Jock Stein phoned me. I was quite friendly with Jock, we got on pretty well. And he said, 'I hear they have offered you the job. I don't want to say too much, but you know the World Cup is on the other side of the world.' He hinted he had been offered the job and turned it down and was giving me a bit of advice to turn it down because the World Cup was on the other side of the world.

After nearly three weeks in South America, MacLeod returns to Scotland looking ill. He has barely slept. He says it upset him when he heard stories of his family, back in Ayrshire, becoming prisoners in their own home; of his daughter Gail being tormented at school; of the windows of the family house being smashed on the night of the Iran débâcle. But he quickly adds that a quick phone call home dispelled the stories as fabrications.

Andrew MacLeod, son: There were stories of me being beaten up, which were complete rubbish. My friends were great about it. There were no smashed windows or anything like that. Who didn't get the odd kick playing football? It was fine. I was 17 at the time. Let's say my interest in my school work waned a little that year, but I picked up in my final year. All I knew was that I was going to go to Argentina had we got through to the next round. Occasionally, you had the press camped outside the house. You grew up quickly. There I was, aged 17, being door-stepped by a journalist, offering money for an exclusive on life as Ally's son. My only regret is I didn't take the money.

Just whose hand? Scotland win a penalty in their crucial World Cup qualifier against
Wales at Anfield in Liverpool. Joe Jordan says it wasn't him.

It began so well! Joe Jordan puts Scotland into the lead against Peru *(left)* and, for a while, it all goes to plan. Final score: Scotland 1, Peru 3.

For Don Masson *(below, left)*, Scotland's game against Peru was a personal disaster.

No crowd, no finesse, can't even score against Iran *(below)*. A comedy of errors by the Iran defence gifts Scotland an own-goal. Final score: Scotland 1, Iran 1.

All this way for SFA. Scotland's 1–1 draw with Iran represents one of the all-time low points in the relationship between the Scots fans and their team.

The recuperation begins. Kenny Dalglish
equalises for Scotland against Holland. Just
before half-time, the score stands at one
apiece.

For a moment, the miracle is on. Archie
Gemmill scores a wonder goal to put
Scotland 3–1 up against the Dutch. Only
one more goal is needed for Scotland to
progress to the next round on goal difference. But Holland score instead. Good,
but not good enough. Final score:
Scotland 3, Holland 2.

'And I took two tablets.' Willie Johnston is sent home in disgrace after testing positive for a banned stimulant. He still protests he was treated unfairly.

Bruce Rioch: I had a real affection for MacLeod. I really liked him very much. He came with great enthusiasm. I had a great affection for Willie Ormond too. Willie gave me my first opportunity in the international team. And MacLeod took over and he came with great enthusiasm, tremendous spirit and was smashing. I really liked him and enjoyed him. I think we all hurt with him.

Don Masson: The big difference between Tommy Docherty [his manager at Derby County] and Ally MacLeod was that Ally was always there and he was happy to let the players decide things, which was good. I used to take all the free-kicks and I would get the players on the training field and we would go through the free-kicks and discuss them.

He treated us like adults. I thought Ally was brilliant, not coaching-wise but for man-management. I would put him on a par with Dave Sexton [Masson's manager at QPR]. He allowed me to dictate the game, which was brilliant, because we got good results. He allowed Martin Buchan and Gordon McQueen to organise at the back, us to organise the midfield and up front they knew what they were doing. He didn't go into detailed analysis of the opposition. Against Peru, we didn't know anything about them.

Ally MacLeod: How was I to see them [Peru and Iran, before the World Cup]? It wasn't as if I could take a quick flight. You're talking about being away a week. I had a lot of things to attend to back home. As Scotland manager, I had to keep up to date on the players already in the squad and also those being recommended to me. At the end of the day, we went on a South American tour in 1977 to prepare for what it would be like over there.

The advertising and endorsements I did was in non-footballing time. It didn't interfere with my football. It was a load of baloney that I made a lot of money out of the advertising. I believe I put more into Scotland than any other manager has done. If a club wrote to the SFA recommending a player, I would be in my car and away to see them. The amount of miles I travelled in my car, checking on players, was unbelievable. Up and down, between Scotland and England, all the time.

This same man, a month earlier, had been relaxing in the warm glow of eulogy. Previewing a five-part feature by him in the *Scottish Daily Express*, an article gushes, 'Ally – the man of the people who speaks to fans in their own words'. It begins: 'Go anywhere in Scotland and mention one name, "Ally", and everyone from five years old upwards will know whom you mean. He no longer needs the MacLeod to complete the identity.'

The series starts in what could hardly be described as low-key fashion:

'You can mark down 25 June 1978 as the day Scottish football conquers the world. For on that Sunday, I'm convinced the finest team this country has ever produced can play in the final of the World Cup in Buenos Aires . . . AND WIN. We have the talent. We have the temperament. And the ambition. And the courage. All that stands between us and the crown is the right kind of luck.

'I'm so sure we can do it that I give my permission here and now for the big celebration on 25 June to be made an annual festival . . . a national Ally-day!

'Over the next few days, I'm going to tell in depth and detail, exclusively for *Express* readers, the answer to that question the Scotland fans have been chanting so long: Why are we so good?

'I'll tell you how this squad of players has developed into the finest ever to represent Scotland. I'll take you behind the scenes, spell out our strong-points. And I'll write about what are sure to be big talking points on the terracings. Like: Why I don't want angels in Argentina. Why I could leave out a great player. Why I chose John Hagart as my World Cup lieutenant. Who I think our key men will be.

'I'll answer the critics who think I'm cashing in on our success — and I'll tell you what I REALLY think of England's football team.'

Even if ghost-written, these are stirring words. Inviting disaster. When it is all over, rival newspapers delight in giving their readers a list of Ally's quotes to throw back at him. A listing in the *Sunday Mail* is typical:

On his decision not to have a contract: 'I have always felt I am good enough to keep a job on my merits, without a piece of paper to protect me.'
One week after his appointment: 'People say Jock Stein is the best manager in Scotland, but I think I am.'
On his appointment: 'I don't visualise any problems, I'm here to do a job for Scotland.'
November 1977: 'Handling the players is no problem. Treat them like men and they'll behave like men.'
When the draw was made in January: 'We really couldn't have asked for a better draw than Peru or Iran.'

During the Home Internationals: 'The midfield holds the key to whether we win or lose in Argentina.'

In May, when he called a halt to commercial dealings: 'The money side of the World Cup is secondary.'

In his column for the Daily Express *newspaper:* 'The World Cup is not about perks or profits, it's about pride.'

During the Home Internationals: 'Willie Johnston can take Argentina by storm.'

In his column for the Daily Express *newspaper:* 'I'm not against earning money.'

On selecting his pool: 'I'm going to Argentina to win the World Cup, that's all that matters and I've got to pick the players I think will do it.'

On selecting his pool: 'One thing is for sure, the form of the players will decide who plays in Argentina. If they are not playing well, they won't play. I don't care who they are.'

In his column for the Daily Express *newspaper:* 'How the SFA can fire the man who wins the World Cup will be their problem.'

Two weeks before the World Cup: 'I don't believe in managers who moan about the pressures.'

After the Peru game: 'Don't blame me.'

Two days after the Peru game: 'I take the blame.'

After the Iran game: 'It would need a miracle for us to qualify.'

Before the Holland game: 'In my heart I haven't a worry in the world.'

A few weeks before departure, the poet Alan Bold wrote of MacLeod:

Despite the elongated shape
Of his weel-kent face
He is a bouncing ball of a man –
Never deflated.
With his head cocked to one side
His sing-song drawl
Describes the game
As a living organism,
Something for the players
To go out and grab
With both feet
(Goalkeepers excepted).
He comes across as such a friendly guy
You wouldn't think he'd harm a fly
But that is the expression
Of an impression;

No flies on Ally
He knows what he's after
So don't let the easy laughter
Disguise the fact;
He is a national
Character, an inspirational
Force for the world of football
To reckon with.
He has his campaign planned
And the whole of Scotland
Wants to shake him by the hand.

(Reproduced by kind permission of Alan Bold)

On his return from Argentina, the words must have felt centuries old.

8. Peru

Saturday, 3 June 1978
PERU: *Quiroga, Diaz, Chumpitaz, Manzo, Duarte, Velasquez, Cueto (Rojas), Cubillas, Munante, La Rosa (Sotil), Oblitas*
SCOTLAND: *Rough, Kennedy, Burns, Forsyth, Buchan, Rioch (Macari), Masson (Gemmill), Hartford, Dalglish, Jordan, Johnston*
REFEREE: *U. Eriksson (Sweden);* LINESMEN: *F. Martinez (Spain), G. Tesfaye (Ethiopia)*
ATTENDANCE: *45,000, Córdoba*

The game. Scotland versus Peru. At last, it is upon us. The moment of truth, though for some it doesn't warrant that level of gravity because, for them, victory is a formality. It is written in the stars and predicted in the tea leaves. And when David Coleman on BBC declares, 'One-nil,' in as matter-of-fact a voice as it is possible to get, it seems that Scotland are to fulfil their calling at a canter.

One-nil. Joe Jordan the scorer. He hasn't scored too often for Scotland these past couple of seasons. But, there he is, rifling the ball home after a shot by Bruce Rioch spills out of the goalkeeper's arms. Ya bass! It's fitting that it is Kenny Dalglish's 55th cap, equalling a record set by Denis Law.

Prior to the game, both Jordan and fellow striker Derek Johnstone are the subject of press reports claiming they are both touch and go for the match – Jordan allegedly suffering from a thigh strain, Johnstone supposedly hobbling about with a sore ankle. For the sake of appearances, it would seem preferable to hide behind an injury – real or fake – than face up to the cold reality of having been overlooked. But Johnstone will have none of it. Today, he says he was fit to play, that Jordan was chosen ahead of him, and that's the end of the matter. Honest words that do nothing to heal the wound. In Argentina, as Johnstone is hurting, many pundits are simply bemused. The striker is on the crest of a wave. He has scored 41 goals that season for Rangers; he has just scored twice during the recent Home Internationals – and he didn't even play against England! He has just been chosen as Scottish Player of the Year by his fellow professionals and, separately, by the Scottish Football Writers' Association.

Derek Johnstone: Around the time, I was getting chest infections quite a lot. A couple of my brothers were asthmatic, I had seen them grow up with it, and I thought I was maybe getting it a bit later in life. So I took an inhaler with me and because of the heat and the humidity, my chest was a wee bit troublesome at times. But it was never ever going to put me off playing. I trained as hard as anyone. I was never injured.

I'd say 1978 was probably the peak of my career. I was scoring goals, Rangers had won the Treble and I was heading to Argentina as part of the Scotland squad. It was the pinnacle of my career. During the Home Internationals, I scored my first goal for Scotland – against Northern Ireland – and followed that up by scoring in the game against Wales. I was on a high.

I was just grateful to get in. Ally MacLeod had to pick me because I had scored so many goals that season – I was the striker on form. But I knew Joe Jordan was the number one and quite rightly so. He was a regular. Perhaps he wasn't the most prolific goalscorer for Scotland, but he always seemed to do a good job. If he wasn't scoring himself, he was creating chances.

But I was disappointed, more than disappointed. I think the biggest kick in the teeth was when Joe Harper was put on as a substitute against Iran when he wasn't even on the bench for the game against Peru. He's a very good pal, Joe, and I'm pleased he can look back and say he has played in a World Cup finals, but it was probably the lowest time in my life. To this day, people remind me mostly of two things: the winning goal I scored against Celtic in the League Cup final when I was 16; and Argentina – why didn't I play? The scars are still there. I still feel as badly now about not getting a game as I did then. But there is no malice towards Ally MacLeod.

Nobody has a divine right to play and, obviously, it is the manager's prerogative to play who he likes. At Dunblane before we left, I took Ally to one side for a couple of minutes to tell him that if there were any problems in defence I could always play centre-back; that if I had to choose between both positions, I would prefer to play at the back. And that probably threw Ally a bit since I was recognised as a centre-forward. It was providing both myself and Ally with an extra option. I wasn't a wee laddie any more. I was providing him and myself options. I had played a few times that season for Rangers at centre-back. If you have aerial strength, you will be a danger no matter what position you are playing. There are always free-kicks and corners to go up for.

I didn't expect to start a game. I felt Jordan was probably the better player – certainly harder working than I was. I assumed that, so long as Joe was fit, he would start and I would be available to change things as a substitute. I was at the peak of my game, enjoying my football, scoring goals. I played against Northern Ireland and Wales only because Joe hadn't been fit. He was fit for the game against England and played. [Johnstone is not strictly accurate. Jordan didn't play against Wales but he did against Northern Ireland and was substituted. MacLeod tried Jordan and Johnstone together in that match, a tactic that, according to pundits, failed miserably].

'If' is a big word. Maybe two big players, Jordan and myself, might have made a difference. Obviously, Ally was looking for Joe to knock down the ball for a sharp little man – Dalglish or Harper – to stick it in the net. But it didn't work. Peru and Iran stuck big defenders on Joe and he wasn't really able to feed the smaller strikers. Maybe two big strikers working in partnership might have asked more questions of the defence.

My forte at the time was just getting my head to a lot of balls punted into the box. Get the ball in the box and I'd attack it. Cut the ball back from the by-line and I'd attack it.

Ally did it his way and it didn't work out and he got a lot of stick for it, which, at the time, I didn't think was justified. A manager can do so many things. But once the players cross the line it's up to them, and if they don't do it there is not an awful lot the manager can do. Against Peru, maybe two or three of the lads got pass marks. It's so easy to criticise managers as being tactically naïve. A manager can be the greatest tactician in the world, but if the players don't play, tactics don't mean a thing. Nobody is tactically naïve. If players don't play, it just looks that way.

Before Argentina, there was a lot of talk that I had put in a transfer request at Rangers, which was wrong. My contract was up and I hadn't spoken to Rangers about renewing it, so the speculation was there. I wasn't the only one out of contract – if I remember right there was also Sandy Jardine and Colin Jackson. Rangers were the only club I wanted to play for. I had never been a Rangers fan when I was growing up, but being at the club for something like nine years meant I had developed a real affection for them. I heard Arsenal and Spurs were interested. But in no time Willie Waddell [the Rangers managing director] called us upstairs, put a piece of paper in front of us, said, 'That's what you are getting,' and all three of us signed, as quickly as that, in a matter of seconds.

The reason the speculation arose was because Jock Wallace left as manager [to go to Leicester City] and it was well known he was a big influence on me. He was like a father to me. We both started at Rangers at the same time. It was him who first saw my potential with my heading ability. He would take me for extra training, where he would swing a ball on the end of a rope on a pole and work on my timing because that is what heading is about, it is about timing, not how big you are. Both Gerd Müller and Lou Macari were excellent headers and neither was very tall. Jock and I grew up together, we saw things together. He was a big, rough man. But if you worked for him and gave your all, you got the same back from him. If you didn't, he would be the first to grab you by the throat. He got 100 per cent out of the players and, even if he was a bit raw for European football, Rangers did as well in Europe under him as under anybody else.

When we played in Europe, he would give each of us cards with pictures, plus a little bit of information, of who we would be up against. He didn't over-fill our heads with tactics and preparation, but you knew enough about who you were up against – what they were good at, what they were not so good at, that sort of thing.

So, anyway, Jock felt he wasn't getting paid what a Rangers manager should be paid. It's all right gaining medals but at the end of the day it doesn't pay the mortgage. I heard about his decision to leave at a stag night, I think it was my own – I had two because I got married after the World Cup – and went straight up to his house to speak to him about it. Leicester were prepared to pay Jock what he was worth and Rangers weren't; that was a problem with Rangers back then. Much though they were a great club, they weren't the greatest payers. It's very different now.

When I got back from Argentina, because I was getting married and my head was full of that, I sort of forgot about the World Cup and feeling down about it all. But at pre-season training, it came back a bit. You had all the lads asking if I had done anything wrong. They would ask, 'Did you have an argument with him? Did you hit him?' There were a lot of rumours at the time. It was nonsense. There were never any fall-outs. Because the Rangers players couldn't believe that I didn't play, it started coming out that I must have had an argument with him, which just wasn't true. It was simply a case of him not picking me.

Ally MacLeod: It was a stupid thing him [Derek Johnstone] suggesting he should play centre-half. He was the best striker in Scotland. There were no fall-outs over it, but I said, 'You will never play centre-half for me.' That was about the only problem I had with the players. In club level, you are sometimes forced to fine a player who steps out of line. But in Argentina, the squad was well behaved. I think the only problem I had was with Derek Johnstone.

One-nil. A glorious moment. Explosions of joy back home. It is an early goal. A goal that has people crowding closer to the TV set and slapping each other on the back. It's a beautifully worked goal. Martin Buchan passes to Kenny Dalglish in the centre circle, who shields the ball with his body before nudging a pass to the left flank for Asa Hartford to send a ten-yard pass down the touchline for Willie Johnston. The pace of the move then quickens. Johnston knocks a diagonal pass to Dalglish who has moved downfield, who lays the ball back to Hartford who first-times his pass to Bruce Rioch at the edge of the box, whose instant left-foot shot is spilled by the goalkeeper, allowing Jordan to pounce.

Who cares that it is an English commentator? It was meant to be the Scots' very own Archie Macpherson but he is somewhere in the stadium cursing gremlins in the system. He isn't being heard. He taps his microphone in disbelief; paces the Córdoba press box like a bear with a sore head.

Russell Galbraith, television producer: Arthur Montford was the commentator lined up for Scottish Television, with Hugh Johns doing the rest of the UK for ITV. And on BBC, Archie Macpherson was doing BBC Scotland with David Coleman commentating for the rest of the UK. But there was a mix-up in line patching, with the Argentinians or Germans or whoever was helping. Hugh Johns' commentary vanished up a pipe somewhere, just got lost. But the converse was that Archie Macpherson's commentary also disappeared up a pipe somewhere. So Arthur's commentary served the whole of the UK on ITV and Coleman's did likewise on the whole BBC network, while Archie paced, po-faced, up and down the corridor. I don't blame him, mind you. We were under pressure to let Hugh Johns into Arthur's seat, which, needless to say, we resisted.

And then Peru equalise. Terror. It's a good-looking goal. They're no' bad, these Peruvians. Been preparing as a squad since February. 'Poor poor

Peru,' wrote poet Alan Bold, 'If you only knew/What the boys in blue/ Are going to do to you/Too true!'

Just before kick-off, the odds are 8/13 for a Scotland win, 9/2 for a Peru win and 5/2 the draw. The odds for the score of 3–1 to Peru are 80/1. That morning, an advert for Ladbrokes bookmakers in a newspaper goes, 'Betcha Scotland Kick Peru Over the Andes'. A lot of the local press, such as *La Razon*, has Scotland down as favourites too.

The Peru manager, the 'roly-poly' Marcos Calderon, is under a bit of pressure, chastened by an expensive trip to Italy supposedly to run the rule over Scotland, only to find the subject of his spying mission is a Scotland select drawn from the domestic league.

Also before the game, in the *Daily Record*, Willie Johnston puts his signature to a letter to the readers: 'We have talked about Peru,' he begins, 'and worked on some ideas on how we might beat them. And the unanimous decision was that it was going to be a very hard match. Starting with a victory would give us qualification. I don't think any of us have doubts about that. We also realise that Peru may try to be defensive against us and the boss has told me to get round behind the defence. The right-back is supposed to be on the slow side – but I won't know that until I've been up against him. I hope it's right.

'It used to worry me when I was younger when a manager suggested I was a key man. This happened in European games during my career with Rangers. Wingers were meant to be the match winners then and I used to be nervous. It doesn't affect me so much now. The boss told me that he wants me to play an important role and I just have to do my best.

'The doubts over Joe Jordan and Derek Johnstone troubled me a bit because it would have meant an alteration to my game. I couldn't be more pleased now about Joe being in the team.

'We know what victory means to the people back home – as well as to the hundreds who have made it here. We will be remembering that send-off we were given. The memory can help inspire us.'

Signed Willie Johnston.

And then comes that equaliser. Indeed, Scotland are fairly relieved to go into the interval at one-apiece. And then the Scots miss a penalty opportunity to make it 2–1. And then Peru score not once, but twice. Is there no mercy in the world?

The game finishes 3–1 for Peru. And in stunned silence, the post-mortems begin. If only. If only Don Masson had scored from the penalty spot to put Scotland 2–1 ahead. If only the Scottish defensive wall had stood up to Cubillas's free-kick which gave Peru an unassailable 3–1 lead. Indeed, if only Cubillas had not conjured that incredible free-kick, delivered with an imperious flick of the outside of his right boot.

Certainly, the Scots are unable to field their strongest possible side following the suspension of Willie Donachie and the injury to Gordon McQueen. But there is more to the outcome than the odd 'If only'. First, Peru are an exceptionally talented side, very quick in attack. Second, because Peru are a good side, Scotland's passing is often broken up and therefore patchy. Scotland look superb for the first 15 minutes – Masson in particular is excellent – but the Peruvians are too good to be denied their moment.

Roughly, the game goes like this: Excellent start for Scotland. A number of opportunities created, mainly by Don Masson and Asa Hartford. Goal. Peru begin to come back, Scotland having to weather pacy attacks. Goal, three minutes before the interval. A bright resumption for Scotland – Joe Jordan heads a Kenny Dalglish lob against the upright and, a few minutes later, is denied by an excellent save by Quiroga. Sustained Scottish pressure. Rioch charges into the box, attempting to control a headed pass. Defender Diaz makes contact. Penalty. Penalty miss. Scotland appear to play through the disappointment. Then the cracks begin to appear. Scotland in retreat. Peru score. Scotland replace Masson and Rioch with Macari and Gemmill. Still, Scotland stretched. Peru score again. Fifteen minutes left. Lots of Scottish huff and puff but it remains 3–1 to Peru.

The Scotland goal is a beauty and owes everything to midfield ingenuity. And then? Too many players are bypassed by events. Willie Johnston admits he was off-form; so too does Bruce Rioch. Johnston is the blunter of the two: 'I was crap.'

Scotland labour; Peru slice through. Too true. Particularly the supposed has-beens, the 'old men' of Hector Chumpitaz, Hugo Sotil and Teofilo Cubillas. The name of Cubillas, in particular, is etched in the Scottish psyche by virtue of the two goals he scores, Peru's second and third.

Cueto scores Peru's equaliser, the result of neat passing and lots of movement on the edge of the Scottish box. It looks like he intercepts a one-two intended for someone else. But the angle of his intervention means he is behind the Scottish defence within just a couple of paces. Clear on goal, Rough, the Scottish goalkeeper, has no chance.

Peru's second further exposes a Scottish weakness for defending deep instead of pressing in midfield. Retreating when they should have harried, Cubillas is invited to bear down to within 20 yards of the Scottish goal. Shot. Slight curl. Goal. Rough? Flat-footed. Leaden, even.

By the time Cubillas scores his second, the Scots are spent. MacLeod's response to Peru's second is the almost immediate replacement of Masson and Rioch. But no sooner has Gemmill touched the ball for the first time than he too is guilty of mis-passing, giving the ball to Duarte on the edge of the Peru box.

Two passes later – one short, the other very long – and Oblitas, goalside of Kennedy, is suddenly charging in on the Scottish goal. At the other end of the park. With the defender trailing in his wake. Though Kennedy gets to his man, it is at the expense of a free-kick 20 yards out. The rest, as they say, is history.

Don Masson: Coming back from Argentina and going back to Derby County was the worst time in my career. I was so low, I wanted to pack up. The missed penalty affected me so badly. I felt terrible, it really affected me. For six months. You can put a brave face on it; it still affects me now. There's not a day goes past when I don't think of it in some way or another. Gary McAllister missing the penalty against England in Euro '96? He'll never forget about it. He'll put it to the back of his mind but it will always be there. Gareth Southgate [missed penalty in Euro '96 semi-final], Stuart Pearce [missed penalty in 1990 World Cup semi-final]? They'll never ever forget about it. You can't dismiss it as though it never happened.

At the time for me, the team were great, Ally was great. But it's an individual thing. I felt I had let everybody down. And after that I came back to Derby, under Tommy Docherty, which was a terrible experience anyway. He used to slaughter Bruce Rioch and me in the papers. We were both at Derby and were captain and vice-captain of Scotland. He would never say anything to our faces but then you would read in the paper him saying we should never be playing for Scotland. It was terrible, really.

After the penalty miss and all the hullabaloo with Willie Johnston being sent home – I was his room-mate – I was just sickened. I always say that if I had scored that penalty, the whole World Cup would have been different. The SFA would not have had to find a scapegoat like Bud [Willie Johnston]. I wouldn't blame Ally – he was just a puppet. But the SFA had to be seen to be doing something. It wasn't as if Johnston was taking something in the same category as athletes taking steroids, where there should be a lifetime ban. He has to live with that as I have to live with the missed penalty.

If I had scored the penalty, it would have been different. It was the only penalty kick I missed for Scotland; I never missed many throughout my career. I remember scoring against Argentina in our

1977 tour of South America and scoring another against Finland when we beat them 6–0. And, of course, there was the one against Wales at Anfield. We needed that goal because the match was going nowhere, we were just cancelling each other out.

The Peru one has to be the most important of course, and I missed. It wasn't the best kick in the world. I have never actually seen it. I avoid watching myself on television. The best game of my career was for Scotland against Czechoslovakia at Hampden during the qualifiers. We absolutely murdered them. And I have never seen that, either. I am hyper-critical.

I would feint a little before taking the kick and would go for the corner. A wee stop and then shoot. Aiming for the side-netting, between the stanchion and the post, and about a foot off the ground. No way the keeper can get these, even if they have moved a bit. Run, stop, pass the ball into the corner. It worked most times. It's a skill, using the instep of the foot. I didn't realise it at the time but it was a gift I had been given from God. Put me on a golf tee in front of a dozen people and I am like jelly. But give me a penalty kick in front of a 100,000 people and I know I can perform. I was in control. But against Peru, the kick was not aimed well enough and the keeper moved. Good luck to him.

The first thing that went through my mind after missing was how I had let everybody down. I stood there and just thought of my wife, my parents, my wife's parents. Right away, people back home in Scotland. I knew the significance of it. I knew immediately the impact it would have on the confidence of the team. It took years before I went back to my parents' house in Banchory, I felt so bad about it. I try to be lighthearted about it now. It's not that easy.

The whole team were very sympathetic. I was inconsolable. After I missed, it was as though everything was going around and I wasn't there. The manager did me a favour by taking me off. There is one wee voice saying, 'Come on, you can make up for it by playing well,' and another saying, 'Get me off the pitch, get me out of here.' It was 1–1. It wasn't the end of the world at that point. Obviously, it changed when they went ahead. I just wanted to be in the shower on my own. I cried in the shower. As I said, I was inconsolable.

I knew what the lads were thinking, and they knew what I was thinking. You didn't need to say anything. When I missed that penalty, I knew I would never play for Scotland again. You live or die by it. I was the penalty-taker. I had assumed the responsibility. If you succeed, you are a hero; if you miss, you are a villain. I could have avoided the risk by letting someone else become the penalty-taker. But I didn't. At that age and with Souness coming through, I knew my time was finished.

What could Ally say about it? He didn't shout and bawl. He had been let down, individually and collectively.

I didn't sleep for a couple of nights afterwards. I usually didn't sleep well after any match – I would relive the game, dissect how I played, analyse what I had done. Not the good things, more the bad things. To learn for the next game. So, after the Peru game, you can imagine how my mind was racing.

So, to go back to Derby, where I didn't want to play for Tommy Docherty anyway, I was all for packing it up. I had a chance to go to Norwich and then Notts County came in. I had been with them before and helped them move from the Fourth Division through to the Second and they said, 'Why don't you finish the job, get Notts County promotion to the First Division?' I was at Notts County from 1968 to 1974, went to QPR, then Derby County and then returned to Notts County for another four seasons during which time we won promotion to the First Division.

Notts County, second time around, was the incentive I needed after the débâcle of the World Cup. After Notts County, I spent some time in the USA, with the Minnesota Kicks. Would you believe it, but Cubillas was playing over there at the same time, for Fort Lauderdale, with Gerd Müller. We beat them.

Bruce Rioch: It is easy to look back and say MacLeod's loyalty to certain players, including myself, was misplaced. Maybe he thought that players doing not so well at club level could still perform at international level. I think the players appreciated his loyalty. But, now, having been a manager myself for many years, while I know loyalty is a great quality and should not be under-estimated, so long as you don't disrupt the balance and harmony of the team you need to pick players on form to win matches.

I had left Derby, went up to Everton for nearly a year, couldn't settle, and returned to Derby. It was a period in my career when I didn't have peace and harmony in myself. I don't mean in my personal life, my family life, but in my football life. I only found it again after I left Derby and set off on my travels [on loan to Birmingham City followed by Sheffield United, starting in December 1978]. I went to America for three years. I would say from the end of '76, for at least two years, maybe longer, I didn't have peace and harmony in my football. Probably still had it at international level; in fact, I welcomed the chance to join up with the international squad. But I didn't find it at club level.

The Scottish midfield had not been functioning as well as it had done. I wasn't playing well at that time, at club level, most certainly not. In saying that, the midfield, myself included, was part of a good performance in the game against Holland. What happened in that game for me was a change in position which gave me more freedom to go into forward positions, knowing full well I had the support behind me of Graeme Souness and the talent of Asa Hartford and Archie Gemmill on the outside.

Ally MacLeod: I don't believe one bad performance is sufficient reason to drop a player. I tried to build a club atmosphere and you had to show a certain loyalty to players to get loyalty back.

Gordon McQueen: You have to remember that three of the regular back four were missing on that opening game against Peru. Danny McGrain wasn't even in Argentina because he was already out through injury. Willie Donachie was suspended and there was me, as it turns out, missing the whole campaign.

We were thought of as a good back four. And then in midfield you had Bruce Rioch and Don Masson having a lot of trouble at Derby County with Tommy Docherty. They had played great in the qualifying matches but, by being in dispute with Docherty and Derby County, they are hardly going to Argentina in the right frame of mind.

Danny McGrain was a fantastic right-back, great to play with. Willie Donachie was a smashing left-back. But, obviously, the most important one for me was Tom Forsyth. I played at club level with some great central defenders such as Norman Hunter and Martin Buchan, but I had as good, if not better, a partnership with Tom Forsyth as I had with any of those other players. I liked his type of player – committed – and I reckon we had a good partnership going. McGrain and Donachie were very comfortable on the ball while Tom and I were both quick, competitive and could win tackles. And there wasn't a lot more asked of us. We would get the ball and it was great to be able to roll the 10- to 15-yard pass to Willie or Danny who would take responsibility, especially if a bit more skill was required. I felt the team that got us through the qualifying stages was a very strong side. And, of course, that team never played again after the qualifiers. For the Home Internationals, because Danny was already injured, we had Stuart Kennedy in at right-back. We also had Sandy Jardine, Martin Buchan and Kenny Burns in. Of course, I was out against England after my injury against Wales.

During the qualifying stages, the back four kept it pretty simple because you had people like Don Masson who would drop deep to collect the ball off us. And there were other players, such as Asa Hartford and Bruce Rioch, who were capable of coming and taking the ball from us. Our job was nice and simple, simply stop the opposition forwards from playing. When I was at Leeds, you had players like Johnny Giles and Billy Bremner dropping from midfield to take the ball; and at Manchester United, it was Ray Wilkins or Bryan Robson who you would roll the ball to.

Martin Buchan: I played left-back and in the match against Peru I was up against a guy, Munante, who was an Olympic 400m runner and I thought I did quite well against him. Unfortunately, there was a guy called Cubillas playing through the middle, up front. He and his team-mate were playing one-twos for fun through our defence. They were quite exceptional. I would have preferred to have played centre-back, but you take any chance to play for your country. I played left-back because Willie Donachie was suspended.

Stuart Kennedy: I was a right-sided full-back and had my hands full in the Peru game with their winger. The research on Peru could certainly have been better. They had two very fast wingers. Oblitas played against me. I'm no slouch myself and I needed all my pace and strength to keep him in check. If anything, the other winger, Munante, was a bit quicker and because of Willie Donachie's suspension for that game, we had Martin Buchan who was not a natural in at left-back. He was no slouch either, but he was a centre-back not a natural left-back. Peru were a very competent side.

I was hyped up for it. I've played league, cup, European and inter-national games, but that one was different. In the dressing-room before the game, I could hardly run. The tension that was in my legs! In my warm-up, I had this incredible tension. It was knowing that there were so many people at home pinning so much on you. I was thinking to myself, 'I'm actually going to be playing in the World Cup,' and I just couldn't get rid of this tension. After the first five to ten minutes of the game I was fine, but that was the most tense I have ever felt.

I was second from the end of the wall when Cubillas bent his free-kick in. Lou Macari was at the end. I couldn't have blocked it, but you'll see me turning my head to see where it was going. There was a lesson there, as far as putting one of your smallest guys at the end of the line. These days, sides like Wimbledon have all their tall players in the wall, rather than in the box trying to defend the cross. Their first priority is to make the shot on goal as difficult as possible.

Asa Hartford: The dressing-room was huge and, instead of bringing the group together at half-time to get his points across, Ally let the players scatter in threes and fours throughout the room. Some managers talk for the whole of the half-time period and the players go out more confused than when they came in. I always remember Brian Clough at Nottingham Forest. He would come in, make a couple of points, and that was it. They were the most relevant points. During one game, he went, 'Hey, fatty. Hey, big head,' referring to Larry Lloyd and Kenny Burns, 'you can't play and you can't run. I'm paying you good money, get out and get tight on these forwards.' And that was it. Point made.

I did feel that Ally could have brought us closer together at half-time. He wasn't a waffler. But he could have sat us down in a small area, so everyone could hear him and everyone could see him.

When you are a midfield player trying to press, you need your defenders quite close behind so that if the opposition try a one-two past you, there is someone there to track the move, to be in contention. But, of course, we were also being turned over by their two fast wide players. It was hard all round. They had good players.

Alan Rough: At the free-kick, I took a wee step to my right because I had a feeling he was going to try and send the ball around the wrong end of the wall. In normal circumstances, taking that step would be fatal, because most free-kicks are curled around the outside of the wall, not squeezed inside.

So stepping to my right was an attempt to get to the inside of the wall quicker than normal. But, of course, I never saw the ball until it was quite late, and I made a late-late dive. He hit the ball with the outside of his foot. I was just inches away because I had done what I shouldn't have. Had I stood my normal ground, I would have seen him kick the ball but I would never have got across. What do you do? I didn't see him kick the ball, but it was the right thing to do if I was going to have any chance of covering the distance. When you are up against players of that ability, you're sometimes saying, 'Just have a penalty.' You have a better chance of saving it, because at least you can see what he is doing.

Television evidence appears to exonerate Macari, posted on the outside of the five-man Scottish wall (from the left: Macari, Kennedy, Gemmill, Dalglish and Burns) and accused of moving out of the way of the shot. While he may have moved slightly, the flight of the free-kick seems to inch past Macari's original position. He looks guilty as sin in photographs taken from side-on and behind the goal. So, too, for that matter, does the next player in the wall, Kennedy. But one person's evasive action is another's curiosity as to where the ball has landed.

As one, the newspapers round on MacLeod. According to them, he is guilty on two counts: firstly, for failing to have researched Peru thoroughly enough and, secondly, for ducking the blame in the immediate aftermath of the game. He is quoted as saying, 'They didn't play as they could. They didn't play to their strengths. And when you have eight players like that you struggle. You couldn't even beat Muirend Amateurs.' He adds that Jordan is the best Scot and gives pass marks to Kennedy, Buchan, Hartford and Rough.

And elsewhere: 'It was not so much what Peru did. It was more what we did not do. We had seven or eight players who did not play well and when you have that many players off form, you will not beat an amateur team. I thought we played well for the first 15 minutes and if we had played like that for another 15 minutes we would have taken care of them. All we had to do was keep finding Jordan. But we failed to do that and started giving the ball away. They ran past us in midfield. If we had gone two-up there was no way Peru would have beaten us. Our fiery temperament was not there. We just did not get stuck in or play with enough force. We were a sloppy side. Why? I don't know – nerves, tension.'

As one, the players, 20 years on, cannot recollect any more than cursory background information on Peru. And Iran. It's clearly an issue at the time. A fortnight before leaving for Argentina, MacLeod feels it necessary to launch a pre-emptive strike in his newspaper column. He takes the readers through his late-night routine of watching videos of the opposition. He is clearly tickled pink by having a video machine at all. 'What I have looked for in my armchair spy sessions has been, basically, the general pattern and rhythm of a side; who their key players are, and how they work the set-pieces and particularly free-kicks. I am convinced that this World Cup will be won from these dead-ball situations.'

That said, he believes in letting the opposition worry about Scotland and not the other way around. He does, however, confess that the Scots were ill-prepared as far as their own set-piece repertoire was concerned in a friendly match against East Germany the previous September. He rates Don Masson as Scotland's key set-piece man.

Ian Archer, from the paper that had earlier given MacLeod his head, joins the chorus of criticism after Peru. He poses six questions: Why were Rioch and Masson playing instead of Souness and Gemmill? Why did it take MacLeod 73 minutes to take Rioch and Masson off? Why were Peru's 'flying wingers' being marked by a novice (Buchan) and an absolute beginner (Kennedy)? Why was Peru's best player, Cubillas, never marked? How much homework was done on Peru? Why was Scotland's traditional fiery play suddenly abandoned after the goal and replaced by a slow pace that was a certain ride to disaster?

Mike Aitken, in *The Scotsman*, thinks Scotland adopted too continental an approach of trying to knock the ball about, and that Munante and Oblitas were too much for Kennedy (inexperienced) and Buchan (stop-gap). He adds that Masson had a nightmare throughout and should never have been given the responsibility for taking the penalty since he was clearly low on self-belief; that Willie Johnston didn't cross a decent ball; that Dalglish had a shocker; that Rioch shone for just 20 minutes; that Hartford was overwhelmed; that Forsyth and Burns were solid but backed off too easily; that Kennedy didn't look international class; that Buchan fared little better as a stop-gap; and, finally, that Rough was blameless in goal. In other words, that the Scots didn't play their normal game, tackled like choirboys and strolled about as if it was a Sunday kickabout.

He declares: 'All the talk of winning the World Cup, all the rabid commercialism and the extraordinary conceit of the Scots blew up in their faces at the very first hurdle.'

Jim Reynolds, in the *Glasgow Herald*, writes: 'I watched in disbelief a Scottish performance so miserable, so dreadfully inept that I just wanted to hide from the local people who have given the Scots such support. When Scotland went one-up, too many players tried to show just how good they were individually, and they eventually paid the price which most show-offs have to pay . . . ignominious defeat.'

The South American press are as unforgiving: *Buenos Aires Herald* – Scotland's tactics were wrong. Cubillas wasn't adequately marked. Also, there was zone marking against a slow but technical team. *Diario Popular* – Scotland had a taste of Peruvian whisky. It made the Scots sick and they lost. *Cronica* – The excessive confidence of the Scots betrayed them. *La Prensa* – Peru were quicker and more clever. *La Nación* – Before the match the Scottish players were seen wandering the streets at all hours of the night. *Clarin* – Lack of Scottish imagination and serious defence problems.

Ian Archer, journalist: Bill Greig [now at the *Express*] was doing a piece for Independent Radio News. He wasn't doing a commentary as such, but an actualité piece. So he's doing this piece, along the lines of, 'We are at the decisive moment of the match and Don Masson, who has never missed a penalty for Scotland, is about to take the penalty. This is the goal that can take Scotland into the quarter-finals. Masson versus Quiroga.' There is then this deathly silence for a moment and then Bill's microphone hurtles past me and he's up there, shouting, 'You bastard, I always knew you would fucking miss!' This whole Scottish madness was there in that ten seconds.

The dug-out and the press box were miles from the pitch. You had your usual half a dozen Scottish dailies, your evening papers, your Sundays, TV, radio. If you leave the English contingent out, I suppose there were about 30 Scots in the press box. There was disappointment but it was recognised that Peru were a decent side, playing in South America. The feeling was not one of calamity. But there was nothing in Scotland's performance that night which indicated that things were going to end in absolute, bloody mayhem, which they did. After the Peru game, there was plenty of time to retrieve things.

Sandy Jardine: Scotland were well capable of beating Peru. If you are asking, 'Did Ally make any tactical mistakes?' then what I'm saying is that it doesn't matter what tactics you are using if the players are not performing. The players didn't play that night. I don't think they knew enough about Peru. It would have helped if we had more information about them. But I don't think you can say it was Ally's fault. We were all responsible.

Alex Smith, then manager of Stirling Albion: We went one-nil up and then the game started to stretch a little, they started to get room to play, to play one-twos and to put us under pressure. It might have helped had Ally had a couple of people in the stand to get a bigger picture of what was going on. There were so few back-room staff and they were down in the dug-out which was eye-level to the pitch.

After the game, Peru manager, Calderon, is quoted as saying: 'Only a baby would leave Cubillas and Cueto unmarked. We have always thought that Scotland played with more brawn that brain, but they did not even have that.'

Peru 3 (Cueto, Cubillas x 2) Scotland 1 (Jordan)

9. The Johnston Affair

The medication known as Reactivan is used to combat fatigue. It is available only on prescription and consists mainly of vitamins such as ascorbic acid, thiamine, pyridoxine and cyanocobalamin. It is neither a decongestant nor a remedy for hay fever. It is a mild stimulant, which works through the presence of the substance fencamfamin. In 1978, as far as football's world governing body, FIFA, was concerned, fencamfamin was a banned substance.

If defeat by Peru is not bad enough, the Scotland camp is dealt another shuddering blow to its morale when, during a post-match doping test, Willie Johnston tests positive for fencamfamin.

It is believed that only one other player has tested positive for substance misuse during a World Cup finals, a Haitian, Ernest Jean-Joseph, who was banned for a year by FIFA for taking drugs before a match against Italy during the West Germany finals in 1974.

The response of the SFA is swift and unequivocal: Johnston is immediately sent home in disgrace, banned from ever again playing for Scotland. A week later, journalist Ian Wooldridge tests Reactivan on himself. In the *Daily Mail* of 9 June, he explains they had precious little effect on him, concluding that what 'oddness' he felt was probably due to missing out on his usual lunchtime drink. (Instead of visiting a bar at lunchtime, he goes to a theatre to see a play, *Gaun ta ra Gemme*, about four Scottish fans making their way to Argentina by submarine. Coincidentally, the same edition of the paper carries a picture of Ally advertising carpets, to illustrate an article about advertisers backing away from the Scotland camp.)

From the start, Johnston makes no attempt to hide what he has done. He freely admits he has taken a couple of pills, equivalent, he believes, to a few cups of coffee. He says they are being taken for hay fever, repeated later in his autobiography in which he adds, crucially, that they were given to him by his club, West Bromwich Albion. He further claims that Reactivan is widely used in English football. Back in 1978, the FA wasn't carrying out drug testing; in other words, Reactivan was *de facto* not a banned medication in English football.

By the time the media begin to get wind of the story, the Scottish team are dressed in their official blazers, guests at an official reception being attended by the UK's Minister of Sport, Denis Howell. ITN's Trevor McDonald gets to within a whisker of asking a daft-grinning Johnston (there are television pictures to prove it) what is happening, when team manager, Ally MacLeod, abruptly jumps in to break the interview up.

It is a moment of unedifying high emotion. It is the storm before the hurricane as, next day, the media descend on the Scottish camp at their headquarters in Alta Gracia.

Russell Galbraith, television producer: Ernie Walker [the SFA secretary] asked me to set up the location for the press conference where he was going to read the formal SFA statement on the Willie Johnston affair. So I got these three chairs out and our cameraman, Varick Easton, positioned himself right in front of Ernie to get the best pictures. Just before, I got hold of [journalist] Doug Baillie, and I said to him, 'Doug, this place is going to go mad, everybody is going to be here, they are all going to be jumping. Can you help?' Sure enough, Ernie appears and sits down and, immediately, this Japanese photographer stands in front of Varick's lens. And you know Doug, he's a big man, and he lifts this photographer by the scruff of the neck. You have never seen anything so funny.

Ernie Walker, SFA Secretary, 5 June 1978: Gentlemen, we know why you are here. I propose to read a prepared statement to you, I don't intend to add to that statement and I don't intend to answer questions on the statement.

It has been agreed that you should be admitted here for the purpose of hearing the statement. It has been arranged with the security forces that the camp will be cleared immediately we have concluded the statement. Your co-operation in this respect will be appreciated. I'll read the statement.

Yesterday afternoon FIFA intimated to the SFA that the doping control test carried out on player William Johnston at the conclusion of the Peru v Scotland match had given a positive result. An immediate investigation was carried out and the player admitted that despite repeated warnings and instructions which were given to all members of the squad collectively and individually by the association medical officer, he had taken prior to the match two stimulative tablets.

During the course of this investigation it was established clearly and positively that no other player in the squad was involved in any way whatsoever.

The association's officials have decided that the player will not take any further part in the World Cup competition, that he will return home as soon as appropriate arrangements can be made, that further disciplinary measures against him will be considered later, and that he will not be selected to represent Scotland again.

The Scottish Football Association has never before been involved in such a matter. The officials concerned here in Argentina are determined that the good name of our country must be protected.

Whatever Scotland's results on the football field might be, they will be achieved fairly. Thank you.

MacLeod, unsurprisingly, is becoming more exasperated, defensive, tetchy, snapping at journalists for pressing him hard on Willie Johnston's sudden exit from camp and, infamously, he has that very public altercation with Trevor McDonald, now anchoring *News at Ten*, then a sports reporter for ITN.

Trevor McDonald: The loss against Peru was a great, great shock to the system. I'll never forget when Martin Tyler, the ITV commentator, and I went to the Peru camp the morning before their game against Scotland and there was a little man who was short and had very stocky legs, all bandaged up. He gave his age as late 20s and Martin said to me, 'Late 20s! more like late 30s. You can never trust these South Americans. Look at all these bandages. Legs gone.'

And then the match starts. And there is this man who is lying about his age by ten years, whose legs have allegedly gone, suddenly giving Kenny Burns about ten yards and going past him like a train. And, like a flash, though I'm no expert, I thought, 'This isn't right.'

And at the end of the game, I went down to see Graeme Souness [who didn't play] whom I knew quite well. It was very difficult to interview people but I managed to ask him, 'What is happening here? Do you think you can come back and win from here?' And he looked at me and smiled and said, 'Trevor, you saw it. What do you think?'

That was the first shock. Then next day, I began to hear rumours that a member of the Scottish contingent had tested positive for drugs. And as the day progressed, the story began firming up and I heard it might be Willie Johnston. I had been due to fly from Córdoba to be in Buenos Aires that evening and had declined an invitation to a party in Córdoba given by, I think, the British

Consul, and being attended by the Scots and the Minister of Sport, Denis Howell.

I got to Córdoba airport and, having just persuaded the airline to put our luggage in the hold as a matter of priority, I got a call from the office saying, 'It's serious, it is Willie Johnston and you have got to get to that party.' So we took the equipment back off the plane and dashed to the party and I arrived and had a brief conversation with Denis and somebody from the Embassy who was saying he hoped we would be doing a respectful job filming the Queen's birthday celebrations in Buenos Aires which we were due to do. And just as Denis was saying to this fellow, 'No, no, Trevor is an immensely decent man who is totally trustworthy,' I saw a BBC man – I can't remember who it was – interviewing Willie Johnston. So I made for him, I told the guys, 'Put the lights on and let's go.' And as I approached, from a long way off, Ally MacLeod saw what was going on and made a beeline for me and absolutely went ballistic and said, 'I thought you were a decent so-and-so and this is what you are trying to do – this is appalling and I want you to leave.' Of course, completely the reverse of what Denis Howell had been saying a few moments before.

I hadn't said a word to Johnston. Ally went absolutely ballistic. What he didn't realise was that while carrying-on for a good 30 or 40 seconds and getting the camera lights switched off, the sound kept running. And when the recording was broadcast, it caused an enormous sensation. Everybody was starting to say that MacLeod had gone mad, was starting to shout at correspondents now. It was considered the moment he lost it, though I must say that is very much on reflection, I didn't feel so at the time.

It was uncomfortable for those of us who had got to know him so well. He was very hurt about it, saying, 'Trevor, to think that you should be doing this.' All I was doing was trying to do a report on a story that was not of my doing, was a *fait accompli*, and was breaking at the time.

It had happened late at night and we next had the problem of getting the tape back to London. One of my colleagues, Stewart Purvis, who is now chief executive of ITN and was producer/fixer in Buenos Aires, somehow managed to get the tape to London via RAI [Italian TV station] and, by the next day, we were splashed everywhere. I never got to interview Johnston and one of the great ironies was that I'm sure the BBC man ahead of me had got a half-decent question in on the drugs allegation but I'm not sure if it ever saw the light of day, partly because they didn't manage to get their tape back to London as quickly as we did and partly because the MacLeod outburst eclipsed everything.

Afterwards, a BBC man came up to me and said, 'Look, I don't want to discuss the fact that you outscooped us, but I'll buy you a decent bottle if you can only tell me how you managed to get the tape so quickly to London.'

It is never very pleasant to be shouted and screamed at like that and I remember leaving in the car, feeling pretty chastened by it. Nobody else at the party would have known what was going on and, at a glance, they would have thought I had done something quite appalling and deserved to have been shouted out. In the car, I didn't fully realise what we had got until we rewound the tape and listened to it. And though I thought, 'Bugger me!' I was still thinking one-dimensionally and saying, 'No pictures, how awful.' It was Stewart who could see what could be done with it.

I have always regretted that Ally and I never really had any further dealings from that point. I believe he was a decent man doing a job that went frightfully badly wrong. I continued to go to press conferences and so on, but relations were a little strained – he didn't put a fraternal hand round me any more.

McDonald, despite his recollections, does get to Johnston. Just. A television camera from elsewhere and trained entirely on Willie Johnston shows McDonald getting only as far as saying, 'You've heard these reports –' Then, MacLeod steps in. Though both men are off camera and McDonald is beyond the range of the microphone, the incident is clear enough. MacLeod: 'There's a time and place to interview the players and it is during the day, not when they are here at the British Embassy. You're pushing your luck. I never thought the day would have to come when I would have to ask you to leave. There's a time and a place to ask people things and this is not it. Now get that straight. [Raising his voice, obviously in response to something McDonald has said] You are stooping to low tactics!'

No one can deny that Johnston, along with the rest of the players, was given repeated warnings about banned substances, told by the doctor with the Scottish party, Dr Fitzsimmons, to report anything, even tablets taken for as minor an ailment as a cold. The FIFA list of proscribed substances is massive. The Scotland officials are determined to take no risks. But it requires the co-operation of the players. Every one of Johnston's colleagues has sympathy for him. One even makes an attempt to take the heat out of the situation by admitting, vaguely, he might have taken something himself. But while many of the players feel Johnston is being harshly treated by the SFA, they also recognise he had his chance to come clean. He might have genuinely believed the pills to be aspirins by another name, but he still hid them from the Scotland doctor. At the very least, he is guilty of misjudgement.

Martin Buchan: I remember Doc Fitzsimmons being distraught because he had gone round every single player, with his clipboard and the FIFA directive, and he asked, 'Are you taking or will you be taking any of these drugs or similar?' I said, 'No, but I will tell you in the last couple of weeks I've taken Clinoril [brand name], I had a problem with my knee and it was to try and reduce the swelling.' And he made a note.

Unfortunately, the doc was told a lie. You have got to say that. The question was asked even if it was supposed that what was taken was harmless. At Manchester United, there were a couple of players when I first joined who had a little mouthful of brandy or whatever before they went out. It was psychological. I never drank until I was 19. I don't think I drank a whisky until I was 36. That was at a friend's house in Alloa, when I was travelling north and stopping overnight. I had one because he had run out of beer.

Joe Harper: It was really very soft what Willie Johnston took. It doesn't make you run any faster, it just makes you feel a bit better. Not that I saw anyone take anything, but maybe as many as five or six players might have taken it on the day Willie got caught. In fairness to the manager, the doctor had gone round everyone warning us not to take any drugs, no matter what, without consulting him first. Because there are drugs within drugs and some of them were banned.

Only England-based players knew of Reactivan. But it wasn't a great deal, players were not having to furtively go into the toilets. The pills were taken quite openly. It wasn't a question of doing it under cover. It wasn't considered a drug. It was considered a bit of a lift, like a vitamin C. Like taking an aspirin if you had a headache. When I was at Everton, before you went on to the park you were handed a bottle of whisky to take a slug if you wanted. I didn't take any, but I didn't need anything to gee me up before a game. Take anything? Stimulants? Never in my life. My boost was waking up on Saturday morning. It couldn't come quickly enough. Some mornings when I was at Aberdeen I'd wake up so early I could play six holes at the golf course next door.

A couple of days after Willie had been caught, Derek Johnstone, Alan Rough and I returned to the room Derek and I were sharing, just to rest in the humid conditions. And the doctor walks in to ask how we are, to ask if we had any injuries. And, next moment, he's going crazy. 'What the fuck is that?' he asks. And Derek, Alan and myself have no idea what he is going on about. And on one of the bedside tables is a nasal spray. And big Derek says, 'It is just a nasal spray doc.' And the doctor says, 'I know it is a fucking nasal spray. Who's using it?' And we are pointing at each other. Derek and I are both pointing at Roughie and he's pointing at us. And, apparently, there was a banned substance in it. That was how scary it was.

Harper will not name names when it comes to his allegation that Willie was caught while a handful of other players were popping a Reactivan. Derek Johnstone echoes Harper's claim and is as reticent about divulging identities. So too is Archie Gemmill. Ditto the rest of them. Their line is consistent: 'There were others, but I'm not going to finger them; if they have any decency, they will admit to it themselves.' Only one does. Twenty years on, the old bonds remain strong. There are certain things in football . . .

Derek Johnstone: Wee Bud got caught for taking Reactivan, but little did they know that a few others had been taking it. But, as usual, no one owned up, so wee Bud carried the can. Willie Johnston was the fastest thing on two legs, so why he needed Reactivan I don't know – obviously just to make him feel better.

I remember the doc coming around the rooms, asking if anyone had any tablets, even headache tablets, and I said, 'I've got this inhaler,' and he actually took it off me. I said, 'But I get a bit chesty at times,' and he said, 'Come and see me if there is a problem.' That's how seriously they were taking it. Anyone who had any tablets whatsoever, they took them off you, just in case they contained a banned substance.

I think it might have got to wee Bud that no one admitted how widespread it was, even when the dust had settled after the World Cup was over. Taken a bit of the pressure off him. Because he became the fall guy, the butt of all these jokes. These players have got to live with that, they all know who they are. It's not as if we are talking hard drugs. Things were exaggerated for effect. It was a banned substance he had taken. But it was all blown out of proportion to make a good news story and Bud has been living with the consequences ever since.

Archie Gemmill: I know of two or three players who flushed them down the toilet in a panic, but I have never taken anything in my life and I never would. To tell you the truth, even cough mixture was high up on the list [of medications containing banned substances]. If you wanted to take an aspirin or anything, it had to be cleared by the doctor. We got a circular with the list and I remember thinking, 'How can cough medicine be so high up?' You won't identify the two or three from me, that's for sure. I don't know if they ever took it, but most certainly it was, let's say, in the party. I had never heard of Reactivan until the World Cup, I had never heard of anything.

I was called with Kenny Dalglish to give a urine sample but they got the numbers mixed up and it was Willie Johnston and Kenny Dalglish they wanted. I went with Kenny and, of course, you struggle sometimes to give a sample. And a while later, I don't know if it was five minutes or twenty minutes, I was told I wasn't required any more. I was, if you remember, a substitute in the game. So I went and told Willie he had to go. I had been and when I gave my name and number it wasn't me they wanted. So I went back and told Willie, 'It is not me, it's you they want.'

Gordon McQueen: I didn't take Reactivan. I had never heard of it. I had not heard of drugs, full stop. I swear on the children's lives that no one at Leeds took anything like that. The only illegal drug that was taken – and it became illegal a few years later when it was discovered kids were taking them for a little bit of a buzz – was Mandrax, a heavy sleeping tablet. I had been in the Leeds United dressing-room which was unbelievably strict and disciplined, and although I had been at Manchester United for just a few months before Argentina, there wasn't a single person there involved in anything like that, because you would know. I smoked cigarettes. Smoked all my life – still do. But drugs were unheard of.

Bruce Rioch: Take Drugs? Absolutely not, guaranteed not. We didn't need stimulants, absolutely not. I learned from discussions that took place in the camp that at one football club in England, some of the players representing that club would take a Reactivan tablet now and again. That was the first time I had heard of it. Absolutely. I never knew about it until the manager told me Willie had been found positive.

In our championship year at Derby County, there was a period when we were doing well and there was a bottle of brandy in the dressing-room and somebody would have a very small nip before a game and then you would win the game and somebody would have a nip after. It wasn't a drink as such and it became a bit of a superstition. I don't think that was uncommon in a lot of football clubs. During that era, I can't recall players being spirit drinkers. They were, if anything, beer drinkers – a pint of beer could be sweated off. I can't remember any whisky drinkers in the squad.

Willie Donachie: Willie Johnston is a great guy but he was very highly strung. You would sit next to him and his feet would be tapping all the time. So the thing he took was the worst thing to take. What Willie needed was to calm down. It wasn't a performance-enhancing substance he took, it was a performance-detracting substance. I didn't know he was taking Reactivan. Had I known, I would have advised him strongly against it, because I had seen it being taken in England. Before a game I wanted to be as quiet and as calm as possible because I could get wound up. So had I known what he was on, I would have advised him against it. I'm not sure whether he knew what it was exactly. What I needed was a massage to calm me down, rather than something like that to make me even more uptight. I don't think Willie would have been the only one in the squad who took it, but I don't think it was widespread.

Kenny Burns: I used to take the odd Mogadon when I was at Birmingham, just to help me sleep on a Friday night. At Forest, I didn't need it, simply because I was pissed up. At Birmingham, they wouldn't allow you to have a drink; at Forest, if you said, 'I'll have a cola,' they'd say, 'He's no' having a cola, give him a beer. A cola is all acid.'

Graeme Souness: I wasn't mixing with senior players, I was not party to what was going on. So, from where I was standing, it was only him [Willie]. There were all sorts of stories afterwards; but at the time, nothing. [Asked if he took anything himself:] No. [And whether it was a widespread practice in the game:] In my experience of football, that wasn't the case.

Johnston's description of events in his autobiography runs, understand-ably, to many pages. There are a number of key points to his summary:

1. 'I had problems of my own before the game, as I was feeling lousy with a stuffed-up nose and a slight chestiness. I put it down to another bout of hay fever, to which I am prone, but it sure wasn't going to stop me playing. Before I left for Argentina, I had taken the precaution of securing some tablets from my own doctor at West Bromwich.'

2. 'Over an hour before the kick-off against Peru I confirmed the time with Sandy Jardine and proceeded to take two of the pills, quite openly, in a last effort to clear the stuffiness.'

3. 'Reactivan couldn't possibly be a drug, as I had used the pills often before at West Bromwich when I had these stuffy symptoms.'

4. 'Reactivan pills didn't pep me up, and of that I was positive. They merely acted as a decongestant for me.'

5. 'Many of the lads were shocked when they discovered that the Reactivan pills were to blame, because some of them had used them before at home, just as I had.'

6. 'The reporter [from the BBC] started firing questions at me . . . I immediately replied with a statement that was to become infamous the world over, and was used to condemn me time and time again. I said I have never taken anything like that in my life.'

7. [After being told he would never be selected to play for Scotland again:] 'The words hit me like a blast from a shotgun. I could feel my legs buckling under me. I was staggered.'

Willie Johnston: I should never have played against Peru. I was ill. I had a cold, I had hay fever, I was dying. I should not have played. But I was 32 years of age and a football player, it was the World Cup, and I wanted to play for my country. I was going to tell MacLeod how I felt, but I thought I would be all right on the night. Every football player is like that. I was crap, contribution nil.

I'd had a knee injury and played a practice game a couple of days or so before. And I thought to myself, 'You are not right here,' but I played. And I took two tablets.

There were four of us ordered to take a urine test: Cubillas, their right-back, Dalglish and myself. Archie Gemmill was selected but he wouldn't go [see Gemmill's version above].

Put it this way, I wasn't the only one on whatever I was supposed to have taken. I admit I took two tablets, I took two tablets called Reactivan. I've never said anything different. It is for other people to say what they did.

In England, in 1976, '77 and '78, most players were taking something, with some of them administered by their club doctors. I had mine prescribed by the doctor, but I can't say who. It was like taking a double brandy before a game. As far as I saw it, it wasn't a drug. In 1978 I could have taken two aspirin and the same thing would have happened. I thought it was all right to take the two tablets. I wouldn't have taken them if I knew it was wrong. I may be stupid, but nobody is going to take a substance that is going to be found out. At that time, every player in England had access to them. I got caught. When you had a touch of cold or the flu, club doctors would get hold of them for you. Ask the others. Ask them to take a look into their own conscience. Ask them. Did you or did you not?

At the urine test, I'll always remember looking at my sample and looking at Kenny's and I'm saying, 'Something funny going on here.' Different colours. It is only my word against somebody else's, but who's to say the samples were not tampered with or swapped around? I wanted an appeal and they wouldn't appeal. I asked Ally MacLeod. I wanted an appeal, but the SFA wouldn't appeal. I was the bad boy of Scottish football, and I was wanted rid of.

Scottish football wanted rid of me. Everyone has a right to an appeal. If it happened now, you would have heard nothing because I would have successfully appealed. Twenty years ago? No chance. I have no idea what they found in the test. To this day, I have never had a letter. If it had happened to anyone else, in the Scottish or any other camp, it would have been kept quiet. If it had happened in other camps, you wouldn't have heard about it. But I was the bad boy. The Scotland team could not refuse to take me to Argentina. They couldn't leave their best player at home, could they?

So I'm denied an appeal. I am being flung out of training camp. I'm being sent home in disgrace. If they had appealed, 24 hours later, they'd know I was clean. I take maybe an aspirin or a paracetamol. If I had taken two paracetamol I still would have been done. Why pick me?

Next morning [Monday morning, two days after the Peru game], I woke up and there were two hundred newspaper men sitting outside my door. I was at a reception the previous night. Trevor McDonald stuck a microphone in my face that night and asked,

'What about this drugs thing?' How quickly can you get a test result and then tell the media? It was a load of shite. They wanted rid of me. I was in the wrong place at the right time as far as they were concerned.

[That Monday morning] I'm sent for by Ally MacLeod. He asks if I had done anything and I say, 'Aye, taken two tablets.' And then we go into another room and an SFA committee are there, waiting for me. And I tell them the same thing and they send me back to my room. I wait a few hours and then they put me in a car, lying down in the back with a coat over my head, and take me out of the camp.

Eight-hour drive to Buenos Aires. Put up in a hotel in Buenos Aires. Left on my own. Next day, a car draws up from the British Embassy. It's a guy from Edinburgh – can't remember his name but I would kiss him if I saw him. He asks, 'Would you like a bottle of beer?' I reply, 'I would love a bottle of fucking beer.' He comes out with these big bottles of beer and we sit there blethering about football. I don't know who he was but he was a godsend.

I wasn't terrified until the boy came on with the machine-gun. By that time I was on the connecting bus on the airport tarmac. I was the only one on it, except for this boy with a gun who's jabbing the front of it in my ribs. I had earlier been in the VIP lounge on my own, now I was on this bus on my own, and I'm thinking, 'This is it, they are going to shoot me.'

Anyway, we get to the aircraft and they put me on it and I'm sitting in there, again on my own. There's nobody else on the plane and I'm thinking, 'What the hell is going on here?' The aircraft eventually fills up. It turns out to be a scheduled flight and we head back to Heathrow, via Rio and Paris. Got into London and Big Ron [Ron Atkinson, WBA manager] is there to meet me and he says, 'I've got you a contract with Boots the Chemist.'

All the press boys had got on at Paris to try and have a word with me. But they went first class, thinking that was how I would be travelling. I was in the baggage hold – well, second class. I was knackered – 21 hours of flying. I hadn't had a drink. It was the only time in my life I thought, 'I wish the plane would go down.' All these people reading their Argentinian newspapers with 'Willie Johnston' in the headline. Got to Paris. Asked if I could phone my wife. Couldn't, wasn't allowed. Into London, a massive scrum. Press boys. And I still didn't get to phone my wife. As it turns out, she has been taken to a hotel in Oxford by Big Ron.

So we are in London and I'm knackered and Big Ron comes up

with the idea of me appearing on this news programme. He's saying to me that Bob Wilson is maybe losing his job and if I give him a scoop interview, I'd be helping him. I'm knackered, I'm asking where my wife is, when can I see her, but I say, 'Fuck it, let's get it over with,' and we go to the studios. I should never have done it. I was knackered. I was used. I did it for Big Ron who was just doing it to get his foot in the TV door and I was his pawn. I was meant to just explain what had happened but I was being accused by this panel of people of taking drugs.

And what happened next? One minute I'm playing in the World Cup and the next minute I'm in the WBA reserves. They would never play me. One day we were playing Tottenham and, again, I'm on the bench. Now, honest, we were a good team – Laurie Cunningham, Cyrille Regis, Ally Brown – a lot of good professionals. And the team keeps winning and they are playing so well I can't get back in the side. But we are playing Tottenham one day at the Hawthorns and Tottenham are one-nil up with 20 minutes to go and Ron says, 'Get warmed up.' Ten minutes later I'm still warming up and the crowd is shouting for me to go on. And I'm saying, 'Give me ten minutes and I might turn it around,' and he's saying, 'I'm not bowing to the crowd.' So I just go up the tunnel for a bath and I'm in the bath when Ron comes in and says, 'Tony Brown is injured, you'll have to go on,' and I just say, 'Fuck off.'

I get grief about it all the time. Every time there's a drug scandal, the media are on to me. The sprinter Ben Johnson gets caught and I'm asked, 'Are you related?' Swear to God, I get stick all the time. I'm supposedly football's junkie. There is only one Scotsman who has scored two goals in a single European final [Johnston as Rangers defeat Moscow Dynamo 3–2 to lift the European Cup-Winners' Cup on 24 May 1972]. But what sells papers? I get called almost every week by the press about drugs, even now.

Anyway, a few months after Argentina and I'm just trying to get away from it all, and especially away from West Brom, and Tony Waiters [former Blackpool and England goalkeeper] asks if I want to spend some time playing in Canada where he is the manager of Vancouver Whitecaps. Lovely man, Tony. And my wife and I think, 'Why not? We could do with the break.' So we are at the press conference in Vancouver, announcing my signing, and up pops Tony, saying, 'Vancouver is, as everyone knows, the drugs capital of the world, so Willie should feel very much at home.'

In the book *Football is Still a Funny Game* by Ian St John and Jimmy Greaves, Ron Atkinson tells a yarn of the journey he and Johnston make from the airport to the television studios. On the M4 motorway out of Heathrow airport into London, Atkinson is going at some speed behind the wheel of his Jaguar and soon spies two motorcycle headlights in his mirror. Believing he is about to be caught for speeding, he tries all sorts of evasive action to shake off his adversaries – he turns sharply off the motorway at Chiswick, he zigzags through a maze of small streets, he does a quick U-turn, he drives up a one-way street, he stops at a green light and drives off when it turns red. He even reverses into the motorcyclists. But they are still on his tail when he arrives at the BBC studios. He's ready to utter, 'It's a fair cop,' when it is revealed the motorcyclists are BBC outriders sent to prevent the car from being followed.

Willie Johnston: I got them at West Brom. I took them with me from the UK. In a wee bottle. I also took salt tablets and vitamin C. But, as I always say, put these pills to the test. How serious a drug were they? The only time you were prescribed them was when you had the cold or the flu. So, if you missed training for two or three days, you would take Reactivan to supposedly give you a lift. You didn't take them on a regular basis, only if you felt a bit under par. And I didn't feel good before the Peru game.

Did I get the chemist's report? Maybe something was found in one of the other samples that was worse than fencamfamin, but I became the fall guy because they had also found fencamfamin in my sample. I don't know. I never got a chance to appeal. I made their life easier by putting my hand up and admitting I'd taken two tablets. If I had kept quiet, I'd at least have got access to the evidence and an appeal.

I was sitting in the bath when Archie got me for the doping test. I could have said no. Do you think that if I knew I had done something wrong I would have gone?

You ask the others. But they are still in football and they don't want to bring up the past. They know what they did. Twenty years on, they're still in football and they're still telling people they did nothing.

Scottish Football Association Annual Report, 7 May 1979: All of the events in Argentina are documented in the association's minutes and there is little point in raking them up in this report. However, one event, the worst of all to befall us, must be mentioned for the record. One of the players was found to be guilty of taking a stimulative drug before our match with Peru. He did so furtively and despite, like all of the players, having been warned and instructed on FIFA regulations in these matters. If the party needed anything else to depress morale after our defeat by Peru and the tidal wave of abuse heaped upon officials and players by a section of the media, nothing could have been better calculated to do the job. The thoughtless and reckless action of one player caused the football world to go into a state of self-righteous shock. Scotland were shown to be cheats and Scots everywhere, who had so recently been flushed with pride, were ashamed. The focal point where that shame was felt most keenly was the battered remnants of the group in Argentina. There was never any serious likelihood of survival after that. The party was over.

At least one player makes a representation on behalf of Johnston, his room-mate, Don Masson. It is a vague and confusing intervention. The SFA's own records take up the tale:

Scottish Football Association Annual Report, 7 May 1979: There was a strange side issue to the Willie Johnston affair. The team manager and the doctor reported that, on two occasions after the Johnston investigation had started, his room-mate, Don Masson, said to them that he had taken the same tablets that Johnston had taken, at the same time as Johnston. Naturally, it was decided immediately that Masson should be interviewed in addition to Johnston.

When this was done, the player emphatically and vehemently denied having taken any drugs, either in Argentina or at any other time during his career. He admitted having misinformed the manager and the doctor, apologised profusely for having done so, and advanced the reason that in a fit of misplaced loyalty he had imagined that by jumping on the bandwagon, as it were, he would, in some way, be helping his pal who was obviously in trouble.

He seemed to be utterly sincere and was certainly very convincing. The president [Willie Harkness] interrogated him closely and at length and finished by having the player utter a categorical assurance of his innocence. He was then advised that no action, meantime at least, would be taken against him. In other words, unlike Johnston, he was not about to be sent home.

Don Masson: He was my room-mate. Obviously, with hindsight, it was the wrong thing to do. But I felt that I should try to support him by saying it could have been anybody. It was a silly thing to say, but your mind is not clear when your mate is being hauled up for doing whatever. Maybe I should have kept quiet and let them get on with it. I didn't take anything myself, I didn't take anything like that in my life. It got all blown out of proportion. It got to the papers. I denied I had taken anything. But I was tainted. You say things to try and help your mate, not thinking they will take it literally.

I was told I wasn't playing in the Iran game because of loss of form. It had nothing to do with my supposed admission. It might have contributed. After the penalty miss against Peru, I wasn't in the right frame of mind, anyway. I wouldn't have done myself or the team justice. Had Ally not said he was going to drop me because of my form, I would have probably volunteered not to play.

Ally MacLeod: Had we qualified from the section, one of the frightening things was the possibility of us being prevented from going through because of the Willie Johnston thing. That would have been a bigger blow to Willie Johnston than it already was. I believe that Willie Johnston didn't think he was taking drugs. At that time, in England, there were certain clubs who did give out so-called pep pills. I don't think he thought they were drugs.

Don Masson I think more or less acted out of loyalty to Willie. I don't believe he had taken anything himself. I said that at the time.

After the thing blew, I said, 'Right, if anyone has got pills, hand them over,' and there were quite a lot. It looks like in England, at that time, certain clubs were definitely giving out these pep pills. We didn't see who put them. We didn't ask people to reveal themselves.

There is the standing joke about the cows. There was this field of cows and, I'm not kidding, they could hardly walk because of the heat. And we just threw the pills in the field, and when we got back about 12 hours later, you want to have seen them, they were fleeing all over the place. That's an absolutely true story. Whether it was the weather that changed them, I don't know.

Ken Gallacher, journalist: I got the only interview with Johnston for a daily [newspaper]. I was a friend of his and got access. He was bewildered by it, shocked. He didn't know he had taken a banned substance. Players are like that, they won't be that exact about the ingredients of what they are taking. It was Reactivan, it was like three or four cups of black coffee. I still think Scotland treated him very badly in the sense that he was made incommunicado, hustled to an airport and shoved on to a plane and sent home on his own. I think someone should have gone with him. It wasn't that he had deliberately done anything. He had made a mistake. He was wrong. He should have read the ingredients, but it was not a wilful thing. It is a fact of life that players tend to have – and therefore expect to have – everything done for them, so maybe the manager and coaching staff should have been even more careful checking what the players had with them.

Asa Hartford: I remember the doctor coming around a few days before the Peru game and unfurling this list of banned substances. Reactivan was a pill supposed to contain caffeine and players had taken it in England. I had taken it, but I took nothing with me to Argentina. It was like a caffeine pill. The way it was blown up in the world's press, you'd think it was a hard drug. Some of the players were critical of the way the SFA handled it. He was gone before anyone realised. Even if we wanted to, we could not make a representation on his behalf. It was as if he was a criminal. He was away in the middle of the night, it seemed. From then on, the atmosphere in the camp wasn't very good.

SFA International Committee, 10 July 1978: The committee continued discussion of the various circumstances of the World Cup, and it was decided that the following statements should be issued:
(1) The committee homologated the decisions taken in Argentina by the office-bearers when it was decided that player, William Johnston (West Bromwich Albion) who had admitted to taking two stimulative tablets prior to the match with Peru, in contravention of the Doping Regulations of the FIFA World Cup
   (a) should be sent home immediately
   (b) should not be selected to represent Scotland again; and
   (c) should be subject to further disciplinary action at a later date, if necessary.
In considering this question of further disciplinary action, the committee came to the conclusion that the steps which had been taken were sufficient to meet the case.
   The secretary intimated that FIFA had advised that the player

had been suspended from all international activity at representative and at club level until 12 June 1979.

(2) It was decided that:

(a) The player, Don Masson, having admitted to the office-bearers that he had given false information to the association's team manager and medical officer on a most important issue in Argentina and having expressed the view publicly that he would prefer not to play for Scotland [reference to Masson's newspaper article on his return], should be accommodated in his desire.

(b) The team manager, when selecting players in the future, should be recommended to bear in mind the vehement complaints of the association and its arrangements publicly expressed by the player, Lou Macari (Manchester United) and should give consideration to the advisability of subjecting the player again to these arrangements, which he professes to find so unsatisfactory.

(3) The committee is of the opinion that the morale of the players was seriously affected by the numerous distractions, exaggerations and, in many cases, quite hysterical comments, by the media. It may well be that certain aspects relating to the players were worthy of criticism but whatever their shortcomings might have been, they did not warrant the savage attack which was mounted against them. It is sad enough that those responsible should have caused almost irreparable damage to Scottish football, but even more serious, and of much greater concern, is that their utterly irresponsible actions should have caused international damage to Scotland as a country.

(4) The secretary was instructed to consult the association's legal agents to determine if one particularly vicious piece of reporting is actionable.

(5) The committee proposes to take steps to ensure that in future international match excursions players be prevented from indulging in journalistic exercises and wishes it to be known that any player found to be in breach of these restrictions must be prepared to face the consequences in terms of future selection for Scotland.

(6) The committee is referring to the Executive and General Purposes Committee the question of doping and recommends that the whole subject, which has never arisen in Scotland before, should be discussed and examined at British level.

10. Iran

Wednesday, 7 June 1978
IRAN: *Hedjazi, Nazari, Kazerani, Abdollahi, Eskandarian, Parvin, Danaiefard (Nhyebagha), Sadeghi, Ghasempour, Faraki (Rowshan), Jahani*
SCOTLAND: *Rough, Jardine, Buchan (Forsyth), Burns, Donachie, Macari, Gemmill, Hartford, Jordan, Dalglish (Harper), Robertson*
REFEREE: *T. N'Diaye (Senegal);* LINESMEN: *N. Rainea (Romania), A. Collho (Brazil)*
ATTENDANCE: *8,000, Córdoba*

Once in a blue moon, you hear it mentioned in an Edinburgh boozer. The one about the Iranian internationalist – one of the side who played Scotland in Argentina – who is now running a newsagent/café/restaurant (delete as appropriate) in the capital, trading on past glories, especially that June day in 1978 when he nutmegged Kenny Dalglish.

Investigations suggest the tale to be a preposterous urban myth. So best assume it is 100 per cent true. And why get upset about it? Better that the city can boast an Iranian internationalist than no internationalists. Three of the 22-man Scotland squad – Jardine, Macari and Souness – were born in Edinburgh. And yet only Jardine remains. And even he commutes to Glasgow every working day.

The result against Peru is a shattering blow. But Willie Johnston's departure from the camp has the effect of relegating the football almost to a sideshow. The players feel they are being vilified on a daily basis by the media. There is an atmosphere of resignation. But the truth of the matter is that a win over Iran is, from a football point of view at least, all that is required to lever the Scotland bandwagon back on to the rails. Rationally, there is still much to play for. If reason can survive the collapse in morale, there is still a chance. Iran have lost their first game, against Holland, 3–0, though two of the Dutch goals come from the penalty spot. They are clearly no pushovers as respectable results against Yugoslavia, Bulgaria and Wales during their World Cup warm-up have proved. But, beat Iran, get a result against Holland and it'll be MacLeod the Master Magician. You know what you can do with your Willie Johnston affair.

The odds of Scotland winning the World Cup are now at 50/1. To win the group, they have fallen from 11/8 on the day before the Peru game to 10/1.

Unlike the Peru game, however, there is really no ebb and flow in the match against Iran, no breaking the game down into phases of changing fortune. It is, from start to finish, simply poor. Scotland kick off with five changes to the team that lined up against Peru. Masson is out for loss of form. Johnston is already back in the UK. Forsyth is relegated to the bench. Kennedy has a stomach bug. Rioch has a leg injury. Donachie is back after suspension. There is a new and untried central defensive partnership of Buchan and Burns.

Two minutes before the interval Scotland go into the lead, but the lack of all-round industry means it is greeted with muted celebration. The goal comes from a marvellous piece of Iranian ineptitude. From almost the edge of the box and with the whole pitch to aim for, an Iran defender, Eskandarian, manages to contrive the ball into his own net. It results from a long ball down the middle from Hartford. The keeper comes out to collect, but as he crashes into the on-rushing Eskandarian and Joe Jordan, he spills the ball. Jordan is pole-axed and there isn't another Scot within five yards. But still the defender panics. And as he falls backwards, he lofts a left-footed shot into the back of his own net. There is little in the way of Scottish crowing.

The Iran equaliser contains bizarre elements too. It arrives on the hour mark. Danaiefard collects the ball on the left edge of the box, cuts outside and round Archie Gemmill, the Scotland captain, to leave a narrow angle for a clear shot. As Jardine tries in vain to cover sufficient ground to block him, Rough suddenly increases the likelihood of a goal by abandoning his near post to allow a clear, albeit slim, channel for the player to steer the ball home. Television pictures show a despairing Kenny Burns. His pained expression and outstretched hands say it all. Aw, for fuck's sake. He knew, everyone knew, this would be a game that was going to live forever in the memory. An indelible stain, later to be joined by the likes of Costa Rica and Estonia, football giants every one.

In fairness, Rough has expertly prevented other goalscoring opportunities for the Iranians, including one in the 12th minute when he has to scramble clear a shot by Faraki, following a break and cut-back by Jahani. Mind you, Scotland have their early chances too. During the first five minutes, Macari and Dalglish are presented with glimpses of goal and in the 17th minute Dalglish cuts a ball back when a shot would have probably been better. During the course of events, Scotland have two strong claims for a penalty. But, overall, the side lack punch. The smell of smouldering cordite is in the air. 'Disastrous, disastrous,' Don Masson tells Trevor McDonald somewhere deep inside the stadium. 'I think this is the worst performance ever by a Scottish team. Everything has gone sour in the camp. It's become a nightmare.'

A little later, Scottish screenplay writer Alan Sharp, domiciled in Hollywood but following the national team, tells a TV documentary crew: 'The blame factor seems to me to be not nearly as interesting as the understanding of that disintegration. Because I think it has something to do with the very essence of being Scottish, something to do with a will to lose or McIlvanney's phrase about "Snatching defeat from the jaws of victory". But that was different because the jaws of victory hadn't opened. So if it was going to be talked about, it would have to be talked about in some recondite terms. It wasn't to do with sport, it was to do with some failure of nerve or some loss of reflex co-ordination. I've never seen the like of it.'

The condemnation appears from all angles. SFA president Willie Harkness says: 'Action has to be taken. This has not been good enough.' The chairman of the Selection Committee, Tom Lauchlan, is quoted as saying: 'There will be an immediate meeting when we return to Scotland.' Joe Jordan: 'We flopped again, emotionally and physically. I don't understand it. I just want to tell the angry millions we know how they feel – no sicker than us.' Derek Johnstone: 'I'm sure I won't play against Holland. For some reason the manager doesn't want me in the team. It's been a waste of time being here. I feel really sick.'

It's enough to send advertisers to flight – kind of difficult for a car company like Chrysler to justify an advert comparing Scotland with one of its models because 'they both run rings around the opposition'. The day after the game, comedian Andy Cameron's World Cup single is allegedly being sold for 1p in a Dundee shop which is also offering the free loan of a hammer. One moment of light relief is a report that TV pictures of the Iran manager Hesmet Mohajerani chain-smoking during the game has earned him an official rebuke from both the country's strong anti-smoking lobby and the Shah.

Andy Cameron, comedian: We were going to release an album of football songs and comedy on the day after the Iran game, because that was when Scotland were meant to qualify for the next round. The last I heard was that there are 10,000 copies of the album lying in a garage in Clarkston [Glasgow]. Or at least the ones that haven't been made into fruit bowls and ashtrays. That's an old line I've used before.

The album went on sale, but I think about three copies and a cover were sold. It was a great cover: my face with a wee drawing of a body, on top of the world.

The single made a wee bit of money – nothing extravagant. I wrote it with another comedian, Clem Dane, and the most popular line was, 'For England cannae dae it 'cos they didnae qualify'. It was to the tune of a Rangers song, by Lex McLean, 'Who's That Team They Call the Rangers?'.

I was booked to do a show on the night of the Iran game. I said to the manager at the venue, 'Look, I'll do the show before the game and then maybe a bit more after we've seen the game on TV.' And he says, 'Naw, don't worry. Do your whole show after.' I think my second line was, 'Start the engine.'

Russell Galbraith, television producer: The obvious other side to Ally giving everybody fun and involvement and high expectation was the palpable disappointment when the roof fell in. I know sensible folk who were in tears after watching our defeat against Peru on the television. You heard of cafés advertising themselves by saying, 'Ally hasn't eaten here.'

Archie Gemmill (captain against Iran): I've said many times that the thing that let us down was the draw against Iran. In those days, a Scotland team would have beaten Iran 99 times out of 100. To draw against them, maybe we didn't deserve to go any further than that. We were poor on the day and Iran played, over the 90 minutes, possibly better than we did. You get things like that happening now and again. I think they played near their maximum but we didn't play anywhere near what we could do. I think if we had played them on another day – a couple of days later perhaps – we would have defeated them quite comfortably. At the time, we were most certainly down.

Martin Buchan: Against Iran, we were one-nil up and I got injured. There was a ball played in between Willie Donachie – who was back playing left-back – and myself. It bisected us. And I thought Willie was going to miss the ball and I stooped down to head clear and Willie, who pirouetted like a ballet dancer, connected with the ball and one of his studs slashed my head open. I have the scar to prove it. So I was led from the field bleeding like a sheep and Dr Fitzsimmons took me into the bowels of the stadium for treatment.

The dressing-rooms in Córdoba were underground. And the doc was stitching my head up and there was a muffled roar. He said, 'I think we have scored, Martin,' and I said, 'Doc, I have a funny feeling they have equalised.' And then we had to endure the taunts from the Scottish fans when we left the stadium. And they were chanting, 'No Mendoza, No Mendoza.'

Willie Donachie: I went to the World Cup in 1974 though I didn't play, and the atmosphere was great. And the atmosphere was great for the match against Peru. But there were only 8,000 people at the game against Iran. And it felt such an anti-climax, especially for all these players used to playing in front of massive crowds. And though we scored, you still sensed things were not right. And a draw was considered a terrible result – which it was, in a sense. But, again, it wasn't as bad as people made out. There are no mugs in the World Cup finals. And Iran had a few very good players – one played in the NASL [North American Soccer League] and played for Cosmos, with Pele and other big players.

Asa Hartford: The stadium had a 40,000 capacity and there were only about 8,000 or so at the game. You just couldn't take in the importance of the game – it was like a reserve-team fixture. It was certainly one of the worst games I have ever played in. I remember actually thinking that during the second half. There was an occasion, when it was 1–1, and a ball was knocked through towards our goal and Kenny Burns turned round to chase it back with this Iranian bearing down on him. And there was that fat arse of Kenny's chasing back and this Iranian player looking as if he was going to beat him to the ball. And I thought, 'This fella could go through and score.' Fortunately, Kenny got the saving tackle in. I thought, 'We could lose this one.'

Alan Rough: When I got to Argentina, I knew, deep inside, that I wasn't playing well, to the top of my form. If you split the season into a beginning, middle and end, you'll find any player will have changing fortunes – maybe a sticky start, then come away in the middle and have a good ending. I was, unfortunately, not playing as well as I thought I could.

I thought Peru's first goal was a good goal from their point of view and it didn't really bother us. It was their second and third that were the problem. Obviously, after Peru, there was a lot of pressure. But, basically, against Iran, I had nothing to do. I don't think I even had a save to make, bar the goal. These are things that happen to a goalkeeper. People were drawing up all these astrological charts on players, saying this player was at his peak, and that one wasn't; you know, your moon and all that. I just knew that, at the end of the season, I wasn't playing well. It's not something you dwell on.

But think of the goals that went in during that World Cup. There were goalkeepers like Dino Zoff [Italy] being beat from 40 yards. If you compiled the top 30 goals from Argentina '78, you would get a shock at the quality and the top keepers being beaten.

The ball was so light. The balls were much lighter than those we were used to over here. I was also the only goalkeeper in the World Cup that never wore gloves, and certainly not those new hi-tech gloves that were starting to appear. I don't think they had even arrived in England; they were certainly not around in Scotland. We still wore these green, gardener's things. We had never heard of those hi-tech gloves. Whether they would have made a difference, I don't know. Mind you, I suppose you would need to get near the ball for them to work.

Gordon McQueen: I couldn't make an objective analysis of the games, (a) because I was young and (b) because all I wanted was a win because there was a chance of playing in the second phase. I was in no state of mind to be over-bothered about anything but wins. I wasn't thinking about tactics, I had tunnel vision at the time. I wanted my leg better and I wanted to play in the second phase. How we won the games I couldn't give a toss.

John Robertson: I didn't feel too bad about the World Cup. After all, I was a new boy in the squad. MacLeod announced the 22 to go to Argentina before the Home Internationals. I'm sure it's something he regretted because I played against Northern Ireland and had a nightmare. It was my début cap and because the squad had already been picked I don't suppose he was able to go back on his word.

Looking back, I was a wee bit overawed by all the names, even though I had just won the League Championship with Nottingham Forest. That's not to say the lads didn't make me feel welcome – they were fine. It was just me, thinking, 'What am I doing with these sort of people?'

I went out there not expecting to play, because Bud Johnston was the kingpin and I went as the understudy. And then, unfortunately, with him being sent home over the drug thing, I got to play. And I had another nightmare.

I had also played against Wales in the Home Internationals, but had come on as a sub. So my first two starts, against Northern Ireland and Iran, were, to say the least, very disappointing. I remember thinking afterwards, 'At least I've done it, my mum and dad can be proud that I played for Scotland.'

I think the manager put a lot of pressure on the squad before we left; I believe his quote was that we were going to come back with a medal. It's all right being optimistic, but that was a very bold statement. There was all the fanfare when we left. There is nothing wrong in being confident, but you can go over the top and it is certainly over the top to say you will be coming back with a medal.

We have a thing in this country: we are always saying we have the best this and the best that. But we are not seeing players in Russia or Uruguay every week. It's a bold statement to say you're the best in the world. There were a lot of good players from other countries at that World Cup.

I didn't enjoy the trip but I can't say the psychological scars didn't heal. Even though I played badly, I don't feel I was to blame. It was the manager's judgement to throw me in and I've got to say I wasn't the only one to play badly against Iran. We were all pretty poor in that game.

At Nottingham Forest, a lot of the play would come through me. With Scotland, there were more areas where an attack might come from, so I didn't get as much of the ball as I was used to. Maybe I tried too hard to impress when I did get the ball. It's hard to remember the details of the Iran game. I didn't particularly enjoy it and I didn't want to remember it. I don't think I should have gone. Looking back, I don't think Ally should have picked me. I was untried, I hadn't really played with the team, and he really should not have taken me.

I remember taking a free-kick very early on in the game that the goalkeeper just tipped around the post – I took it quickly. Had that gone in, it might have been an entirely different approach. But we scored through an own-goal and then, in the second half, they get an equaliser and, by the end, they could have won it.

Joe Harper: Thirteen minutes against Iran: that was my say in the World Cup. There were only a few of us who returned to Glasgow after the tournament and, although there weren't many people there to meet us off the plane, I remember being heckled and spat at. And I'm thinking, 'Thirteen minutes at the end of a game against Iran for this?' It's easier to say than do, but had I been in the frame for the next World Cup I would seriously have thought twice before saying yes.

I came on against Iran to replace Kenny Dalglish. I had been taken along as Kenny's understudy. I was in superb form that season – every Saturday I went all-out to impress. My first touch [against Iran] was getting the ball in the inside-left position. And I saw Sandy Jardine going down the right wing and I sent a 30-yard half-volleyed pass straight to his feet. And I thought, 'That's exactly the sort of start I need.' And that was about all I did. It had got to the stage when hopeful long balls were being pumped to Joe Jordan. We were desperate. I got one half-shot in. We had a corner and I said to Joe – who was being constantly marked by two defenders – 'When this corner is taken, just take these two guys out of the road. Run away and take them with you.' So the corner is taken and Joe starts running away. But he can't resist coming back in. So, though the ball is at my feet about eight yards out, I'm surrounded by defenders and it becomes a scramble and nothing comes of it. Coming off the park was pretty rough, with the fans giving us a very hard time.

Ian Archer, journalist: You couldn't believe how impossibly badly Scotland played against Iran. They were so flat. It wasn't a Scotland team. I have only ever seen it three or four times in over 30 years of journalism when you feel there is something wrong with a team. Whatever you get with Scotland in terms of talent, you do get passion, heart, fight and they are up for it. But on that night, they were just not up to playing. It was a stunning thing; something went badly wrong. It was an inexplicable performance. The last match was an irrelevance. Something had gone wrong in that week up at Alta Gracia. Not the match against Peru. That was not a dishonourable defeat and the situation was still retrievable.

Leaving aside anything more sinister, the thing was compounded by bizarre team selections. We picked rotten teams. No one knew quite where they stood, who was playing in the next match.

Against Iran, one of the factors has to be complacency – has to be. It was a watershed. Everyone – the hacks, the fans, everybody – left that game and for a long time afterwards we couldn't trust a

Scottish football team. To have invested so much, it just felt like it wasn't worth it any more.

Four years later, we go to Spain and there's 20,000 Scots on the Costa del Sol. We play average but there's 20,000 people who have been on holiday, got a sun tan, had a drink, been out there with the family. And they are saying to themselves, 'This is great. We can support Scotland, have a good holiday, and though the team didn't do as well as we had hoped, they tried hard.' I'd say 1978 removed the panic of thinking we could do well.

Straight after the Iran game, the team came out on one level [of the stadium] and the fans were on another and, though they were close, they were kept apart by being on separate levels. I've always thought that had the fans got to the players, they would have lynched them. The atmosphere was not the kind of mindless hooliganism that haunted the game during that era; this was so many hundred people who had spent a fortune getting there who felt, utterly, that they had been let down. I've never seen people more angry in my life. It was complete and utter anger.

Adrian Haren, fan: The lowest ebb in the relationship between team and supporters came immediately after the 1–1 draw with Iran. Scotland shirts and scarves were hurled at the players as they made for the tunnel. When the team bus began to leave the stadium it got bombarded by coins and spittle. A few fans even attempted to turn the bus over on its side as the driver tried to negotiate a corner. But there was no way the bus could be turned over, due in no small part to the heavy police presence. Nonetheless, the players on the bus looked genuinely alarmed, and so they deserved to be.

Brian Fleming, fan: Basically, everyone seemed to go for the team bus. You are talking about maybe 40 people surrounding the bus who were hysterical and really pissed off. The police turned up, and I think they might have had a water cannon with them. But I don't think they knew what to make of it. They didn't know whether the fans were being friendly or angry. I wasn't involved in any charge on the bus. My pal, Robbie, had a great big Lion Rampant flag and I took the pole off him because I didn't want some nutter trying to take it off him or anything. So I just watched things from a distance, holding this pole. I don't think it was ever going to turn nasty, though there were a few who seemed to lose it and then said afterwards they felt stupid. There were quite a few Argentinians there too, just watching. One guy went down to the front and started calling the players wankers – he'd had a drink – and he got tapped on the shoulder by this wee girl about seven years old who asked him for his autograph. And he stopped, signed the autograph and then turned back at the players to keep having a go at them.

Sandy Jardine: Asa Hartford and I got drug tested after the Iran game. I remember getting pelters for keeping the bus waiting. But it was so warm and I was so exhausted I couldn't pee. And I'd be drinking and drinking and still I couldn't pee. And I would give a wee trickle and the boy would say, 'No, No, more.' It took at least half an hour, maybe three-quarters of an hour, and when we were eventually able to go to the bus, we got pelters from the players because they had been given grief from the supporters.

John Duffy, fan: Some of us only saw the second half of the Iran game because we were lifted by the police a couple of hours before kick-off because we had a banner with 'All this Way for SFA [Scottish Football Association or Sweet Fuck All, take your pick]' on it. We did feel a bit let down. The SFA could have at least given us a couple of free tickets. The players didn't want to know. They had already made their money – it cost them nothing to get there. The SFA had all their perks. For some fans, their life savings had gone into the trip.

So we were thrown into jail for a couple of hours. The Argentinian police could not speak much English and we couldn't speak much Spanish. I think they thought the banner was a political thing, against the Junta. But eventually they let us out at half-time. They drove us to the stadium for the second half in a Black Maria. There were about 17 of us. They let us in, just opened up a gate.

After the game, it was like a death in the family. We had nothing to do with the attack on the team bus. I was too gutted, too shell-shocked. There weren't that many fans involved, only a few were throwing things at the bus and trying to roll it over. But it was just a few – there was no chance of the situation becoming dangerous. It was just frustration.

Myself and two other guys, John McK and Rab R, began hitching from Córdoba to Mendoza for the Holland game. And we got dropped off in the middle of the pampas. So we put up the tent, in the middle of nowhere. Not a soul and a beautiful, starry night. So I pull out this unopened bottle of Glenfiddich, which I had been keeping for the final. And Rab just says, 'Let's get intae this, there's no way we'll be in the final now.' It was just a superb moment, us under the stars drinking Glenfiddich and singing in the wilderness. Next day, we got a lift right through to Mendoza and what happens? It's a great match against Holland.

Russell Galbraith, television producer: After the Iran game we are in this great horseshoe-shaped bar in the hotel, where the Scots media crowd used to gather. This great circle of journalists. It was probably quite late, after the copy had been filed. And Ron Greenwood [the England manager] appeared, beaming, and he said, 'I just don't understand you Scots. All you have got to do is beat Holland by three clear goals and you're through.' I think it was Hughie Taylor – a big, big sportswriter of over 30 years in the business, who had worked for everybody including the *Evening Times*, *Evening Citizen*, *Daily Record*, a very, very popular man – who lifted his eyes and said, 'Beat Holland? We couldn't ★!!?★★ beat you.'

Alex Smith, then manager of Stirling Albion: It was a very unreal atmosphere, with so few people watching. I was sitting on this concrete seat, with my hands in my pockets, thinking, 'This is like a Sunday League game.' I think the atmosphere got to the players slightly.

I met a guy and his wife who spent all their life savings, their endowments, and so on, to get to Argentina. I can't remember his surname, I only know him as 'Davie Dunbar' because he comes from Dunbar [in East Lothian]. I have seen him at every World Cup finals Scotland have since played in. After the Iran game, he and his wife waltzed into this bar. We were obviously disconsolate, and in he came, this fella with a kilt on and a wee button accordion. First thing you know, there's a real rip-roaring ceilidh going on. It was a great night.

There is a rumour that some of the media are encouraging the Scots fans to lose their temper. Meanwhile, back inside the stadium, at the post-match press conference, Ally MacLeod has to sit way back in his seat, such are the number of microphones being pressed into his face. The words are strained, delivered slowly and in pain: 'Individually, each player possibly didn't play well. They gave everything they had. It wasn't a lack of fight or a lack of fire but I don't think that the teamwork was as we have come to expect of Scotland. All in all, I just felt it was a poor performance by us.'

Iran 1 (Danaiefard) Scotland 1 (Eskandarian, o.g.)

II. Politics

It is entirely consistent with the era that the last letter ever written to *The Scotsman* newspaper by the poet Hugh MacDiarmid should be in defence of a collection of poems celebrating football. Scotland's World Cup campaign has become public property, touching almost every aspect of society, not least politics and the arts. And this is a time when domestic politics, like the football, are in a ferment. MacLeod has struck a chord with the people. It isn't just football people who are won over by his charm and enthusiasm. The irony, however, is that while he appears to represent a longing for national identity, the tide has already begun to turn against nationalist politics as represented by the Scottish National Party.

MacDiarmid's letter is published on 8 May. A week before, Rangers have secured the Premier Division title, with Aberdeen a close second. Clydebank and Ayr United are relegated from the Premier Division. And just two days previously, the Scottish Cup has been won by Rangers, with Aberdeen again the runners-up.

The letter is in support of Alan Bold, author of *Scotland, Yes!*, a collection of poems inspired by Argentina '78 and published in *The Scotsman* of 29 April. A front-page splash includes 'Prologue: The Vision, Rhetorical Questions' (Who's the greatest, then?), a 'Peruvian Nursery Rhyme' (Poor poor Peru, If only you knew . . .) and individual eulogies of Alan Rough, Joe Jordan and Kenny Dalglish. Plus an appreciation of Ally himself.

The poison pours in first. A D.M.N. Boyd of Edinburgh writes to say how 'astounded' he is to learn the poems are the work 'not of a talented ten-year-old schoolboy but a 35-year-old "poet and critic with 20 books to his credit".' In a similar vein, a Christine Creech from Wigtownshire blasts: 'Sir, he is an embarrassment to the good name of your paper, this scribbler who would see himself in the First Division with George Mackay Brown and Norman MacCaig. He is not yet in the Sunday Afternoon League.'

The counter follows. MacDiarmid is not alone. 'As for the sneerers and cynics who will accuse Mr Bold of having jumped on to a bandwagon,' begins a Tony McGowan of Leith in Edinburgh, 'let them stop pontificating about poetry being for certain subjects and certain subjects only.'

But MacDiarmid is the big cheese. Given it is the last letter he will write to the paper (he died on 13 September 1978), it has an eerie, valedictory quality:

> In all countries today, there is a conflict between what has generally been regarded as poetry in the past and certain modernist tendencies. Admirers of the former have usually little or no regard for the latter. Their attitude is well shown in Christine Creech's letter on Alan Bold's football poems.
>
> I belong to the opposite camp and think that in these poems Bold has scored a real triumph. High intelligence and football fanaticism seldom go together. It would have been easy to write 'pop' poems on the subject – to write on the level of most discussions of football matters. Bold instead invests his subject-matter with an unwonted dignity. His poems are all intelligent commentaries, stated with a fine directness and economy. Those of us who have followed Bold's career have been wondering what line of development he would take.
>
> Years ago I said that Scotland had in Burns a grand popular poet, and I thought it was time it had a great unpopular one, a role I thought might be mine. Unlike Bold, I have no use whatever for anything that commands a great public following, but with his qualifications it now seems that Bold will assume the role I had thought might be mine.
>
> I would like to congratulate him on a splendid achievement and *The Scotsman* on giving him such a splendid spread. I do not say this in any patronising way. Bold and I are in many respects polar opposites but while these football poems in subject-matter and treatment are beyond my scope, I think I can recognise good poetry when I see it, no matter how different it may be from anything I have written or could attempt, and it is in this spirit that I venture to applaud Alan Bold's achievement.
>
> C.M. Grieve, 'Hugh MacDiarmid'

Barely a day goes by when football, politics and the arts aren't welded together. But *The Scotsman* of 8 May seems particularly symbolic. While MacDiarmid is being published on page 11, two pieces on the opposite page provide telling political slants. Under the logo of the Scottish Argentina Campaign (Football Yes, Torture No), columnist Julie Davidson is providing a trenchant and moving description of human rights abuses in Argentina. The logo, consisting of a skull and crossbones with barbed wire, is in the shape of the official symbol of the World Cup. 'At one time we did think of asking the Scottish squad and the SFA officials to make some kind of public statement on human rights in Argentina,' Davidson quotes the campaign secretary Jackie Roddick as saying. 'But the STUC and the National Union of Mineworkers warned us off that one. They said the consequences might be pressure applied to individual Scots players, which would prejudice their chances in the competition.' All the players confirm that, while their match against Chile in Santiago in 1977 resulted in some protest, no one attempted to dissuade them from playing in Argentina on political grounds.

On the same page, lower down, the international politics give way to domestic politics in the shape of the devolution debate. At a snail's pace, the Scotland Bill is making its way through Parliament, prompting a summary of its progress through the committee and report stages.

Cultural politics, domestic politics, international politics. Football is not quite at the heart of the mélange, but it isn't that far away either. Yet, while it is being assimilated into society, it continues to practise the dark arts of anti-social behaviour. In the same paper on the same day, the game's age-old capacity to sicken is still very much in evidence. 'Policeman hurt as rival football rowdies clash in the streets,' declares a front-page headline. Hibernian have defeated Hearts 1–0 in the final of the East of Scotland Shield and the capital's Princes Street has been turned into a battleground as a result.

The nationalist drum is, however, beginning to sound increasingly hollow. The SNP locomotive is starting to run out of steam as MacLeod leads his merry band of bravehearts on to a DC-10 at Prestwick airport. In fact, as Alan Bold's critics are having their day in the letters page of *The Scotsman*, the front page is reporting major setbacks for the party during the previous day's regional council elections. It is, for the SNP, the second electoral blow in almost as many months. MacLeod's chirpy 'Here's to us, wha's like us?' stands in stark contrast to a by-election failure at Garscadden. Despite wall-to-wall SNP councillors in the Glasgow constituency, Labour (in the shape of Donald Dewar, now Secretary of State for Scotland) manages to hold firm. 'It had been a Labour seat but Labour were becoming increasingly unpopular,' says Stephen Maxwell, one of the local councillors to lose his seat. 'There was growing unemployment caused by the oil price rises of 1973 and 1974, plus the deflationary policies enacted by the chancellor Denis Healey at the behest of the International Monetary Fund. But, still, the SNP could not command a big enough swing.'

On the same day the Scotland squad are departing for Argentina, the

SNP has gathered in sombre mood at Edinburgh's Usher Hall for its annual conference. There are rumblings that the leader, William Wolfe, might be ditched. Worse is to come. On Wednesday, 31 May, George Robertson (now Defence Secretary) defeats Margo MacDonald at a by-election in Hamilton.

'The SNP had started to go off the boil,' continues Maxwell. 'Twelve months previously, the Labour government would not have dared call a general election for fear of what the SNP might achieve. By May 1978, the threat was receding.'

Crude though the comparison is, the SNP's decline mirrors that which is to befall MacLeod. Bombast followed by failure and recrimination. It won't be too long before the SNP begin to splinter, with Maxwell joining with Alex Salmond, Roseanna Cunningham and a handful of others in forming the socialist '79 Group, expelled from the party in 1982.

Maxwell is no great football enthusiast, though he can often be seen on a Saturday morning in the Meadows in Edinburgh kicking a ball about with his young son. But he clearly remembers a 'cold feeling of dread' in the wake of the defeat by Peru. 'There was definitely a feeling that, oh God, a political balloon had burst with the defeat against Peru,' said Maxwell.

The devolution vote takes place on 1 March 1979 and though a majority of those who vote say Yes, Scotland loses out because of an amendment requiring approval from 40 per cent of the electorate. It is commonly espoused that the devastating blow to the country's self-esteem rendered by the Argentina experience has a significant bearing on the outcome of the vote. Then again, the collapse might have been brought about by the internal wranglings at Westminster which allows the original devolution proposal to become so watered down by amendments that it is hardly worth the paper it is written on.

Ian Archer, journalist: We all talked about the impact it might have on devolution; it wasn't just the Edinburgh chattering classes. But now I just see it as rank, bad management of a football team. No more, no less. When you strip it away, the team wasn't well enough managed.

In Argentina, however, the political situation is much, much worse.

Trevor McDonald, journalist: I remember interviewing a woman in the square [Plaza de Mayo], dressed all in black. It was very moving. They marched silently. I interviewed one woman, who responded to me in Spanish and I had to get it translated. You could film from a distance and, being on their best behaviour, the security forces would stay away. But if you got closer to try to interview, they would try to break up the march. Instead of attacking the journalist, they would turn their attention on to the march. I never forget that woman's comment. She said, 'Every mother has a right to know where her son is.' I thought it was brilliantly stated. I can see her face now: an old woman, in her 60s or 70s, a very creased, very lined, large-hipped woman walking with about a dozen others saying, 'Every mother has a right to know where her son is.'

There is no question that it felt as if the people we spoke to had been screened beforehand. It was a great example of how an authoritarian régime can marshal a country. In the UK, if we were to host the World Cup, we could never say to people, 'Be on your best behaviour, entertain visitors.' It takes a special kind of authoritarian régime to do that and to make it happen and they did it. They swept the place – there was never any trouble at any of the games. And, of course, as it became clearer that the Argentinian team were doing not badly, faith in the government's wisdom in doing whatever was required to make the World Cup possible began to grow.

The end of the World Cup was a scene I have never witnessed before. I have never seen people going as mad, pleasantly, as then. In the final piece I did, I kind of shared in their delight, because we had done all these pieces about what a shower of bastards they were. And, finally, in rather great style, their team had won it. And I sought, in my last piece, to separate the political from the feelings of the ordinary, decent people who were just delirious with joy that their team had won. By that time, you did want to separate how nasty the government was from the ordinary people, like the ones who drove us around and so on and who, when we left, wept uncontrollably on our shoulders at the airport.

Russell Galbraith, television producer: We knew it was going to be seat-of-the-pants stuff. We did the draw in Buenos Aires [in early 1978] and we were due to do the draw live on air. Chris Allen, the director, and I went out to Argentina. Once there, we met Ian Archer off the plane who thought it was a nice gesture us meeting him until we told him he was doing the commentary because broadcaster Arthur Montford was ill.

This was the first time colour pictures were coming out of

Argentina. They had built this new TV centre for the World Cup. Argentina didn't do much television anyway and what they did was in monochrome. And we were doing the draw live, we had cleared a big slot in the schedule. We arrived at this centre and all the machinery was in bits, on the floor. This video tape machine was in bits. Producers' hearts always sink when they see technicians at the back of machines. But these machines were in bits. There was a Scots lad working on the machines, saying, 'Don't worry, it'll be all fixed in time.' And, sure enough, it was. But it felt like seat-of-the pants.

In fairness, the authorities pulled out a lot of stops to make the tournament work. When we arrived there, we were treated awfully well. I remember we were at a party in somebody's house and they opened the front and back doors for the whole street to parade through just to have a look at us.

You have to bear in mind the enormous public relations exercise involved. When we arrived in Córdoba straight after the draw, we got there and found machine-gun posts in the main square. And by the time we returned in May for the tournament itself, they were all gone, the streets had been cleared.

The inflation was raging – you know the old gag about the food being dearer at the end of the meal than it was when you started. You would get a taxi in Buenos Aires and the driver would have this big book which he would use to calculate the fare. What the meter said had only a partial bearing on how much you paid.

Notwithstanding the goings-on in the Scotland camp, there is no shortage of controversy elsewhere during the finals themselves. And most of it revolves around the Argentinian team. In their first-round game against France, the Swiss referee, Dubacha, fails to call a blatant penalty against them and then adds insult to injury by awarding Argentina a soft penalty when, clearly, the ball 'plays the hand' of a French defender crashing to the deck. And during the second stage, on the very day that will determine the actual finalists, Argentina's game against Peru is allowed to take place after their nearest rivals in the group, Brazil, have completed their programme. What this means is that the home side have a clear target to aim for. Since Brazil have defeated Poland 3–1, the target is victory by four goals. To reach the final itself. A tall order, you might think. But, in the end, comfortably achieved.

Is it at all relevant that the Peruvian keeper, Quiroga, is actually Argentinian? That the Argentinians are able to play in the same area throughout the course of the tournament? That there are complaints, from Brazil, that their hotel is being barracked at night by noisy Argentinian fans?

Argentina sweep along on a wave of tickertape emotion. And the whiff of corruption. Bravely, on 22 June 1986 in the *Sunday Times*, journalist Maria-Laura Avignola writes of alleged bribery involving 35,000 tons of free grain and the sudden unfreezing of $50 million worth of Peruvian credits by the Argentinian central bank. The go-between is allegedly Admiral Carlos Lacoste, a World Cup organiser and at the time vice-president of FIFA. Against the hosts, Peru field a team which includes four reserves, a defender playing as a striker and, of course, Quiroga. They lose 6–0. And, for her troubles, Avignola is tried in Argentina for 'moral turpitude' – though she is acquitted when it becomes clear she has impeccable sources.

Dubacha isn't the only referee to come under fire. Garrido of Portugal appears to favour Argentina in their opening match against Hungary, which sees Hungary's Torocsik (billed as the new Puskas) and Nyilasi sent off, but only after 'extensive provocation'. Likewise, Rainea of Romania and Barreto of Uruguay appear to lean in favour of Italy, again against Hungary and France.

There are tackles that should have been punished. There is cynicism. In the second round match between Brazil and Argentina, there are 14 fouls in the first 16 minutes, yet Karoly Palotai of Hungary – supposedly one of the better referees of his day – chooses not to issue a single yellow card. And, incredibly, in the match between Brazil and Sweden, Welsh referee Clive Thomas blows for full-time just as a Brazilian corner is in mid-flight from which Zico heads home what appears to be a perfectly legitimate winner. Brazil's poor start to the competition costs the manager his job.

By all accounts, Scotland's representative among the refereeing fraternity, John Gordon, passes muster. He referees the Group One game between Tunisia and Mexico (which Tunisia win 3–1) and the second-round Group A match between Holland and Austria (won 5–1 by Holland).

There are doubts raised about the method of choosing the referee for the final. It goes to a casting vote of a FIFA special committee. In the frame is Barreto – who seems qualified enough, despite having sent off Holland's Nanninga for laughing and his seeming bias in favour of Italy during round one. His problem is that he is from Uruguay, too close for comfort for Argentina. Also in the frame is Israel's Abraham Klein. He has handled superbly the first-round match between Argentina and Italy.

According to reports, Argentina view him as too strict and have duly let it be known to FIFA that they will protest against Klein's appointment on the grounds that Holland are, politically, in dispute with Israel.

Eventually, Italy's Sergio Gonella is appointed. But his weakness is exposed when he fails to penalise the Argentinians for keeping the Dutch waiting for five minutes before kick-off. To make matters worse, he entertains Argentinian protests about a bandage around the wrist of Rene van de Kerkhof, who has to leave the field, only to return with a bigger (but apparently acceptable) bandage. A joke.

During the game, Argentinian defender Luis Galvan is permitted repeatedly to handle through-passes by Holland and even manages to avoid censure for a rough tackle on Johan Neeskens. The Dutch are allowed to be pretty brutal themselves. They are clearly irritated by the farce of the kick-off.

Gonella's handling of the final is lambasted by the world's press. Patrick Mahé in *Le Figaro* writes: 'What Gonella did was worse than awarding a penalty, which was unjust. Little by little he allowed Argentina to prevent Holland from playing.'

The Argentinian side does, however, bring colour and an almost reckless sense of adventure to the tournament. If, as has often been claimed, a World Cup-winning side needs a minimum of five world-class players, Argentina passes the test in goalkeeper Fillol, the *libero* or sweeper Passarella, the creative midfielder Ardiles, the quick and sharp-shooting striker Luque and, finally, the inspirational and explosive striker Kempes. Bertoni and Ortiz are fair wingers and manager Cesar Menotti might have had a stronger defence had Rene Houseman not been struggling for form and had the team not been denied the services of Enrique Wolff of Real Madrid (problems in getting clearance) and Osvaldo Piazza of St Etienne (forced to return to France when his family are involved in a car accident).

Kempes puts Argentina into the lead, with Dutch substitute, Nanninga, coming on to level towards the end. The consensus view is that the Dutch are the best football team of their time, but they waste too many clear-cut chances during the final. Their agony is compounded by the fact that, in the last minute of normal time, they even manage to hit the woodwork, Rensenbrink prodding a deep free-kick from Krol on to the keeper's right-hand post.

After 90 minutes, the game ends 1–1.

During extra time, Argentina, and particularly Mario Kempes, run riot. He makes it 2–1 with a surging run into the box, where he passes two defenders and is rewarded with a kind bounce of the ball. He then assists Bertoni to end the game 3–1 to Argentina. Their two extra-time goals are perhaps a little fortuitous. But fortune favours the brave and there was a lot of pressure on this side to succeed.

Clearly angered by the Argentinians' gamesmanship, the Dutch boycott the after-final banquet.

12. Holland

Sunday, 11 June 1978
HOLLAND: *Jongbloed, Suurbier, Krol, Poortvliet, Rijsbergen (Wildschut), Neeskens (Boskamp), Jansen, W. van de Kerkhof, R. van de Kerkhof, Rep, Rensenbrink*
SCOTLAND: *Rough, Kennedy, Buchan, Forsyth, Donachie, Rioch, Hartford, Gemmill, Souness, Dalglish, Jordan*
REFEREE: *E. Linemayr (Austria);* LINESMEN: *K. Palotai (Hungary), H. Seoudi (Tunisia)*
ATTENDANCE: *40,000, Mendoza*

With the fans' chant of 'No Mendoza, No Mendoza' ringing in his ears, Ally MacLeod pretty much goes to ground after Scotland's bedraggled draw against Iran. It has been open season for too long. Gone is the fresh-faced optimism of a fortnight previously. It was during the Iran game that he was frequently captured on television looking thoroughly depressed, at one point dropping his head into his hands. It is one of the enduring images of sport.

It feels like an eternity before Scotland's final group game against Holland. They still have a chance of qualifying for the second round. To go through, they have to achieve a minor miracle: beat the Dutch by at least three goals. If they do so, it will be Peru and Scotland (on goal difference) who will progress to the next round, involving another set of round-robin matches.

'What we need is players, after playing their worst two games, to play the best game of their lives, and then we could still win,' says MacLeod in *The Scotsman* of 9 June.

The odds of Scotland winning the World Cup have now reached 500/1, well behind Tunisia – who are reported to have complained about the Scots' drinking when both squads were at Alta Gracia – at 200/1. The odds of beating Holland are 4/1; of Holland beating Scotland 8/13; 11/4 the draw.

The despair is at least lifted by a change of venue. Since the game is being played in Mendoza, the Scotland camp has to ship out of Alta Gracia and The Sierras Hotel. The change is, for some, as good as a rest. The new hotel is called the San Francisco. There are three full days to fill between the Iran game on the Wednesday and the Holland game on the Sunday. The interim is relatively quiet. Although the media coverage continues to be harsh, it has less of a sting to it. To all intents and purposes, Scotland are already down and out.

A quick fast-forward to the Mendoza stadium sees Scottish Secretary of State, Bruce Millan, arrive for the game, along with a few other dignitaries, including Lieutenant-General Jorge Rafaél Videla, the head of Argentina's military Junta, and Sir Stanley Rous, past president of FIFA.

The Scotland team bus arrives to a fanfare of indifference or morbid fascination. MacLeod asks the officials to leave the coach before he addresses the players. He has his team line-up. Graeme Souness gets a midfield berth, long overdue in the opinion of many. Kenny Burns is out. So too are Sandy Jardine, John Robertson and Lou Macari. Jim Blyth is still on the bench, despite Alan Rough's part in gifting Iran their equaliser. Stuart Kennedy has recovered from a stomach bug. Bruce Rioch is back. Once again, Joe Jordan is preferred to Derek Johnstone.

Martin Buchan: It was touch and go as to whether I would make it for the Holland game. For three days before it I went about with an ice pack [on his cut head from the Iran game] to reduce the swelling. I'm glad to say I made the game.

Stuart Kennedy: I missed the Iran game because of sickness. And before the Holland game the manager asks me if I am okay. I say I am and he says to the whole squad that he is picking the team to play Holland on the basis of the performances in a practice match he wants us to play. I play okay and am convinced I'll be picked.

But so too is Bobby Clark who, because we had three keepers, played centre-half, which he often did, very competently, for Aberdeen reserves. Bobby has played a blinder in the practice match. Doesn't give Joe Harper a sniff. He wants to play centre-half for Scotland. 'I had a great game, I'm playing for Scotland,' he would keep saying. And I'm saying, 'I don't think the manager quite meant that he was picking the team solely on the performances in the practice match.' And he is saying, very much tongue-in-cheek, 'I had a great game, I'm a better centre-half than the other boy. I'm taking him to the wire on this one.' I tell him, 'Don't be too disappointed when the team is actually chosen.'

Bobby doesn't like sarcasm. Cultured chap. Queen's Park, 50 press-ups, cold showers. That's Bobby. He's a Corinthian. I see

Chariots of Fire, I see Clarky. Takes a Collins dictionary with him everywhere. One day, Clarky has a neck-collar on because of an injury. Doesn't need to train. But he runs that cross-country race. Comes last but finishes. That's Clarky.

Kenny Burns: Football? It was just like going to work for me. Joe Jordan takes his teeth out and is a nasty bastard on the park. But, off the park, if you were in a pub you'd find him sitting in a corner drinking half a lager and lime, quiet as a lamb. He goes to work and does his job. And it was the same with me. You have somebody trying to score a goal and if I stop him we have a chance of getting a bonus, and if he scores he is maybe taking money from my pocket. So I try and stop him. It was just a job. I may have had to kick him. That was my job. You would try to get away with what you could. That's life – fiddle a little bit here and there. I played the game and tried to get away with what I could. That was football and I loved football, loved it.

What you see is what you get with me, I'm no fancy tails. I like to think I tell the truth. If I think you are a ****, you're a ****. I had plenty of faith in my own ability. If you don't have faith in your own ability, how can you expect your team-mates to have faith? I was confident. I wouldn't say I was cocky.

I remember after the Iran game – I didn't have a good game, I know – and Archie Gemmill pops up at a meeting and says, 'He doesn't do that at Forest,' and I'm thinking, 'Thanks Archie,' and sure enough I got dropped for the third game. You know Ally, he wants you to play your club football. I played the first two games. I don't think it was down to me that we didn't do well. I blame the goalie for conceding goals at the near post. We scored in every game and never kept a clean sheet. You've got to ask what was going on. I feel I was a fall guy. Archie played, and he scored a great goal. I don't regard him as a team man, he looks after himself. I don't owe him anything, he doesn't owe me anything.

Archie Gemmill: The manager takes the captaincy off me and I can still persuade him to leave somebody out of the team? Have you ever heard anything so daft? I have no recollection. But next time I see Kenny I'll tell him how exceptionally glad I was that I didn't get him picked for the game.

And I can't remember making that [now famous] remark that if Graeme Souness was a chocolate soldier he would eat himself. I'd tell you if I did. But I most certainly know that he was a very conceited person, but, to be fair, he deserved to be. He was suave, good-looking, well built and a particularly good player. So I might have said something at some time but where it came from I couldn't tell you. I like to win so I might have told some people what I thought of them.

Graeme Souness: I was happy with the 'chocolate soldier' remark, even at the time. He might have been right as well. Maybe I had a higher opinion of myself than I should have, but I don't think I was alone in that. I was like a lot of young people. I think footballers today are the same. They have people telling them how wonderful they are, they have things being written about them, and it is very easy to get carried away with your own importance. I think I was guilty of that, to some extent. I wasn't the worst by any stretch, in my opinion, but I was guilty of it. I was happy with the line, it was funny.

Sandy Jardine: A lot of people have the misconception that foreign trips are the icing on the cake for a footballer. That going to Argentina with Scotland is like them going to Spain for a holiday. They have no understanding of what it is really like. You are straight on to a bus from the flight and then straight in to the hotel and locked up. Which is partly why if footballers have a night out they might go off the rails a bit. If you are a football player, you have to get used to boredom. You hang around for ages and then you have this nervous tension before a game and then you have to come down from it after the game.

I did get absolutely pissed on one occasion. You're okay, it was after the Iran game, a few days before the Holland match. Joe Jordan and I went for a meal with a photographer from one of the newspapers. It was so cheap. And next day we were flying from Córdoba to Mendoza and Joe and I were struggling a wee bit, I can tell you. It was one of these 'never again' feelings. And we got on to this plane and it was an Argentinian airforce plane. It was basic – and I mean basic. It was a propeller job. Me and Joe struggled, that's for sure.

I missed the Peru game because of an injury I picked up during the Home International against Northern Ireland. I wanted to come off. But a couple of others had already been injured and substituted. I remember thinking, 'Hold on, I've got a World Cup coming, I'll get off the park.' But I played on with an injury, which didn't do me any favours, because I couldn't train for a fortnight afterwards.

I played against Iran but not against Holland. I was gone. My enthusiasm had gone. I think Ally's had gone as well – he didn't come out of his room for three days. I remember the doc saying to us he was worried about Ally's health and us feeling it wasn't quite our place to go troubling him; that it was probably more the doc's responsibility.

We didn't really see him after the Iran game until he appeared on the bus on our way to the Holland game. I found out on the bus that I wasn't playing against Holland but by that stage I wasn't too bothered whether I was playing or not.

I've kept quiet about it until now. There was nothing to be gained from speaking about it even straight after the World Cup. Will anybody be interested in this book? At the time, I honestly thought there was nothing more to be said. I certainly wasn't into criticising other people, especially since I felt I never gave of my best.

Asa Hartford: We were told there was going to be an Olympic-sized swimming-pool at the hotel [in Alta Gracia]. That pool had a big crack in it and there was never any water. In the reception, there was this ancient switchboard – you know the type, when there's an operator and plugs you pull in and out. I don't know who was in the room above, but whenever they went to the toilet and you happened to be sitting in the toilet at the same time, you would get soaked from above. We started training in the grounds and I think it was Derek Johnstone who twisted an ankle, the surface was so bad. So, we ended up travelling 30km every day to train. That was a last-minute arrangement.

So, by the time we were 3–1 up against Holland, you can understand why a few players in the stand went, 'Oh no,' and got out of their seats to have a drink.

Jim Blyth: At one stage we were 3–1 up against Holland. They were on their knees, limping and arguing with each other – they were there for the taking. And then [Holland's] Johnny Rep picks up the ball some distance out and fires one and it's 3–2. Against Holland, I wasn't, unlike some of the players, of the attitude, 'Let's get home'. When we went 3–1 ahead, I was the first off the bench, thinking, 'We are going to do this.'

Derek Johnstone: I think everyone was looking forward to playing against the Dutch because they were a side who set the World Cup alight. And it was going to be a good tester and they had good fans there, like the Scots, so it was going to be a great atmosphere. And I'll always remember the coach drawing up to the ground and Ally putting the SFA officials off the bus and us sitting at the back wondering what was coming. And he said, 'Right, here's the team.' And he named the team and he named the subs. And all he then said was, 'Right, just go out and fucking play. It's our last game, go out and play.'

And that was it. And it was the best game we played. We'd got so much stick from the press that none of the lads could really give a toss, to be perfectly honest. But then we just decided to give it one last shot.

The game is a joy. Scotland play well. Short, accurate passes in the midfield. Cohesion from top to bottom. Holland, being more than capable themselves, make a game of it, but are possibly not as mentally attuned as they might be, given the knowledge that all they have to do is keep the score within reasonable limits. Reports also suggest their squad is riven with disharmony. Over money. And, for one reason or another, various players, including the inimitable Johan Cruyff, didn't even go to the World Cup.

They go into the lead. Stuart Kennedy concedes a penalty. Rensenbrink scores. It is the 1,000th goal in World Cup history.

Stuart Kennedy: Nobody wins World Cups except Germany, Argentina, Brazil and Italy. But Holland went close twice, losing the 1974 and 1978 finals narrowly, on both occasions to the host nation. We play them and play well. Our midfield is excellent, their passing was outstanding. Just short, clever passes. They are so good the Dutch are forced to play the long ball over the top.

I felt I had a good solid game, especially after being adjudged to have given away a penalty from which Rensenbrink scored. I made a mistake. I took a casual touch of the ball from a return pass by Graeme Souness and was dispossessed. But I got back and got my tackle in. I rectified the situation. But Rough has come out, made the situation look horrible and, bang, a penalty. I clearly kicked the ball away for a corner, I had rectified my error and, knowing my pace, Roughie should have stayed on his line.

But he came out, obviously trying to help me out. But while I redeem myself, kicking the ball for a corner with my left foot, we are in a pile-up, the three of us. Penalty. I felt terrible, obviously. In fact, I have never felt as bad in my life. My mouth is dry. I've just given away a penalty in a crucial game from which they go one-up. It was a great tackle and I can hardly believe it. But I went on to have an outstanding game. I was taken on many times by one of the van de Kerkhof brothers, the paciest guy in their team, and I think I handled him quite competently.

The setback of losing the penalty – in the 34th minute – is only temporary. It's long overdue for Scotland to show some character. Earlier in the game, they have been lifted by a Rioch header that hits the crossbar. Holland lose the influential Johan Neeskens, stretchered off after an accidental clash in midfield. And just before the interval, Scotland level the score. Souness sends a deep cross from the left which Jordan meets with his head to return the ball back towards the six-yard box. Dalglish, unmarked, hooks it home. Into the second half and Scotland are awarded a penalty. Dalglish plays a short corner on the right with Kennedy and immediately receives the ball back to cross. Again the cross is deep and this time it is nodded down for the on-rushing Souness. He goes to ground, bundled over by Willy Van de Kerkhof. Gemmill, from the spot, is clinical. Up goes that raised fist of his. There is more, much more, to come from him.

> *Bruce Rioch*: There were some good players in the national squad and that came to light in the balance of the team for the last game against Holland. The balance was found that, had the team qualified for the latter stages, would have been stuck to.
>
> The Dutch were not playing with any recognised centre-forward. They were playing two wide players and an overloaded midfield. And we felt that to play the way we did during the previous two games, we would get overrun in the middle of the park. Therefore, through discussion with the manager, we decided to play a flat back four and to bring Graeme Souness in to play as a controlling mid-fielder in front of the back four. It was really the 'diamond formation' with two strikers. That gave us the solidity in the middle of the park that was necessary against the Dutch. I think it was a well-balanced team. There was Hartford on one side, Gemmill on the other and myself playing a freer role, in behind the two strikers. And I think the balance was good, very good. It was also a strong side as far as individual flair was concerned.

Who, honestly, can say they weren't out of their seats when Archie Gemmill scored that wonderful goal to make it 3–1 for Scotland? Was giving it laldy as the wee man clenched his fist in majestic defiance, having scored one of the greatest goals in World Cup history. We have all seen it. It is shown so often on television. And it deserves to be. Dalglish had controlled a longish pass down the touchline from Kennedy, composed himself and tried to dribble his way past three tightly packed defenders. He is blocked but the loose ball falls to Gemmill, who is on to it in a flash at the right edge of the box. He beats one defender (No.6), then another (No.5), then another (No.2 – nutmegs). Only the goalkeeper to beat. Yeeeeeeeeeessss! 3–1. Just one more goal and Scotland are through. It isn't even a Scottish thing. The entire UK looks on with utter astonishment. And supporters of the underdog the world over are no doubt cheering with equal relish.

It isn't quite enough to bury all the traumas of the previous few days. But if ever a goal in a simple football match can assist in a nationwide recovery of morale, Gemmill's is it. That said, the scrappiest, ugliest goal this side of the Mississippi to make it 4–1 would have sparked even greater delirium.

But what a sublime moment, nonetheless.

The all-important fourth goal never materialises. In fact, just as John Robertson is saying to his gaffer, 'Someone up there likes you,' Holland's Johnny Rep carves an opening through the middle of the park and unleashes a shot from 25 yards that sizzles past Rough. It is barely three minutes since Gemmill sent the pulse racing.

Archie Gemmill: There's not a great deal to say about the goal, it is just one of those things that happen every now and again in people's careers. It is not planned, it just happens and I was very fortunate that it should happen to me when it did. I don't know if it was the best goal I have ever scored but it is certainly the most talked about. Every goal has its significance at the time, it is just unfortunate that, at the end of the day, we couldn't get another one to qualify for the later stages.

There was nothing special going through my mind at the time. You have opponents in front of you and, luckily, you manage to get clear of them. When I went past the last defender, the goalkeeper made it a lot easier for me – he decided to dive before I even considered what I was going to do. He dived one way and it was relatively easy to put it in the other corner. If he had stood his ground then I would have to have made a decision what I was going to do. But the decision was made by the goalkeeper diving too early.

I can't really remember any club goal that I would say was a particular favourite. The one against Holland I remember simply because it's shown so often on the television – as simple as that. When I scored, we thought we had a chance of getting through.

We were fighting for a little bit of pride; we didn't feel we could qualify because Holland were a particularly good team. I don't think anyone thought we could beat them by the three goals needed to go through, but as it transpired we could quite easily have done it. Although we won 3–2, overall we had the chances to make it 4–2 or even 5–2. We did play exceptionally well on the day. We were a lot stronger in midfield and had a little bit more movement and flair up front. No professional likes to go to any competition and get stick. At the end of the day, we came out with a small amount of credit for our performance against the Dutch.

Don Masson: It's an awful thing to say, but when Archie scored that goal, there was no response from the Scottish players in the stand. Because it meant possibly staying out another week. That's how bad it was. That's unbelievable, isn't it? But it's true. I spoke to some Dutch lads afterwards, and they wanted to go home straightaway too.

Alan Rough: I actually got most of my fingers to Johnny Rep's goal. And when I turned round and saw the ball in the back of the net, I couldn't believe it. I thought I had put it well over the bar. The ball was so light and the atmosphere so thin you had to get everything behind a save. You had to punch the ball. I knew what it was going to be like after playing in the tour of South America the year before. Before our first game, I asked the ref for a feel of the ball and when I bounced it on the floor, it sprang back above my head. Right up to the ceiling. It was like a volleyball, it was just air. For people who could control and kick a ball, it was fantastic. But of course we just returned to Scotland and practised with the same old heavy balls.

I never went to catch Rep's shot, I just went to touch it. And I thought I had got enough on it. I didn't see the shot as it left his boot, there were quite a few people in front of me. And just before the ball got to me, it moved a bit. I got a lot of hand to it and I just couldn't believe it was in the net when I turned around.

I got a bronze plaque commemorating the first Holland goal, a penalty by Rensenbrink, which was the 1,000th World Cup goal, and which I proceeded to lose on the way home.

Ally MacLeod: Afterwards, Ernst Happel, the Holland manager, knocked on the dressing-room door and said, 'All I would like to say, Ally, is "There, but for the grace of God, go I".' He realised we were so much on top during the game and it could have been him returning home in disgrace. We were so much on top, I remember sitting in the dug-out and thinking, 'Oh God, we are going to make it.'

Holland 2 (Rensenbrink (pen), Rep) Scotland 3 (Dalglish, Gemmill 2 (1 pen))

13. Going Home

A win against the eventual finalists. It is enough to restore some pride, slightly change the tune of the media (who remain convinced Ally MacLeod is soon for the chop). But there is still time for one last calamity as the Scots prepare for departure from Mendoza. The flight to Buenos Aires is fog-bound but that is only the half of it. Once in the Argentinian capital, the hotel assigned to the Scots is the worst they've endured. So bad, indeed, the squad refuse to have anything to do with it. A search party locates a much plusher establishment.

Only a handful make the journey all the way back to Glasgow. Most disembark in London. Jim Blyth recollects a torrid connecting flight to the Midlands on a four-seater plane.

The return across the Atlantic is in second class, contrasting somewhat with the first-class flight fit for heroes on the way out to South America nearly three weeks previously. When the optimism was at its height, in the lead-up to the Hampden send-off of 25 May, the annual report of the SFA – submitted to its AGM on 8 May 1978 – noted: 'It is doubtful if any single event since the last war has had the impact on the Scottish people that our qualifying to play in Argentina has had.' Come mid-June, the world was a completely different place.

> *Tom Forsyth*: After the Holland game, we had to leave the hotel early in the morning and go to Mendoza to fly to Buenos Aires. Fog means three hours in the airport. Eventually we fly to Buenos Aires. Know the Great Eastern Hotel in Glasgow [a dilapidated hostel for homeless people]? That was five-star compared to the hotel [that either FIFA or the Argentinian FA had] booked for us when we arrived at Buenos Aires.
>
> I remember to this day what it was like when we walked in. Rust came out of the taps. Martin Buchan spoke a bit of Spanish and he went with SFA officials and interpreters to the World Cup head-quarters. The rest of us went shopping and when we came back we were transferred to, I think, the Sheraton. It was like a palace.
>
> We let so many people down. It was shocking, hard to recover from. I went on holiday straight after we got back, though not out

of the country. We went to Arran, we had a caravan there. The kids were young, the golf was great, it was lovely. Maybe it would have been harder if I was living in Glasgow, but I was in a small town where I had been brought up since I was one (which means I was an incomer). The people never really said anything, though I'm sure they were thinking things.

It was the worst part of my career. I remember sitting on a bench with a few players, and all we were doing was pinging these stones, wishing we were home. Just killing time, just wanting to be home. Words can't describe it, really. The results. We were really sickened. We got lifted a bit by the Holland game. I try not to think about it. If it crops up in conversation, I say, 'Don't talk about it.' When you phoned about it, I don't know why I said, yes. It was the worst moment in my career. I'm sure quite a few others feel the same way.

SFA Annual Report, 8 May 1978: Traditionally, Scots have tended to associate their worth as a nation with the exploits of their international team, and in these days when, rightly or wrongly, strong feelings of nationalism sweep the country and protests against repression, real or imaginary, are heard on all sides, this strange mixture of events has produced a situation where a quite unprecedented volume of support for the team is exhibited, the very fervency of which could, involuntarily, prove to be one of the most difficult psychological barriers which the team will have to clear.

Whatever happens in Argentina, win or lose, to have qualified again is an accomplishment of which, justifiably, the association and all who are interested in Scottish football may be proud.

In addition to paving the way in June 1977, when the international team toured South America, extensive and thorough preparations have been made, including two visits to Argentina by the secretary and team manager. All that reasonably can be done at this stage has been done and we must now await events. Exciting times!

SFA Annual Report, 7 May 1979: Such was the disappointment at our failure to advance past the initial stages and such was the clamour for a scapegoat that, not surprisingly, the team manager, Mr Alistair MacLeod, moved back to the less hysterical waters of club football before the year was out. He left of his own volition, although such were the pressures, not only from outwith the association, that his departure came as no surprise.

Not all the players are phlegmatic about 1978. Some still carry deep psychological scars. For many, though, the experience has not put them off the idea of following MacLeod into management and coaching. Today, almost three-quarters of the squad remain in football. There are those, like Rioch, who set out to learn from every experience, positive or negative.

Twenty-two players were taken to the World Cup by MacLeod and football remains in the blood of all of them, even Kenny Burns who is now a giftware salesman but who did all he could to keep his swansong on hold by playing for years in non-league, winding down to pub-league, football.

As at 1 January 1998, Martin Buchan is a football promotions manager with a sports equipment manufacturer, while Tom Forsyth is a market gardener having previously managed Dunfermline and been assistant manager at Motherwell and Heart of Midlothian. Archie Gemmill is currently out of work having, a year previously, been co-manager at Rotherham United and, before then, coach at Nottingham Forest for ten years.

Joe Harper has a career in the media, as has his pal Derek Johnstone, who briefly managed Partick Thistle.

Sandy Jardine is a director with the Rangers commercial department while Willie Johnston and Stuart Kennedy are both publicans. Burns was a publican for a while; so too was Jim Blyth, now a goalkeeping coach. Alan Rough is an events promoter, and also manages junior [non-league], Glenafton Athletic.

Don Masson is a hotelier in Nottingham. Lou Macari is also out of work, but he deliberately stepped down from the manager's post at Stoke City to pursue a compensation claim against Celtic where he was manager for a few months. Bobby Clark is a director of soccer at Stanford University in California, with a curriculum vitae that includes the manager's post with the New Zealand national side.

Asa Hartford is first-team coach at Manchester City while Willie Donachie, assistant manager at Everton until March 1997, is first-team coach at Sheffield United. Gordon McQueen, who has managed Airdrie and been a television pundit, is now reserve team coach at Middlesbrough. John Robertson is assistant manager at Leicester City.

Joe Jordan was at Bristol City twice and has also been manager at Stoke and Hearts. He was, very briefly, an assistant at Celtic. He is also out of work at the time of writing, though is an occasional pundit on Channel Four's *Football Italia*.

The boys that have 'done especially good' in football management (this is not a value judgement, simply a statement based on the status of clubs they are or have been with) are the trio of Kenny Dalglish (Liverpool,

Blackburn Rovers, Newcastle United), Graeme Souness (Rangers, Liverpool, Galatasaray, Southampton, Torino, Benfica) and Bruce Rioch (recently sacked as assistant manager at Queens Park Rangers, previously manager at Torquay United, Middlesbrough, Millwall, Bolton Wanderers and Arsenal).

It would be a mistake to assume that the magic had completely vanished from the relationship between the players and the fans by the time the squad wend their weary way home. While a few fans were permanently disillusioned, there were more than enough new recruits to take their place in the ranks of the Tartan Army. Fans such as Ronnie McDevitt from Dunfermline, who has missed fewer than a dozen games played abroad by Scotland since 1978.

Ronnie McDevitt, fan: I was 16 when Scotland played England at Wembley in 1977 and was too young to go to Argentina. And I have to say I felt guilty about not going. It was agony hearing the fans sing, 'Que sera, sera, we're going to the Argentine'. Scotland's first match after the World Cup was in Vienna and about 3,000 Scotland fans travelled. And among them there were quite a few, like me, making their first trip abroad with Scotland.

After Vienna [MacLeod's last game in charge], Scotland played Norway at home. On a wet Wednesday night, 65,000 people turned up. I don't think the bubble burst for a full year after Argentina, and it was, ironically, against Argentina [2 June 1979, Scotland lose 3–1, Maradona plays], in a friendly at Hampden, that people started venting their frustration.

Sandy Jardine: It wasn't down to one individual that things went wrong. If we are honest with ourselves, we could all have done better. I stress it was not down to an individual. I would never want it to be said that it was one person. But we got into this situation that when one thing went wrong, another thing followed, and then another. And so on. It imploded, if you like. I imagine it wasn't a nice experience for anyone. The only person whose reputation was enhanced by it was Danny McGrain who was prevented from going because of injury. We were all tarnished by it.

Bruce Rioch: It would be wrong to blame an individual [Ally] when he has shown loyalty to you as a person. It is a combination of reasons as to why it didn't go right. Who was responsible for not resolving the financial side? Who was responsible for finding but not checking the facilities? The manager was not responsible, for example, for my loss of form.

Alan Rough: Ally was probably the best PR guy to hit Scottish football and he had the track record of being a good manager at club level, but he came up against players who didn't know him. He might not admit it, but I thought he maybe felt inferior to them. He never had that Jock Stein I-don't-give-a-shit-who-you-are style. There was a lot of time during training sessions when we would do light-hearted things, like you would have to tig somebody before you were allowed to pass the ball, and a lot of them didn't like it and would walk off. I always got on well with him. He went into it knowing what his limitations were and did it to the best of his ability.

Jim Blyth: The fans let us know we had let them down. They were quite savage in their criticism. Ally got slaughtered. He lost about a stone and a half in weight. There is that famous television shot that is shown again and again of him holding his head in his hands. He put himself under so much pressure with his promises.

Graeme Souness: I wouldn't criticise the organisation of it. It was the first experience of newshounds rather than just football writers going out to a World Cup. They were being paid to go out to Argentina for three weeks and they had to come up with the goods. They have got to find a story, even if the story wasn't exactly as they had printed it.

I was very much the outsider looking in, I was the new boy. I kept out of it and I escaped, as far as I remember, without anything being written about me. [When reminded of a story where he is quoted claiming at least one member of the squad turned Ally MacLeod against him, he replies:] I can't remember saying that, I can't remember that happening. I was 25 at the time and Scotland had a very strong midfield going into the competition. It was a bonus to be on the trip. If my transfer to Liverpool hadn't happened earlier in the year, I wouldn't have gone. I went there knowing they had a settled side, so to get any game was a bonus. I was a young boy. In relation to the players who had got Scotland to the finals, I was the new boy.

Joe Harper: One thing that has always stuck in my mind since the moment I arrived in Argentina was the contrast in wealth. You would be travelling on the coach and, one minute, seeing all these big houses and the lovely countryside and thinking, 'Brilliant'. Then, just a couple of hundred yards down the road, the place would suddenly become masses of tin huts, smoke, poverty – horrendous. On our first day there, we saw these two dead horses on the roadside and, a fortnight or so later, as we were returning to take the plane home, the horses were still there. That was how dirty it could be in places.

Don Masson: In a way, looking back on it, I feel a little detached. That was a part of my life that is in the past. I was very, very privileged to be doing what I loved, which was playing football. But now, I feel very lucky what I am doing now – running a hotel. Through a lot of adversity, I became a Christian. I lost my mum, dad and first wife in the space of three years. But through that adversity, I have come out a stronger person. So Argentina, relatively, is nothing. My life is now getting up in the morning and serving people. Then it was take, take, take. As far as I'm concerned, I have been given a second chance. I was a horrible person when I was a footballer. I am married again, to Brenda, and I have a purpose, serving people. And I think I'm the luckiest person in the world.

Lou Macari (to journalist Hugh McIlvanney, The Observer, *11 June 1978*): If clever people had been in charge, they would have taken the pressure off by telling us we were coming to play the best players in the world. Instead, we were bombarded with crap about beating the rest of the world into the ground. How could anyone be so optimistic about our chances? When did you last see Scotland play really good football, play with a positive rhythm and a consistent pattern? In the Home Internationals and the qualifying rounds before them it was a fight, a case of charge, a battering-ram job. It was a fight when we beat the Czechs and a fight when we beat the Welsh at Anfield. Meanwhile, the likes of Tunisia and Iran would be slogging away in their little training camps for the last two months with the World Cup as their only target. Tunisia and Iran are better prepared than we are. In our last match before coming here the lads exhausted themselves trying to beat England. It couldn't be any other way with 85,000 mad Scotsmen yelling, 'Gie us an English heid.'

Lou Macari (to a television documentary crew, 1978): The 22 players who came here rightly or wrongly regard themselves as a better squad than England, as better players than England. I mean, in Scotland that's what it is all about: Scotland and England. And you come here and you think, 'This is it, this is the biggest occasion in your life.' And I don't think you're in the same league as England. Unfortunately, we came here and we couldn't lace England's boots as far as being treated off the pitch, as far as the rewards at the end of the day are concerned.

Lou Macari: I think you have to bear in mind that in a competition like that you are surrounded, daily, by 60 or 70 journalists. When I spoke to the television cameras and made what were perceived to be critical remarks, I didn't seek out the cameras, I didn't have any contract to appear. I was just a player who was grabbed. It turned out to be good television. I thought I was just telling the truth about how it had gone wrong for us. I must say, looking back, that was all I did say. I don't think there is anything wrong in telling the truth. If anyone thinks Scotland went there and everything was well organised and well planned, they were mistaken. Obviously, at the time, it went down badly with the SFA.

I took the view that if you can't pass any comment about a competition you have been involved in and people have asked you about, then if that is such a big deal, so be it. I don't think it would have been such a big deal in England, not then and certainly not nowadays when there is much more being said that could be construed as being critical. In Scotland you can still make a comment that I would consider very trivial and still have your knuckles rapped by the SFA. If I had said I had enjoyed myself, then there would have been something wrong with me. We come back disappointed, dejected, feeling we have let everyone down – and they are expecting me to say it is wonderful?

I found Ally MacLeod a decent fella, a genuine fella. I'll stick by that. I'm in a much better position to make a comment on that now, having met so many different managers and footballers. And Ally MacLeod definitely falls into the category of being a decent fella. I think the problem you can have in any competition is that the majority of players will look for an excuse if it starts to go wrong. Ally MacLeod wasn't the excuse for us doing badly. And the pressure heaped on him certainly got the players off the hook.

Out of that campaign came all these supposedly controversial things happening. If you had a World Cup next week and a team like Scotland went there full of hope and it all fell apart, all the same type of stories would be coming out. The manager would be under pressure, the players would be having their knuckles rapped for saying this and saying that. It would be no different. It comes with any competition when a team is perceived to have flopped. Scotland only 'flopped' because they were expected to win the World Cup.

Ian Archer, journalist: It was never right from the start, but it all took some time before it started to come out. There were, for example, no training facilities – the Scots trained on the grass at the bottom of the hotel gardens. But you have to remember the media, because we were based about 30 miles away from Alta Gracia, were only out there for an hour and a half or so per day. Any journalist who says the players were bevvying like mad and getting up to no good is a false witness. But there did come a time when there was a collective loss of will, a time when the players didn't want to be there. Of course, they were hearing things whenever they phoned home, about how they were being knocked down having been built up previously. Mind you, they were happy to be built up, they colluded in the fiction, but when it all went wrong it was everybody else's fault.

Archie Gemmill: I've been a manager myself and all you can do is pick the best eleven players you think are right for whatever game you are going to play. So I have no criticism of the manager. I wasn't a raw player at the time. I was captain of Scotland before Ally MacLeod came and he took the captaincy off me and played other people in midfield before me. But you have just got to bite the bullet and try and prove to whoever is picking the team that they are wrong. At the end of the day, I think I certainly proved that to Mr MacLeod.

Had Scotland qualified for the next round you would not have heard anyone complain about bonuses or lack of water in the swimming-pool or whatever. These are things people will use for excuses. At the end of the day, we weren't good enough. Whether you're living in a five-star hotel or a one-star boarding-house, you should be able to do the job better than we did. It is as simple as that.

At the end of the day, it was a wonderful experience. There are an awful lot of people who would like to represent their country. I was lucky to do it once at a World Cup and I thoroughly enjoyed the experience. If people have a lot of moans about this and that, it is because we didn't do as well as we maybe should have. You'll find there is always trouble within other camps but it doesn't stop these squads getting to cup finals. It's because they want to win and maybe we just didn't have enough people who wanted to win.

Ally MacLeod: Contrary to what some people might think, I got on pretty well with Ernie Walker. It was one of these things that happens, things just not going right. Maybe if we hadn't done so well in the 1977 tour of South America, we might have gone out thinking it was going to be very hard.

Alan Sharp, novelist and scriptwriter (to a television documentary crew in Argentina in 1978): I think the best bit is a number of Scottish guys have visited places they've never come to before. I've heard of boys saying, 'We were on the beach in Ecuador, we were singing songs,' and that kind of thing. And that will be more valuable to them 20 years from now than any fitba' memory because it's got to do with a larger world.

I feel sorry for the guys who just flew in and flew out. What do they remember? Disasters in spades. But for the guys who have to get back [hitch-hiking], it'll be a hard trip but they'll be better when they get back.

John Duffy, fan: On reflection, it was the trip of a lifetime. I know that the joke going around when the team were doing so badly was 'All this way for SFA [Sweet Fuck All]'. But the people made it so good. They would say, 'Come to my house, come to my house.' There were barbecues and bottles of wine, a lot of bevvying. We lived like kings. It was pennies for a big steak and a bottle of wine.

Everything happened too quick. When we got there we were also, of course, a bit travel-shagged. The Holland game made up for a lot of the earlier blows.

After the Holland game, I decided I wanted a run for my money. So I stayed in Argentina. We had a chance to go to a match involving Poland but decided to stay in the wine bar and watch it on telly. I just had a bevvy with the boys.

Brian Fleming, fan: I felt a wee bit let down at the time. But, then again, had it not been for Scotland I would never have got to

Argentina. So I owe them a hell of a debt, because it was fantastic. I'm not sure what Argentina would be like normally, but because it was hosting the World Cup it was a great place to be. I've asked a few journalists and most of them say that Argentina during the World Cup was the best time they've had.

People would just invite you into their house. You couldn't get peace, even if you wanted it, for people saying, 'Come into my house.' It was just unbelievable, it was so friendly. It was just one long party. Pint cocktails, gallon-bottles of wine.

It also made you realise how lucky you were to be living in Scotland. Right through South America, I've never seen so many amputees. There was a lot of poverty in some of the places – people begging basically for food. Small coffins, everywhere you went. You had to take a couple of risks yourself. We were hitching in Mexico and hanging around for ages and I took water from a wee laddie. I knew not to drink the water. But what do you do – die of typhoid or dehydration?

There was also the political thing, but it was mostly Scots guys asking Argentinians what was happening than Argentinians trying to bend your ear. You would be drinking in the same place as the reporters, so you would get bits of information. Trevor McDonald was there and must have been the only black guy in Argentina. He came in and did a report from the bar, then bought everyone a drink and was fine. Some of the fans would speak to the players. I wasn't keen on that, but I did speak to Ally MacLeod once. He was leaning out of the window of a bus and was great to speak to. I didn't go to Anfield [for the crucial qualifying game against Wales]. I couldn't be bothered going to the Holland game, but I went to the World Cup final. Best game I've ever been to. The atmosphere was incredible. I wore my kilt at the game.

Trevor McDonald, journalist: It was an example of how authoritarian governments can will things to happen. For example, the stadium in Córdoba. If you can imagine a virgin forest about 50 miles from the city centre. And in the middle of a clearing made in the forest, there was a stadium built there. You looked at it and thought, 'My God, will this ever be used again? It is too far from anywhere.' But it had been willed that this was going to be part of Córdoba's drive to get the thing.

I had a great time, but when it was all over I wanted to go. My colleagues lingered at the airport talking to the people who'd driven us about and so on. And they couldn't extricate themselves from these rather lachrymose embraces – they were really, really tearful. There was a great juxtaposition. I thought the Argentines could be quite a peculiar race. They could be quite brutal at times, and I thought there were elements of racism. It was difficult to explain to them I was covering Scottish football, especially with a name like 'McDonald'. You didn't feel there were lots of blacks on the streets and I didn't think they were terribly tolerant. Argentina is a country in South America which has distinct European pretensions. They want to be somewhere in the middle of Europe. Anybody black was from Brazil, their sworn enemies. Not that anybody was nasty – quite the contrary.

Martin Buchan: Are there emotional scars? Not really. I was philosophical rather than suicidal. I did my best. I believe that if you do your best, you're entitled to go out after a game and have a beer. I had no problems reconciling myself; I had played to the best of my abilities. I knew my contribution to the games – against Peru, Iran and Holland – was the best I could give.

Russell Galbraith, television producer: I don't think anyone should forget how much good fun the run-up was. Ally was a real tonic. An awful lot of folk will tell you, stirringly, that the hype was over the top while they were happy to generate the hype at the time. Ally was very forthcoming and very friendly to everybody.

He got an awful bruising at the end of it all, an awful bruising from some folk who he might have thought were better-disposed towards him than they turned out. His sheer effervescence carried him and everyone else on this great wave.

It was much more interesting and exciting than almost anything that came afterwards, in World Cup terms. Spain in 1982 was dull, frankly. Jock Stein was determined he was not going to follow that path of raising people's hopes. But you could argue that he dampened people's expectations maybe a bit too much. It's entertainment, after all. What I think Ally was trying to do was get folk involved, enjoy it. Although we had been in the 1974 World Cup and done very well, we'd gone through the 1960s and not qualified for any of the World Cup finals. We had Denis Law and Jim Baxter and failed to qualify. We failed to qualify when the World Cup was on our doorstep [England in 1966] and we probably had the best team then that we've ever had.

Ernie Walker: The SFA never uttered one public breath of criticism about MacLeod and I am not going to start now. The SFA did not jump on the bandwagon of slaughtering him. I was never aware he lacked support from the SFA. They maybe lacked support from him.

Fraser Elder, journalist, 11 June 1978: Perhaps history will say he [Ally MacLeod] was a man who did the right things at the wrong time, the wrong things at the wrong time and nothing at all at the crucial time.

SFA International Committee, 10 July 1978: It will be obvious to everyone that the association's image has been badly dented. It was never particularly high in the eyes of the football public, and there can be little doubt that it will be a long uphill struggle to restore whatever prestige we had.

Self-pity. The Scots are good at that. Just as they are good at being twice shy when once bitten. Another World Cup beckons. But this time, the devolution debate has been signed, sealed and delivered in advance of a 90-minute game of football. If that's a sign of increasing maturity, it reflects the changing demeanour of the Scotland team manager. MacLeod's successors have been decent men preaching pragmatism. Does the World Cup do it for Scotland any more? We'll see.

Appendix 1   How Scotland Qualified

Prague, 13 October 1976
Czechoslovakia 2 (Panenka, Petras) Scotland 0
Attendance: 38,000
CZECHOSLOVAKIA: Vencel, Biros, Ondrus, Capkovic (Jurkemic), Goegh (Kroupa), Dobias, Panenka, Pollak, Masny, Nehoda, Petras
SCOTLAND: Rough, McGrain, Donachie, Buchan, McQueen, Rioch, Dalglish (Burns), Masson (Hartford), Jordan, A. Gray, Gemmill (capt)

Hampden, 17 November 1976
Scotland 1 (Evans o.g.) Wales 0
Attendance: 63,000
SCOTLAND: Rough, McGrain, Donachie, Blackley, McQueen, Rioch (Hartford), Burns, Dalglish, Jordan, Gemmill (capt), E. Gray (Pettigrew)
WALES: Davies, Page, J. Jones, Phillips, Evans, Griffiths, M. Thomas, Flynn, Yorath, Toshack, James (Curtis)

Hampden, 21 September 1977
Scotland 3 (Jordan, Hartford, Dalglish) Czechoslovakia 1 (Gajdusek)
Attendance: 85,000
SCOTLAND: Rough, Jardine, McGrain, Forsyth, McQueen, Rioch (capt), Dalglish, Masson, Jordan, Hartford, Johnston
CZECHOSLOVAKIA: Michalik, Paurik, Capkovic, Dvorak, Goegh, Dobias (Gallis), Gajdusek, Moder (Knapp), Pollak, Masny, Nehoda

Liverpool, 12 October 1977
Wales 0 Scotland 2 (Masson (pen), Dalglish)
Attendance: 51,000
WALES: Davies, R. Thomas, J. Jones, Mahoney, D. Jones, Phillips, Flynn, Sayer (Deacy), Yorath, Toshack, M. Thomas

SCOTLAND: Rough, Jardine (Buchan), Donachie, Masson (capt), McQueen, Forsyth, Dalglish, Hartford, Jordan, Macari, Johnston

Other matches: Wales 3 Czechoslovakia 0; Czechoslovakia 1 Wales 0

Group table

Team	P	W	D	L	F	A	Pts
Scotland	4	3	0	1	6	3	6
Czechoslovakia	4	2	0	2	4	6	4
Wales	4	1	0	3	3	4	2

Players representing Scotland during the qualification matches:
John Blackley (Hibernian)
Martin Buchan (Manchester United)
Kenny Burns (Birmingham City)
Kenny Dalglish (Celtic, then Liverpool before Scotland's second game versus Czechoslovakia)
Willie Donachie (Manchester City)
Tom Forsyth (Rangers)
Archie Gemmill (Derby County)
Andy Gray (Aston Villa)
Eddie Gray (Leeds United)
Asa Hartford (Manchester City)
Sandy Jardine (Rangers)
Willie Johnston (West Bromwich Albion)
Joe Jordan (Leeds United)
Lou Macari (Manchester United)
Don Masson (Queens Park Rangers)
Danny McGrain (Celtic)
Gordon McQueen (Leeds United)
Willie Pettigrew (Motherwell)
Bruce Rioch (Derby County, then Everton before Scotland's second game versus Czechoslovakia)
Alan Rough (Partick Thistle)

Appendix 2   1978 Qualifying Competition*

EUROPE

Group One
23 May 1976 Cyprus 1 Denmark 5
16 October 1976 Portugal 0 Poland 2
27 October 1976 Denmark 5 Cyprus 0
31 October 1976 Poland 5 Cyprus 0
17 November 1976 Portugal 1 Denmark 0
5 December 1976 Cyprus 1 Portugal 2
1 May 1977 Denmark 1 Poland 2
15 May 1977 Cyprus 1 Poland 3
21 September 1977 Poland 4 Denmark 1
9 October 1977 Denmark 2 Portugal 4
29 October 1977 Poland 1 Portugal 1
16 November 1977 Portugal 4 Cyprus 0

Team	P	W	D	L	F	A	Pts
Poland	6	5	1	0	17	4	11
Portugal	6	4	1	1	12	6	9
Denmark	6	2	0	4	14	12	4
Cyprus	6	0	0	6	3	24	0

Poland qualify for Finals

Group Two
13 June 1976 Finland 1 England 4
22 September 1976 Finland 7 Luxembourg 1
13 October 1976 England 2 Finland 1
16 October 1976 Luxembourg 1 Italy 4
17 November 1976 Italy 2 England 0
30 March 1977 England 5 Luxembourg 0
26 May 1977 Luxembourg 0 Finland 1
8 June 1977 Finland 0 Italy 3
12 October 1977 Luxembourg 0 England 2
15 October 1977 Italy 6 Finland 1
16 November 1977 England 2 Italy 0
3 December 1977 Italy 3 Luxembourg 0

Team	P	W	D	L	F	A	Pts
Italy	6	5	0	1	18	4	10
England	6	5	0	1	15	4	10
Finland	6	2	0	4	11	16	4
Luxembourg	6	0	0	6	2	22	0

Italy qualify for Finals

Group Three
31 October 1976 Turkey 4 Malta 0
17 November 1976 East Germany 1 Turkey 1
5 December 1976 Malta 0 Austria 1
2 April 1977 Malta 0 East Germany 1
17 April 1977 Austria 1 Turkey 0
30 April 1977 Austria 9 Malta 0
24 September 1977 Austria 1 East Germany 1
12 October 1977 East Germany 1 Austria 1
29 October 1977 East Germany 9 Malta 0
30 October 1977 Turkey 0 Austria 1
16 November 1977 Turkey 1 East Germany 2
27 November 1977 Malta 0 Turkey 3

Team	P	W	D	L	F	A	Pts
Austria	6	4	2	0	14	2	10
East Germany	6	3	3	0	15	4	9
Turkey	6	2	1	3	9	5	5
Malta	6	0	0	6	0	27	0

Austria qualify for Finals

Group Four
5 September 1976 Iceland 0 Belgium 1
8 September 1976 Iceland 0 Holland 1
13 October 1976 Holland 2 Northern Ireland 2
10 November 1976 Belgium 2 Northern Ireland 0
26 March 1977 Belgium 0 Holland 2
11 June 1977 Iceland 1 Northern Ireland 0
31 August 1977 Holland 4 Iceland 1
4 September 1977 Belgium 4 Iceland 0
21 September 1977 Northern Ireland 2 Iceland 0
12 October 1977 Northern Ireland 0 Holland 1
26 October 1977 Holland 1 Belgium 0
16 November 1977 Northern Ireland 3 Belgium 0

Team	P	W	D	L	F	A	Pts
Holland	6	5	1	0	11	3	11
Belgium	6	3	0	3	7	6	6
Northern Ireland	6	2	1	3	7	6	5
Iceland	6	1	0	5	2	12	2

Holland qualify for Finals

Group Five
9 October 1976 Bulgaria 2 France 2
17 November 1976 France 2 Eire 0
30 March 1977 Eire 1 France 0
1 June 1977 Bulgaria 2 Eire 1
12 October 1977 Eire 0 Bulgaria 0
16 November 1977 France 3 Bulgaria 1

Team	P	W	D	L	F	A	Pts
France	4	2	1	1	7	4	5
Bulgaria	4	1	2	1	5	6	4
Eire	4	1	1	2	2	4	3

France qualify for Finals

Group Six

16 June 1976 Sweden 2 Norway 0
8 September 1976 Norway 1 Switzerland 0
9 October 1976 Switzerland 1 Sweden 2
8 June 1977 Sweden 2 Switzerland 1
7 September 1977 Norway 2 Sweden 1
30 October 1977 Switzerland 1 Norway 0

Team	P	W	D	L	F	A	Pts
Sweden	4	3	0	1	7	4	6
Norway	4	2	0	2	3	4	4
Switzerland	4	1	0	3	3	5	2

Sweden qualify for Finals

Group Seven

13 October 1976 Czechoslovakia 2 Scotland 0
17 November 1976 Scotland 1 Wales 0
30 March 1977 Wales 3 Czechoslovakia 0
21 September 1977 Scotland 3 Czechoslovakia 1
12 October 1977 Wales 0 Scotland 2
16 November 1977 Czechoslovakia 1 Wales 0

Team	P	W	D	L	F	A	Pts
Scotland	4	3	0	1	6	3	6
Czechoslovakia	4	2	0	2	4	6	4
Wales	4	1	0	3	3	4	2

Scotland qualify for Finals

Group Eight

10 October 1976 Spain 1 Yugoslavia 0
6 April 1977 Romania 1 Spain 0
8 May 1977 Yugoslavia 0 Romania 2
26 October 1977 Spain 2 Romania 0
13 November 1977 Romania 4 Yugoslavia 6
30 November 1977 Yugoslavia 0 Spain 1

Team	P	W	D	L	F	A	Pts
Spain	4	3	0	1	4	1	6
Romania	4	2	0	2	7	8	4
Yugoslavia	4	1	0	3	6	8	2

Spain qualify for Finals

Group Nine

9 October 1976 Greece 1 Hungary 1
24 April 1977 USSR 2 Greece 0
30 April 1977 Hungary 2 USSR 1
10 May 1977 Greece 1 USSR 0

18 May 1977 USSR 2 Hungary 0
25 May 1977 Hungary 3 Greece 0

Team	P	W	D	L	F	A	Pts
Hungary	4	2	1	1	6	4	5
USSR	4	2	0	2	5	3	4
Greece	4	1	1	2	2	6	3

Hungary qualify for play-off with winners of Play-off Group Two (South America)

SOUTH AMERICA

Group One

20 February 1977 Colombia 0 Brazil 0
24 February 1977 Colombia 0 Paraguay 1
6 March 1977 Paraguay 1 Colombia 1
9 March 1977 Brazil 6 Colombia 0
13 March 1977 Paraguay 0 Brazil 1
20 March 1977 Brazil 1 Paraguay 1

Team	P	W	D	L	F	A	Pts
Brazil	4	2	2	0	8	1	6
Paraguay	4	1	2	1	3	3	4
Colombia	4	0	2	2	1	8	2

Brazil qualify for Play-off Group

Group Two

9 February 1977 Venezuela 1 Uruguay 1
27 February 1977 Bolivia 1 Uruguay 0
6 March 1977 Venezuela 1 Bolivia 3
13 March 1977 Bolivia 2 Venezuela 0
17 March 1977 Uruguay 2 Venezuela 0
27 March 1977 Uruguay 2 Bolivia 2

Team	P	W	D	L	F	A	Pts
Bolivia	4	3	1	0	8	3	7
Uruguay	4	1	2	1	5	4	4
Venezuela	4	0	1	3	2	8	1

Bolivia qualify for Play-off Group

Group Three

20 February 1977 Ecuador 1 Peru 1
27 February 1977 Ecuador 0 Chile 1
6 March 1977 Chile 1 Peru 1
12 March 1977 Peru 4 Ecuador 0
20 March 1977 Chile 3 Ecuador 0
26 March 1977 Peru 2 Chile 0

Team	P	W	D	L	F	A	Pts
Peru	4	2	2	0	8	2	6
Chile	4	2	1	1	5	3	5
Ecuador	4	0	1	3	1	9	1

Peru qualify for Play-off Group

Play-off Group
10 July 1977 Brazil 1 Peru 0
14 July 1977 Brazil 8 Bolivia 0
17 July 1977 Peru 5 Bolivia 0

Team	P	W	D	L	F	A	Pts
Brazil	2	2	0	0	9	0	4
Peru	2	1	0	1	5	1	2
Bolivia	2	0	0	2	0	13	0

Brazil and Peru qualify for Finals
Bolivia to play winners of Group Nine (Europe)

29 October 1977 Hungary 6 Bolivia 0
30 November 1977 Bolivia 2 Hungary 3
Hungary qualify for Finals

CENTRAL & NORTH AMERICA

Sub-Group One
24 September 1976 Canada 1 USA 1
3 October 1976 USA 0 Mexico 0
10 October 1976 Canada 1 Mexico 0
15 October 1976 Mexico 3 USA 0
20 October 1976 USA 2 Canada 0
27 October 1976 Mexico 0 Canada 0

Team	P	W	D	L	F	A	Pts
Mexico	4	1	2	1	3	1	4
USA	4	1	2	1	3	4	4
Canada	4	1	2	1	2	3	4

Play-off for second place (in Haiti)
22 December 1976 Canada 3 USA 0
Mexico and Canada qualify for Play-off Group

Sub-Group Two
4 April 1976 Panama 3 Costa Rica 2
2 May 1976 Panama 1 El Salvador 1
11 July 1976 Costa Rica 3 Panama 0
1 August 1976 El Salvador 4 Panama 1
17 September 1976 Panama 2 Guatemala 4
16 September 1976 Guatemala 7 Panama 0
1 December 1976 El Salvador 1 Costa Rica 1
5 December 1976 Costa Rica 0 Guatemala 0
8 December 1976 Guatemala 3 El Salvador 1
12 December 1976 Guatemala 1 Costa Rica 1
17 December 1976 Costa Rica 1 El Salvador 1
19 December 1976 El Salvador 2 Guatemala 0

Team	P	W	D	L	F	A	Pts
Guatemala	6	3	2	1	15	6	8
El Salvador	6	2	3	1	10	7	7
Costa Rica	6	1	4	1	8	6	6
Panama	6	1	1	4	7	21	3

Guatemala and El Salvador qualify for Play-off Group

Sub-Group Three
Preliminary Round
2 April 1976 Dominican Republic 0 Haiti 3
17 April 1976 Haiti 3 Dominican Republic 0
Haiti qualify for Round One

Round One
4 July 1976 Guyana 2 Surinam 0
29 August 1976 Surinam 3 Guyana 0
Surinam qualify for Round Two

31 July 1976 Netherlands Antilles 1 Haiti 2
14 August 1976 Haiti 7 Netherlands Antilles 0
Haiti qualify for Round Two

15 August 1976 Jamaica 1 Cuba 3
29 August 1976 Cuba 2 Jamaica 0
Cuba qualify for Round Two

15 August 1976 Barbados 2 Trinidad & Tobago 1
31 August 1976 Trinidad & Tobago 1 Barbados 0
14 September 1976 Barbados 1 Trinidad & Tobago 3
Trinidad & Tobago qualify for Round Two

Round Two
14 November 1976 Surinam 1 Trinidad & Tobago 1
28 November 1976 Trinidad & Tobago 2 Surinam 2
18 December 1976 Surinam 3 Trinidad & Tobago 2
(played in French Guyana)
Surinam qualify for Play-off Group

28 November 1976 Cuba 1 Haiti 1
11 December 1976 Haiti 1 Cuba 1
29 December 1976 Cuba 0 Haiti 2 (played in
Panama)
Haiti qualify for Play-off Group

Group Finals
8 September 1977 Guatemala 3 Surinam 2
8 September 1977 El Salvador 2 Canada 1
9 September 1977 Mexico 4 Haiti 1
12 September 1977 Canada 2 Surinam 1
12 September 1977 Haiti 2 Guatemala 1
12 September 1977 Mexico 3 El Salvador 1
15 September 1977 Mexico 8 Surinam 1
16 September 1977 Canada 2 Guatemala 1
16 September 1977 Haiti 1 El Salvador 0
19 September 1977 Mexico 2 Guatemala 1
20 September 1977 Canada 1 Haiti 1
20 September 1977 El Salvador 3 Surinam 2
22 September 1977 Mexico 3 Canada 1

23 September 1977 Haiti 1 Surinam 0
23 September 1977 Guatemala 2 El Salvador 2

Team	P	W	D	L	F	A	Pts
Mexico	5	5	0	0	20	5	10
Haiti	5	3	1	1	6	6	7
Canada	5	2	1	2	7	8	5
El Salvador	5	2	1	2	8	9	5
Guatemala	5	1	1	3	8	10	3
Surinam	5	0	0	5	6	17	0

Mexico qualify for Finals

AFRICA

Preliminary Round
7 March 1976 Sierra Leone 5 Niger 1
21 March 1976 Niger 2 Sierra Leone 1
Sierra Leone qualify for Round One

13 March 1976 Upper Volta 1 Mauritania 1
28 March 1976 Mauritania 0 Upper Volta 2
Upper Volta qualify for Round One

Round One
1 April 1976 Algeria 1 Libya 0
16 April 1976 Libya 0 Algeria 0
Algeria qualify for Round Two

12 December 1976 Morocco 1 Tunisia 1
9 January 1977 Tunisia 1 Morocco 1
Tunisia qualify for Round Two 4–2 on penalties

17 October 1976 Togo 1 Senegal 0
31 October 1976 Senegal 1 Togo 1
Togo qualify for Round Two

10 October 1976 Ghana 2 Guinea 1
24 October 1976 Guinea 2 Ghana 1
16 January 1977 Guinea 2 Ghana 0 (in Togo)
Guinea qualify for Round Two

Zaire v Central African Republic (CAR withdrew)
Zaire qualify for Round Two

16 October 1976 Sierra Leone 0 Nigeria 0
30 October 1976 Nigeria 6 Sierra Leone 2
Nigeria qualify for Round Two

17 October 1976 Congo 2 Cameroon 2
31 October 1976 Cameroon 1 Congo 2 (match
abandoned in the 82nd minute)
Congo qualify for Round Two

4 September 1976 Upper Volta 1 Ivory Coast 1
25 September 1976 Ivory Coast 2 Upper Volta 0
Ivory Coast qualify for Round Two

29 October 1976 Egypt 3 Ethiopia 0
14 November 1976 Ethiopia 1 Egypt 2
Egypt qualify for Round Two

Kenya v Sudan (Sudan withdrew)
Kenya qualify for Round Two

Uganda v Tanzania (Tanzania withdrew)
Uganda qualify for Round Two

9 May 1976 Zambia 4 Malawi 1
30 May 1976 Malawi 0 Zambia 1
Zambia qualify for Round Two

Round Two
6 February 1977 Tunisia 2 Algeria 0
28 February 1977 Algeria 1 Tunisia 1
Tunisia qualify for Round Three

13 February 1977 Togo 0 Guinea 2
27 February 1977 Guinea 2 Togo 1
Guinea qualify for Round Three

13 February 1977 Ivory Coast 3 Congo 2
27 February 1977 Congo 1 Ivory Coast 3
Ivory Coast qualify for Round Three

6 February 1977 Kenya 0 Egypt 0
27 February 1977 Egypt 1 Kenya 0
Egypt qualify for Round Three

13 February 1977 Uganda 1 Zambia 0
27 February 1977 Zambia 4 Uganda 2
Zambia qualify for Round Three

Nigeria v Zaire (Zaire withdrew)
Nigeria qualify for Round Three

Round Three
5 June 1977 Guinea 1 Tunisia 0
19 June 1977 Tunisia 3 Guinea 1
Tunisia qualify for Group Finals

10 July 1977 Nigeria 4 Ivory Coast 0
21 July 1977 Ivory Coast 2 Nigeria 2
Nigeria qualify for Group Finals

15 July 1977 Egypt 2 Zambia 0
31 July 1977 Zambia 0 Egypt 0

Egypt qualify for Group Finals

Group Finals
25 September 1977 Tunisia 0 Nigeria 0
8 October 1977 Nigeria 4 Egypt 0
21 October 1977 Egypt 3 Nigeria 1
12 November 1977 Nigeria 0 Tunisia 1
25 November 1977 Egypt 3 Tunisia 2
11 December 1977 Tunisia 4 Egypt 1

Team	P	W	D	L	F	A	Pts
Tunisia	4	2	1	1	7	4	5
Egypt	4	2	0	2	7	11	4
Nigeria	4	1	1	2	5	4	3

Tunisia qualify for Finals

ASIA/OCEANIA

Oceania Sub-Group
13 March 1977 Australia 3 Taiwan 0 (in Fiji)
16 March 1977 Taiwan 1 Australia 2 (in Fiji)
20 March 1977 New Zealand 6 Taiwan 0
23 March 1977 Taiwan 0 New Zealand 6 (in NZ)
27 March 1977 Australia 3 New Zealand 1
30 March 1977 New Zealand 1 Australia 1

Team	P	W	D	L	F	A	Pts
Australia	4	3	1	0	9	3	7
New Zealand	4	2	1	1	14	4	5
Taiwan	4	0	0	4	1	17	0

Australia qualify for Group Finals

Asian Sub-Group One (all matches in Singapore)
27 February 1977 Singapore 2 Thailand 0
28 February 1977 Hong Kong 4 Indonesia 1
1 March 1977 Malaysia 6 Thailand 4
2 March 1977 Hong Kong 2 Singapore 2
3 March 1977 Indonesia 0 Malaysia 0
5 March 1977 Thailand 1 Hong Kong 2
6 March 1977 Singapore 1 Malaysia 0
7 March 1977 Thailand 3 Indonesia 2
8 March 1977 Malaysia 1 Hong Kong 1
9 March 1977 Indonesia 4 Singapore 0

Team	P	W	D	L	F	A	Pts
Hong Kong	4	2	2	0	9	5	6
Singapore	4	2	1	1	5	6	5
Malaysia	4	1	2	1	7	6	4
Indonesia	4	1	1	2	7	7	3
Thailand	4	1	0	3	8	12	2

Hong Kong and Singapore qualify for Sub-Group Final

Sub-Group Final
12 March 1977 Singapore 0 Hong Kong 1
Hong Kong qualify for Group Finals

Asian Sub-Group Two
27 February 1977 Israel 0 South Korea 0
6 March 1977 Israel 2 Japan 0
10 March 1977 Japan 0 Israel 2 (in Israel)
20 March 1977 South Korea 3 Israel 1
26 March 1977 Japan 0 South Korea 0
3 April 1977 South Korea 1 Japan 0
North Korea withdrew

Team	P	W	D	L	F	A	Pts
S Korea	4	2	2	0	4	1	6
Israel	4	2	1	1	5	3	5
Japan	4	0	1	3	0	5	1
N Korea	0	0	0	0	0	0	0

South Korea qualify for Group Finals

Asian Sub-Group Three
12 November 1976 Saudi Arabia 2 Syria 0
26 November 1977 Syria 2 Saudi Arabia 1
7 January 1977 Saudi Arabia 0 Iran 3
28 January 1977 Syria 0 Iran 1
8 April 1977 Iran v Syria (Syria did not appear, forfeit 0–2)
22 April 1977 Iran 2 Saudi Arabia 0

Team	P	W	D	L	F	A	Pts
Iran	4	4	0	0	8	0	8
Saudi Arabia	4	1	0	3	3	7	2
Syria	4	1	0	3	2	6	2

Iran qualify for Group Finals

Asian Sub-Group Four
(all matches in Qatar)
11 March 1977 Bahrain 0 Kuwait 2
13 March 1977 Bahrain 0 Qatar 2
15 March 1977 Qatar 0 Kuwait 2
17 March 1977 Bahrain 1 Kuwait 2
19 March 1977 Qatar 0 Bahrain 3
21 March 1977 Qatar 1 Kuwait 4
United Arab Emirates withdrew

Team	P	W	D	L	F	A	Pts
Kuwait	4	4	0	0	10	2	8
Bahrain	4	1	0	3	4	6	2
Qatar	4	1	0	3	3	9	2
UAE	0	0	0	0	0	0	0

Kuwait qualify for the Group Finals

Group Finals

19 June 1977 Hong Kong 0 Iran 2
26 June 1977 Hong Kong 0 South Korea 1
3 July 1977 South Korea 0 Iran 0
10 July 1977 Australia 3 Hong Kong 0
14 August 1977 Australia 0 Iran 1
27 August 1977 Australia 2 South Korea 1
2 October 1977 Hong Kong 1 Kuwait 3
9 October 1977 South Korea 1 Kuwait 0
16 October 1977 Australia 1 Kuwait 2
23 October 1977 South Korea 0 Australia 0
28 October 1977 Iran 1 Kuwait 0
30 October 1977 Hong Kong 2 Australia 5
5 November 1977 Kuwait 2 South Korea 2
11 November 1977 Iran 2 South Korea 2
12 November 1977 Kuwait 4 Hong Kong 0

18 November 1977 Iran 3 Hong Kong 0
19 November 1977 Kuwait 1 Australia 0
25 November 1977 Iran 1 Australia 0
3 December 1977 Kuwait 1 Iran 2
4 December 1977 South Korea 5 Hong Kong 2

Team	P	W	D	L	F	A	Pts
Iran	8	6	2	0	12	3	14
S Korea	8	3	4	1	12	8	10
Kuwait	8	4	1	3	13	8	9
Australia	8	3	1	4	11	8	7
Hong Kong	8	0	0	8	5	26	0

Iran qualify for Finals

Argentina (hosts) and West Germany (holders) are exempt from the qualifying rounds

Appendix 3 1978 World Cup Results

Group One

2 June Mar del Plata Italy 2 (Rossi, Zaccarelli)
France 1 (Lacombe) attendance 42,373
2 June Buenos Aires Argentina 2 (Luque, Bertoni)
Hungary 1 (Csapó) att 77,000
6 June Mar del Plata Italy 3 (Rossi, Bettega,
Benetti) Hungary 1 (Tóth pen) att 32,000
6 June Buenos Aires Argentina 2 (Passarella pen,
Luque) France 1 (Platini) att 77,216
10 June Mar del Plata France 3 (Lopez, Berdoll,
Rocheteau) Hungary 1 (Zambori) att 28,000
10 June Buenos Aires Italy 1 (Bettega) Argentina 0
att 77,260

Team	P	W	D	L	F	A	Pts
Italy	3	3	0	0	6	2	6
Argentina	3	2	0	1	4	3	4
France	3	1	0	2	5	5	2
Hungary	3	0	0	3	3	8	0

Italy and Argentina qualify for next round

Group Two

1 June Buenos Aires West Germany 0 Poland 0 att
77,000
3 June Rosario Tunisia 3 (Kaabi, Goummidh,
Dhouib) Mexico 1 (Vasquez) att 25,000
6 June Rosario Poland 1 (Lato) Tunisia 0 att 15,000
6 June Córdoba West Germany 6 (D. Müller, H.
Müller, Rummenigge 2, Flohe 2) Mexico 0 att
46,000
10 June Rosario Poland 3 (Boniek 2, Deyna)
Mexico 1 (Rangel) att 25,000
10 June Córdoba West Germany 0 Tunisia 0 att
35,000

Team	P	W	D	L	F	A	Pts
Poland	3	2	1	0	4	1	5
W Germany	3	1	2	0	6	0	4
Tunisia	3	1	1	1	3	2	3
Mexico	3	0	0	3	2	12	0

Poland and West Germany qualify for next round

Group Three

3 June Buenos Aires Austria 2 (Schachner, Krankl)
Spain 1 (Dani) att 49,371
3 June Mar del Plata Brazil 1 (Reinaldo) Sweden 1
(Sjöberg) att 38,000

7 June Buenos Aires Austria 1 (Krankl pen)
Sweden 0 att 46,000
7 June Mar del Plata Brazil 0 Spain 0 att 40,000
11 June Buenos Aires Spain 1 (Asensi) Sweden 0
att 48,000
11 June Mar del Plata Brazil 1 (Roberto) Austria 0
att 40,000

Team	P	W	D	L	F	A	Pts
Austria	3	2	0	1	3	2	4
Brazil	3	1	2	0	2	1	4
Spain	3	1	1	1	2	2	3
Sweden	3	0	1	2	1	3	1

Austria and Brazil qualify for next round

Group Four

3 June Córdoba Peru 3 (Cueto, Cubillas 2)
Scotland 1 (Jordan) att 45,000
3 June Mendoza Holland 3 (Rensenbrink 3, 2 pens)
Iran 0 att 45,000
7 June Córdoba Scotland 1 (Eskandarian o.g.) Iran
1 (Danaiefard) att 8,000
7 June Mendoza Holland 0 Peru 0 att 30,000
11 June Córdoba Peru 4 (Velasquez, Cubillas 3,
2 pens) Iran 1 (Rowshan) att 25,000
11 June Mendoza Scotland 3 (Dalglish, Gemmill 2,
1 pen) Holland 2 (Rensenbrink pen, Rep) att
40,000

Team	P	W	D	L	F	A	Pts
Peru	3	2	1	0	7	2	5
Holland	3	1	1	1	5	3	3
Scotland	3	1	1	1	5	6	3
Iran	3	0	1	2	2	8	1

Peru and Holland qualify for next round

Group A

14 June Buenos Aires West Germany 0 Italy 0 att
60,000
14 June Córdoba Holland 5 (Brandts, Rensenbrink
pen, Rep 2, W. van de Kerkhof) Austria 1
(Obermayer) att 15,000
18 June Buenos Aires Italy 1 (Rossi) Austria 0 att
60,000
18 June Córdoba Holland 2 (Haan, R. van de
Kerkhof) West Germany 2 (Abramczik, D.
Müller) att 46,000

21 June Buenos Aires Holland 2 (Brandts, Haan)
Italy 1 (Brandts o.g.) att 70,000

21 June Córdoba Austria 3 (Vogts o.g., Krankl 2)
West Germany 2 (Rummenigge, Hölzenbein) att
20,000

Team	P	W	D	L	F	A	Pts
Holland	3	2	1	0	9	4	5
Italy	3	1	1	1	2	2	3
West Germany	3	0	2	1	4	5	2
Austria	3	1	0	2	4	8	2

Holland qualify for the final; Italy qualify for the third-place play-off

Group B

14 June Mendoza Brazil 3 (Dirceu 2, Zico pen)
Peru 0 att 40,000

14 June Rosario Argentina 2 (Kempes 2) Poland 0
att 40,000

18 June Mendoza Poland 1 (Szarmach) Peru 0 att
35,000

18 June Rosario Argentina 0 Brazil 0 att 46,000

21 June Mendoza Brazil 3 (Nelinho, Roberto 2)
Poland 1 (Lato) att 44,000

21 June Rosario Argentina 6 (Kempes 2, Tarantini,
Luque 2, Houseman) Peru 0 att 40,567

Team	P	W	D	L	F	A	Pts
Argentina	3	2	1	0	8	0	5
Brazil	3	2	1	0	6	1	5
Poland	3	1	0	2	2	5	2
Peru	3	0	0	3	0	10	0

Argentina qualify for the final; Brazil qualify for the third-place play-off

Third-place

24 June Buenos Aires Brazil 2 (Nelinho, Dirceu)
Italy 1 (Causio) att 76,609

Final

25 June Buenos Aires Argentina 3 (Kempes 2,
Bertoni) Holland 1 (Nanninga) (after extra time)
att 77,260

ARGENTINA: Fillo, Olguín, Galván, Passarella,
Tarantini, Ardiles (Larrosa), Gallego, Kempes,
Bertoni, Luque, Ortíz (Houseman).

HOLLAND: Jongbloed, Krul, Pootvliet, Brandts,
Jansen (Suurbier), W. van de Kerkof, Neeskins,
Haan, Rep (Nanninga), Rensenbrink, R. van de
Kerkof.

OTHER TOURNAMENT FACTS

Leading scorers

6	Kempes (Argentina)
5	Cubillas (Peru)
	Rensenbrink (Holland)
4	Luque (Argentina)
	Krankl (Austria)

Total goals: 102

Average per game: 2.7

Sendings-off: 3

Torocsik (Hungary) v Argentina

Nyilasi (Hungary) v Argentina

Nanninga (Holland) v West Germany

Cautions: 58

Goals from a penalty: 12 (from 14 awarded)

Own goals: 3

Appendix 4 The Scotland Squad (I)

THE PLAYERS

Name	Position	Club	Age	Caps	Goals
Alan Rough	goalkeeper	Partick Thistle	26	18	0
Jim Blyth*	goalkeeper	Coventry City	23	2	0
Bobby Clark*	goalkeeper	Aberdeen	32	17	0
Sandy Jardine	full-back	Rangers	29	34	1
Stuart Kennedy	full-back	Aberdeen	24	3	0
Willie Donachie	full-back	Manchester City	26	30	0
Martin Buchan	central defender	Manchester United	29	28	0
Tom Forsyth	central defender	Rangers	29	19	0
Gordon McQueen**	central defender	Manchester United	25	20	3
Kenny Burns	central defender	Nottingham Forest	24	11	1
Bruce Rioch	midfielder	Derby County	30	22	6
Don Masson	midfielder	Derby County	31	16	5
Archie Gemmill	midfielder	Nottingham Forest	31	26	2
Graeme Souness	midfielder	Liverpool	24	6	0
Asa Hartford	midfielder	Manchester City	27	24	3
Lou Macari	midfielder	Manchester United	28	22	5
Willie Johnston	winger	West Bromwich Albion	31	21	0
John Robertson	winger	Nottingham Forest	25	2	0
Joe Jordan	forward	Manchester United	26	30	7
Kenny Dalglish	forward	Liverpool	27	54	18
Joe Harper	forward	Aberdeen	30	3	2
Derek Johnstone**	forward	Rangers	24	13	3

RESERVES (NOT CALLED UPON)
Jim Stewart (Middlesbrough), Willie Miller (Aberdeen), John Blackley (Newcastle United), Andy Gray (Aston Villa), Arthur Graham (Leeds United), Ian Wallace (Coventry City)
* Players who would not appear in the World Cup finals, nor play for Scotland again
** Players who would not appear in the World Cup finals

Average age of squad, excluding uncalled reserves: 27.8 years
Average number of caps in squad, excluding uncalled reserves: 19.2

MAIN TOUR PARTY
Ally MacLeod – Manager
John Hagart – Assistant Manager (former manager of Heart of Midlothian)
Andy Roxburgh – Technical
Donny McKinnon – Trainer (Partick Thistle)
Hugh Allan – Trainer (Kilmarnock)
Jim Steel – Masseur (Celtic)
Ernie Walker – Secretary of the Scottish Football Association
Willie Harkness – President of the Scottish Football Association (from Queen of the South)
Tom Lauchlan – President of the Scottish League and Chairman of the SFA International Committee (from Kilmarnock)

Appendix 5 The Scotland Squad (2)

FULL NAME: **James Anton Blyth**
POSITION: goalkeeper
BORN: 2 February 1955, Perth
CLUBS (PLAYER): **Preston North End** (October 1972, one league appearance), **Coventry City** (£22,500, October 1972, 151 league apps, including a loan spell at Hereford United – March 1975, seven league apps), **Birmingham City** (free transfer, August 1982, 14 league apps), **Nuneaton Borough** (July 1985 – May 1986, 21 apps). He was an apprentice at Preston and as soon as he turned professional, having played just one league game, he moved to Coventry
CAPS: 2; 1977–78 season versus Bulgaria, Wales
SCOTLAND CLEAN SHEETS: none
ARGENTINA – QUALIFYING ROUNDS PLAYED: none
ARGENTINA – WORLD CUP MATCHES PLAYED: none
CURRENT OCCUPATION: Coventry City goalkeeping coach
OTHER: Blyth was unfortunate with injuries. A £440,000 move to Manchester United in 1978 was scuppered by a back injury. He moved to Hereford United, where ex-Coventry player John Sillett was manager. He had joined Coventry aged 17 and gained the chance to establish himself as the first-choice keeper after an injury to Bryan King, a big-money signing from Millwall. In September 1979, his recurring back problem forced him to leave the pitch during the warm-up before a game against Norwich City. Blyth was Coventry's Player of the Year in 1976–77. He ran a pub, The Plough Inn, in Nuneaton, while playing for the local side.

FULL NAME: **Martin McLean Buchan**
POSITION: central defender
BORN: 6 March 1949, Aberdeen
CLUBS (PLAYER): **Banks O'Dee** (n/a), **Aberdeen** (August 1966, 130+3 league appearances, nine goals), **Manchester United** (£125,000, February 1972, 376 league apps, four goals), **Oldham Athletic** (free transfer, August 1983 – October 1984, 28 league apps, no goals, retired through injury); (MANAGER): **Burnley** (June 1985 – October 1985)
CLUB HONOURS (PLAYER): Aberdeen: Scottish Cup winners' medal, 1970. Manchester United: Division Two Champions medal, 1975; FA Cup winners' medal, 1977; FA Cup runners-up medal, 1976, 1979; OTHER HONOURS: Scottish Youth international; Scottish Under-23 international (three appearances); Aberdeen club captain aged 20; Scottish Player of the Year, 1971
CAPS: 34; 1971–72 season versus Portugal, Belgium, Wales, Yugoslavia, Czechoslovakia, Brazil; 1972–73 versus Denmark (x2), England; 1973–74 versus West Germany, Northern Ireland, Wales, Norway, Brazil, Yugoslavia; 1974-75 versus East Germany, Spain, Portugal; 1975–76 versus Denmark, Romania; 1976–77 versus Finland, Czechoslovakia, Chile, Argentina, Brazil; 1977–78 versus East Germany, Wales, Northern Ireland, Peru, Iran, Holland; 1978–79 versus Austria, Norway, Portugal

SCOTLAND GOALS: none

ARGENTINA QUALIFYING ROUNDS PLAYED: versus Czechoslovakia (away), Wales (away)

ARGENTINA WORLD CUP MATCHES PLAYED: versus Peru, Iran and Holland

CURRENT OCCUPATION: Football Promotions Manager, Puma UK

OTHER: Buchan spent 11 years at Old Trafford, having been signed by Frank O'Farrell. Famously, he snuffed out Kevin Keegan when United won the FA Cup in 1977. In total, he played three FA Cup finals. He was in the side that lost 1–0 to Southampton in 1976 when clear favourites and was a losing finalist in 1979 when United lost 3–2 to Arsenal. He captained United for six years. A low point was when he was alleged to have caused irreparable damage to Colin Bell's knee in the Manchester derby on 12 November 1975. Supposedly there was a collision but Buchan cannot recollect making contact. Bell played on for a couple more years but was never the same player after his injury. The resulting furore influenced his decision not to go to Manchester City when offered a contract by them when he left United.

FULL NAME: **Kenneth Burns**

POSITION: central defender

BORN: 23 September 1953, Glasgow

CLUBS (PLAYER): **Rangers groundstaff** (n/a), **Birmingham City** (July 1971, 163+7 league appearances, 45 goals), **Nottingham Forest** (£150,000, July 1977, 137 league apps, 13 goals), **Leeds United** (£400,000, October 1981, including loan spell at Derby County, March–May 1983; at Leeds, 54+2 league apps, two goals; at Derby, six league apps, one goal), **Derby County** (March 1984, including loan spell at Notts County, February–March 1985; at Derby, 30+1 league apps, one goal; at Notts County, two league apps, no goals), **Barnsley** (non-contracted, August 1985, 19+2 league apps, no goals), **Sutton Town** (August 1986, including co-manager from March 1987), **Stafford Rangers** (July 1988), **Grantham Town** (July 1988), **Ilkeston Town** (July 1989)

CLUBS (CO-MANAGER): **Sutton Town** (March 1987 – July 1988)

CAPS: 20; 1973–74 season versus West Germany; 1974–75 versus East Germany, Spain (x2); 1976–77 versus Czechoslovakia, Wales (x2), Sweden; 1977–78 versus Northern Ireland, Wales, England, Peru, Iran; 1978–79 versus Norway; 1979–80 versus Peru, Austria, Belgium; 1980–81 versus Israel, Northern Ireland, Wales

SCOTLAND GOALS: 1, versus East Germany

CLUB HONOURS (PLAYER): Nottingham Forest: European Cup winners' medal, 1979, 1980; League Championship medal,1978; League Cup winners' medal, 1978; League Cup runners-up medal, 1980; OTHER HONOURS: Scottish Youth international; Scottish Under-23 international (two appearances); FA Footballer of the Year, 1978

CURRENT OCCUPATION: Giftware sales rep

ARGENTINA QUALIFYING ROUNDS PLAYED: versus Czechoslovakia (away), Wales (home)

ARGENTINA WORLD CUP MATCHES PLAYED: versus Peru and Iran

OTHERS: Burns was a talented but fiery centre-forward with Birmingham City. He starred as a central defender for Nottingham Forest under Brian Clough and Peter Taylor and was Footballer of the Year in 1977–78 when Forest won the League Championship and the League Cup. He was reunited with Peter Taylor at Derby County and with ex-Forest team-mate Martin O'Neill at Grantham

FULL NAME: **Robert Brown Clark**

POSITION: goalkeeper

BORN: 26 September1945, Glasgow

CLUBS (PLAYER): **Queen's Park** (July 1962, 83 league apps), **Aberdeen** (May 1965, 434+1 league apps), **Clyde** (June 1982, no league apps); (MANAGER): **Bulawayo Highlanders**, Zimbabwe (January 1983 – January 1984), **Dartmouth University Men's Soccer Coach**, New Hampshire (June 1985 – April 1994), **New Zealand national team** (April 1994 – February 1996)

CAPS: 17; 1967–68 season versus Wales, Holland; 1969–70 versus Northern Ireland; 1970–71 versus Wales, Northern Ireland, England, Denmark, Portugal, USSR; 1971–72 versus Belgium, Northern Ireland, Wales, England, Czechoslovakia, Brazil; 1972–73 versus Denmark, England

SCOTLAND CLEAN SHEETS: 7; versus Holland, Northern Ireland (x2), Wales (x2), Belgium, Czechoslovakia

CLUB HONOURS (PLAYER): Aberdeen: League Championship medal, 1980; Scottish Cup winners' medal, 1970; Scottish Cup runners-up medal, 1967, 1978; Scottish League Cup winners' medal, 1977; Scottish League Cup runners-up medal, 1979, 1980; (MANAGER): Dartmouth University: won three Ivy League titles; OTHER HONOURS: Scottish Under-23 international (two appearances), Scottish Under-21 international (three appearances), Scottish League (one appearance)

ARGENTINA QUALIFYING ROUNDS PLAYED: none

ARGENTINA WORLD CUP MATCHES PLAYED: none

CURRENT OCCUPATION: Director of Soccer, Stanford University, California

OTHER: The son of a Clyde director who went on to become treasurer at the Scottish Football Association, Bobby played for Scotland at every level, including amateur and youth. When he signed for Aberdeen's manager Eddie Turnbull in May 1964, he was studying at Jordanhill College to become a PE teacher. He played over 500 games – in all competitions – for Aberdeen, including a few as an outfield player. He was mostly first-choice keeper for Scotland between 1967 and 1973, vying for the position with Ronnie Simpson, Jim Herriot, Jim Cruickshank, Bob Wilson and Ally Hunter. His last game was in a 5–0 crushing by England, the SFA Centenary match of February 1974. He briefly looked to be out in the cold at Aberdeen when Ally MacLeod become Scotland boss, taking goalkeeper Ally McLean with him. However, Clark bounced back to reclaim the number-one jersey. At one stage he looked set to join Stoke City for £100,000, which would have been the highest transfer fee in Britain for a goalkeeper.

FULL NAME: **Kenneth Mathieson Dalglish**

POSITION: forward

BORN: 4 March 1951, Dalmarnock, Glasgow

CLUBS (PLAYER): **Celtic** (August 1967, 200+4 league appearances, 112 goals), **Liverpool** (£440,000, August 1977 – February 1991, though played last game in May 1990, 342 league apps, 118 goals); (MANAGER): **Liverpool** (June 1985 – February 1991), **Blackburn Rovers** (October 1991 – June 1995; director of football, June 1995 – August 1996), **Newcastle United** (January 1997 – present)

CAPS: 102; 1971–72 season versus Belgium, Holland; 1972–73 versus Denmark (x2), England (x2), Wales, Northern Ireland, Switzerland, Brazil; 1973–74 versus Czechoslovakia (x2), West Germany (x2), Northern Ireland, Wales, England, Belgium, Norway, Zaire, Brazil,

Yugoslavia; 1974–75 versus East Germany, Spain (x2), Sweden, Portugal, Wales, Northern Ireland, England, Romania; 1975–76 versus Denmark (x2), Romania, Switzerland, Northern Ireland, England; 1976–77 versus Finland, Czechoslovakia, Wales (x2), Sweden, Northern Ireland, England, Chile, Argentina, Brazil; 1977–78 versus East Germany, Czechoslovakia, Wales (x 2), Bulgaria, Northern Ireland, England, Peru, Iran, Holland; 1978–79 versus Austria, Norway, Portugal, Wales, Northern Ireland, England, Argentina, Norway; 1979–80 versus Peru, Austria, Belgium (x2), Portugal, Northern Ireland, Wales, England, Poland, Hungary; 1980–81 versus Sweden, Northern Ireland, Israel; 1981–82 versus Sweden, Northern Ireland (x2), Portugal, Spain, Holland, Wales, England, New Zealand, Brazil; 1982–83 versus Belgium, Switzerland; 1983–84 versus Uruguay, Belgium, East Germany; 1984–85 versus Yugoslavia, Iceland, Spain, Wales; 1985–86 versus East Germany, Australia, Romania; 1986–87 versus Bulgaria, Luxembourg

SCOTLAND GOALS: 30; versus Denmark, Northern Ireland, West Germany, Wales, Norway, East Germany, Northern Ireland, Denmark, Northern Ireland, England, Finland, Sweden, Northern Ireland (x2), England, Chile, Czechoslovakia, Wales, Holland, Norway (x2), Norway, Portugal, Israel, Holland, New Zealand, Belgium (x2), Yugoslavia, Spain

CLUB HONOURS (PLAYER): Celtic: Scottish Championship medal, 1972, 1973, 1974, 1977; Scottish Cup winners' medal, 1972, 1974, 1975, 1977; Scottish Cup runners-up medal, 1973; Scottish League Cup winners' medal, 1975; Scottish League Cup runners-up medal, 1972, 1973, 1974, 1977. Liverpool: European Cup winners' medal, 1978, 1981, 1984; European Cup runners-up medal, 1985; League Championship medal, 1979, 1980, 1982, 1983, 1984; League Cup winners' medal, 1981, 1982, 1983, 1984; League Cup runners-up medal, 1978; (PLAYER-MANAGER): Liverpool: League Champions, 1986, 1988, 1990; FA Cup winners' medal, 1986, 1989; (MANAGER): Blackburn Rovers: Premiership Champions, 1995; OTHER HONOURS: Scottish Youth international; Scottish Under-23 international (four appearances); Football Writers' Player of the Year, 1979 and 1983; PFA Player of the Year, 1983; Manager of the Year, 1986, 1988, 1990, 1995; first player to score more than 100 league goals in Scotland and England; in the World Cup match versus Peru, in 1978, he equalled Denis Law's appearance record for Scotland; in March 1986, he became the first Scot and fifth Briton to complete a century of caps; awarded MBE in 1985; made Freeman of Glasgow in 1985

CURRENT OCCUPATION: manager of Newcastle United

ARGENTINA QUALIFYING ROUNDS PLAYED: versus Czechoslovakia (home and away), Wales (home and away)

ARGENTINA WORLD CUP MATCHES PLAYED: versus Peru, Iran, Holland

OTHER: Dalglish moved from Celtic to Liverpool between 1978 World Cup qualifying games against Wales (at Hampden) and Czechoslovakia (also at Hampden). As a manager, he notoriously finds press conferences a bore, famously replying to the question, 'How did you see the match, Kenny?' with a curt, 'From the dugout.' He followed Kevin Keegan at Liverpool (as a player) then at Newcastle United (as manager). Before joining Newcastle, he was briefly a scouting advisor at Rangers.

FULL NAME: **William Donachie**
POSITION: full-back
BORN: 5 October 1951; Castlemilk, Glasgow
CLUBS (PLAYER): **Glasgow Amateurs** (n/a), **Manchester City** (apprentice October 1968, pro December 1968, 347+4 league appearances, two goals), **Portland Timbers**, USA (£300,000,

March 1980, 93+2 apps, two goals, including loan spell at **Norwich City**, September 1981
– February 1982, 11 league apps, no goals; moved to and from Norwich for £200,000),
Burnley (November 1982, 60 league apps, no goals), **Oldham Athletic** (July 1984 –
November 1994, 158+11 league apps, three goals) ; (ASSISTANT MANAGER/ FIRST-TEAM
COACH): **Oldham Athletic** (after initially joining as a player in July 1984), **Everton**
(November 1994 – May 1997), **Sheffield United** (July 1997 – present)

CAPS: 35; 1971–72 season versus Peru, Northern Ireland, England, Yugoslavia, Czechoslovakia,
Brazil; 1972–73 versus Denmark, England, Wales, Northern Ireland; 1973–74 versus
Northern Ireland; 1975–76 versus Romania, Northern Ireland, Wales, England; 1976–77
versus Finland, Czechoslovakia, Wales (x2), Sweden, Northern Ireland, England, Chile,
Argentina, Brazil; 1977–78 versus East Germany, Wales (x2), Bulgaria, England, Iran,
Holland; 1978–79 versus Austria, Norway, Portugal

SCOTLAND GOALS: none

CLUB HONOURS (PLAYER): Manchester City: League Cup winners' medal, 1976; League Cup
runners-up medal, 1974; (ASSISTANT MANAGER/FIRST-TEAM COACH): Oldham Athletic: FA
Cup semi-finalists, 1990; League Cup runners-up, 1990; Second Division Champions,
1991. Everton: FA Cup winners, 1995; OTHER HONOURS: Scotland Under-23 international
(two appearances)

ARGENTINA QUALIFYING ROUNDS PLAYED: versus Czechoslovakia (away); Wales (home and
away)

ARGENTINA WORLD CUP MATCHES PLAYED: versus Iran and Holland

CURRENT OCCUPATION: First-team coach, Sheffield United

OTHER: Towards the end of his career Donachie spent two spells at Portland Timbers in the
NASL in the USA. An ankle injury against Northern Ireland in 1974 temporarily
interrupted his career; when he recovered, he found he was up against Danny McGrain
and Sandy Jardine for the full-back spot. He had moved to full-back from midfield during
his first season at Manchester City, the same season he was capped as a 20-year-old. He
succeeded Glyn Pardoe (victim of a broken leg) to join Tony Book in the Manchester
City defence and was an ever-present in 1973–74 (when they reached League Cup final)
and in 1976–77. He missed the Scotland game against Czechoslovakia at Hampden in
September 1977 because of a wrist injury, and was suspended for Scotland's first game of
the World Cup finals, against Peru, because of two bookings picked up during qualifying.

FULL NAME: **Thomas Forsyth**

POSITION: midfield/defence

BORN: 23 January 1949, Glasgow

CLUBS (PLAYER): **Motherwell** (July 1967, 150 appearances, 17 goals), **Rangers** (£40,000, October
1972 – March 1982, 218 league apps, two goals; retired due to injury); (MANAGER):
Dunfermline Athletic (September 1982 – May 1983); (ASSISTANT MANAGER): **Greenock
Morton** (1983–84), **Motherwell** (July 1984 – May 1994), **Heart of Midlothian** (July 1994 –
July 1995)

CAPS: 22; 1970–71 season versus Denmark; 1973-74 versus Czechoslovakia; 1975–76 versus
Sweden, Northern Ireland, Wales, England; 1976–77 versus Finland, Sweden, Wales,
Northern Ireland, England, Chile, Argentina, Brazil; 1977–78 versus Czechoslovakia,
Wales (x2), Northern Ireland, England, Peru, Iran, Holland

SCOTLAND GOALS: none

CLUB HONOURS (PLAYER): Rangers: League Championship medal, 1975, 1976, 1978; Scottish

Cup winners' medal, 1973, 1976, 1978, 1981; Scottish Cup runners' up medal, 1977, 1980; Scottish League Cup winners' medal, 1978; (ASSISTANT MANAGER): Morton: First Division Champions, 1984. Motherwell: Scottish Cup winners, 1991; OTHER HONOURS: Scottish Under-23 international (one appearance); Scottish League (two appearances).

ARGENTINA QUALIFYING ROUNDS PLAYED: versus Czechoslovakia (home), Wales (away)

ARGENTINA WORLD CUP MATCHES PLAYED: versus Peru, Iran and Holland

CURRENT OCCUPATION: market gardener

OTHER: Forsyth won his first Scotland cap while at Motherwell and, after moving to Rangers in a £40,000 move, captained Scotland in only his third international (against Switzerland in April 1976). He was nicknamed 'Jaws' because he was considered a ferocious tackler. He was also a skilful player and scored the winning goal in Rangers' 3–2 win over Celtic in the final of the Centenary Scottish Cup, in 1973. He won 14 of his 22 caps under Ally MacLeod, who believed him to be one of the most consistent of players. Injury forced him to retire from football in March 1982.

FULL NAME: **Archibald Gemmill**

POSITION: midfield

BORN: 24 March 1947, Paisley

CLUBS (PLAYER): **Drumchapel** (n/a), **St Mirren** (July 1964, 65 league appearances, 9 goals), **Preston North End** (£13,000, May 1967, 93+6 league apps, 13 goals), **Derby County** (£66,000, September 1970, 261 league apps, 17 goals), **Nottingham Forest** (£25,000 + player [John Middleton, equivalent to £160,000], September 1977, 56+2 league apps, four goals), **Birmingham City** (£150,000, August 1979, 97 league apps, 12 goals), **Jacksonville Teamen**, USA (March 1982, 32 apps, two goals), **Wigan Athletic** (non-contracted, September 1982, 11 league apps, no goals), **Derby County** (November 1982 – May 1984, 63 league apps, eight goals); (COACH): **Nottingham Forest** (August 1985 – May 1994); (CO-MANAGER, with John McGovern): **Rotherham United** (September 1994 – September 1996)

CAPS: 43; 1970–71 season versus Belgium; 1971–72 versus Portugal, Holland, Peru, Northern Ireland, Wales, England; 1975–76 versus Denmark, Romania, Northern Ireland, Wales, England; 1976–77 versus Finland, Czechoslovakia, Wales (x2), Northern Ireland, England, Chile, Argentina, Brazil; 1977–78 versus East Germany, Bulgaria, Northern Ireland, Wales, England, Peru, Iran, Holland; 1978–79 versus Austria, Norway (x2), Portugal; 1979–80 versus Austria, Portugal, Northern Ireland, Wales, England, Hungary; 1980–81 versus Sweden, Portugal, Israel, Northern Ireland

SCOTLAND GOALS: 7; versus Northern Ireland, Bulgaria (penalty), Holland x 2 (one a penalty), Norway (penalty), Austria, Portugal (penalty)

CLUB HONOURS (PLAYER): Derby County: League Championship medal, 1972, 1975. Nottingham Forest: League Championship medal, 1978; League Cup winners' medal, 1979; (CO-MANAGER): Rotherham United: Auto Windscreen Shield winners, 1996; OTHER HONOURS: Scottish Under-23 international (one appearance)

ARGENTINA QUALIFYING ROUNDS PLAYED: versus Czechoslovakia (away), Wales (home)

ARGENTINA WORLD CUP MATCHES PLAYED: versus Peru, Iran and Holland

CURRENT OCCUPATION: unemployed

OTHER: Gemmill was the first-ever substitute to appear in Scotland, for St Mirren versus Clyde, on 13 August 1966. He joined Derby County from Preston NE to take over from Willie Carlin in midfield, Derby manager Brian Clough staying overnight in the Gemmill household to make sure the deal was completed. In the absence of Roy McFarland, he skippered Derby to the league title in 1975. He was on the coaching staff at Forest for nine years, but was disappointed to be left out of Forest's 1979 European Cup final team. He starred as Birmingham City regained top-flight status at the first attempt in 1979–80. He was Peter Taylor's first signing for Derby in November 1982 after a spell at Wigan (under ex-Forest team-mate, Larry Lloyd). At Rotherham, his co-manager was ex-Forest team-mate, John McGovern.

Gemmill scored one of the all-time great goals and the widely accepted best goal of the 1978 World Cup when he weaved his way through the Dutch defence to put Scotland 3–1 up. His son, Scot, is also a Scotland international.

FULL NAME: **Joseph Montgomery Harper**
POSITION: centre-forward
BORN: 11 January 1948, Greenock
CLUBS (PLAYER): **Greenock Morton** (July 1963, n/a), **Huddersfield Town** (£30,000, March 1967, 26+2 league apps, four goals), **Greenock Morton** (£15,000, August 1968, n/a), **Aberdeen** (£40,000, October 1969, 101+1 league apps, 68 goals), **Everton** (£180,000, December 1972, 40+3 league apps, 12 goals), **Hibernian** (£120,000, January 1974, 69 league apps, 26 goals), **Aberdeen** (£40,000, July 1976 – May 1981, 99+6 league apps, 57 goals); (PLAYER-MANAGER): **Peterhead** (July 1982 – July 1985, n/a); (MANAGER): **Huntly** (July 1985, n/a), **Deveronvale** (July 1990 – May 1993, n/a)
CAPS: 4; 1972–73 season versus Denmark (x 2); 1975–76 versus Denmark; 1977–78 versus Iran
SCOTLAND GOALS: 2; versus Denmark (x 2)
CLUB HONOURS (PLAYER): Aberdeen (first and second spells): League Championship medal, 1980; Scottish Cup winners' medal, 1970; Scottish Cup runners-up medal, 1978; Scottish League Cup winners' medal, 1977; Scottish League Cup runners-up medal, 1979; Drybrough Cup winners' medal, 1971. Hibernian: Scottish League Cup runners-up medal, 1975; OTHER HONOURS: Scotland Youth international; Scotland Under-23 international (two appearances); Scottish League (one appearance)
ARGENTINA QUALIFYING ROUNDS PLAYED: none
ARGENTINA WORLD CUP MATCHES PLAYED: versus Iran
CURRENT OCCUPATION: media pundit
OTHER: When he joined Hibernian, it was for a record fee paid by a Scottish club. His international career was interrupted when he was implicated in a fracas in a Danish nightclub – part of the infamous 'Copenhagen Five' – but he was later exonerated. He scored a hat-trick for Hibs in the 1975 League Cup final, but was still on the losing side as Celtic won 6–3. After finishing his senior career with Aberdeen, Harper moved into Highland League football.

FULL NAME: **Richard Asa Hartford**
POSITION: midfield
BORN: 24 October 1950, Clydebank
CLUBS (PLAYER): **Drumchapel Amateurs** (n/a), **West Bromwich Albion** (amateur April 1966, professional November 1967, 206+8 league appearances, 18 goals), **Manchester City** (£225,000, August 1974, 184+1 league apps, 22 goals), **Nottingham Forest** (£500,000, June 1979, three league apps, no goals), **Everton** (£400,000, August 1979, 81 league apps, six goals), **Manchester City** (£350,000, October 1981, including on loan to Fort Lauderdale,

USA. At City, 75 league apps, seven goals. At Fort Lauderdale May 1984, n/a), **Norwich City** (free, October 1984 – May 1985, 28 league apps, two goals), **Bolton Wanderers** (free, as player-coach July 1985, 81 league apps, eight goals), **Stockport County** (free, as player-manager June 1987, 42+3 league apps, no goals), **Oldham Athletic** (free, March 1989, three+4 league apps, no goals), **Shrewsbury Town** (free, as player-coach then player-manager, July 1989 – January 1991, 22+3 league apps, no goals), **Boston United** (free, February 1991 – May 1991, 15 apps, no goals); (PLAYER-MANAGER): **Stockport County** (June 1987 – March 1989), **Shrewsbury Town** (January 1990 – January 1991; was player-coach from July 1989); (COACH, THEN RESERVE-TEAM MANAGER): **Blackburn Rovers** (August 1992 – November 1993); (EITHER ASSISTANT MANAGER OR CARETAKER MANAGER): **Stoke City** (November 1993 as assistant to Joe Jordan; caretaker, September 1994; assistant to Lou Macari, October 1994), **Manchester City** (as assistant to Alan Ball, July 1995; caretaker August 1996 – September 1996); (FIRST-TEAM COACH): **Manchester City** (September 1996 – present)

CAPS: 50; 1971–72 season versus Peru, Wales, England, Yugoslavia, Czechoslovakia, Brazil; 1975–76 versus Denmark, Romania, Northern Ireland; 1976–77 versus Czechoslovakia, Wales (x2), Sweden, Northern Ireland, England, Chile, Argentina, Brazil; 1977–78 versus East Germany, Czechoslovakia, Wales (x2), Bulgaria, England, Peru, Iran, Holland; 1978–79 versus Austria, Norway (x2), Portugal, Wales, Northern Ireland, England, Argentina; 1979–80 versus Peru, Belgium; 1980–81 versus Northern Ireland (x2), Israel, Wales, England; 1981–82 versus Sweden, Northern Ireland (x2), Portugal, Spain, Wales, England, Brazil

SCOTLAND GOALS: 4; versus Sweden, Chile, Czechoslovakia, Wales

CLUB HONOURS (PLAYER): WBA: League Cup runners-up medal, 1970. Manchester City: League Cup winners' medal, 1976; Norwich City: League Cup winners' medal, 1985; Bolton: Freight Rover Trophy runners-up medal, 1986; OTHER HONOURS: Scottish Youth international; Scottish Under-21 international (one appearance); Scottish Under-23 international (five appearances)

ARGENTINA QUALIFYING ROUNDS PLAYED: versus Czechoslovakia (home and away), Wales (home and away)

ARGENTINA WORLD CUP MATCHES PLAYED: versus Peru, Iran and Holland

CURRENT OCCUPATION: First-team coach, Manchester City

OTHER: One November morning in 1971, when Asa was 21, a dream £177,000 transfer to Leeds United from West Bromwich Albion was suddenly terminated after the standard pre-signing medical showed up a tiny hole in his heart. He had been due to make his début against Leicester when the news came, not long after he had promised his fiancée, Joy, that he would be able to bring their wedding forward six months and buy a fine house in Yorkshire on the back of the lucrative contract being offered by Leeds manager, Don Revie. On the same morning of that intended début, he was informed he had just been included in the Scotland squad for the coming week's match against Belgium. That piece of news was followed by a trip to the doctor and the damning X-ray results. He spent that afternoon in the directors box at WBA, before the emotion got too much and he broke down in tears with his team-mate, Len Cantello, in the home dressing-room.

Medical opinion soon consoled him as far as his football future was concerned. Though the move to Leeds was off, he was still able to play, the hole between two sections of the heart unlikely to grow or place him in any danger. The following weekend, he was playing versus Nottingham Forest and about to be picked by Tommy Docherty for Scotland.

Three years later, in 1974, after having played 140 games for WBA since the Leeds incident, he signed for Manchester City in a £250,000 move. Between Norwich and Bolton, he briefly coached in Norway.

FULL NAME: **William Pullar ('Sandy') Jardine.**
POSITION: right-back/midfield
BORN: 31 December 1948, Edinburgh
CLUBS (PLAYER): **United Crossroads** (n/a), **Edinburgh Athletic** (n/a), **Rangers** (451 league appearances, 42 goals), **Heart of Midlothian** (as player-assistant manager, July 1982 – September 1987, 184 league apps, three goals) (CO-MANAGER, WITH ALEX MACDONALD): **Heart of Midlothian** (November 1986 – November 1988)
CAPS: 38; 1970–71 season versus Denmark; 1971–72 versus Portugal, Belgium, Holland; 1972–73 versus England, Switzerland, Brazil; 1973-74 versus Czechoslovakia (x2), West Germany (x2), Northern Ireland, Wales, England, Belgium, Norway, Zaire, Brazil, Yugoslavia; 1974–75 versus East Germany, Spain (x2), Sweden, Portugal, Wales, Northern Ireland, England; 1976–77 versus Sweden, Chile, Brazil; 1977–78 versus Czechoslovakia, Wales, Northern Ireland, Iran; 1979–80 versus Peru, Austria, Belgium (x2)
SCOTLAND GOALS: 1; versus Wales
CLUB HONOURS (PLAYER): Rangers: European Cup Winners' Cup winners' medal, 1972; European Cup Winners' Cup runners-up medal, 1967; League Championship medal, 1975, 1976, 1978; Scottish Cup winners' medal, 1973, 1976, 1978, 1979, 1981; Scottish Cup runners-up medal, 1969; 1977, 1980, 1982; Scottish League Cup winners' medal, 1971, 1978, 1979, 1982; Hearts: Scottish Cup runners-up medal, 1986; (ASSISTANT AND LATER CO-MANAGER) Hearts: Lost out on League Championship in 1986 on goal difference; Scottish Cup runners-up, 1986; OTHER HONOURS: Scotland Under-23 international (four appearances); Scottish League (two appearances); Scottish Football Writers' Player of the Year, 1975, 1986
ARGENTINA QUALIFYING ROUNDS PLAYED: versus Czechoslovakia (home), versus Wales (away)
ARGENTINA WORLD CUP MATCHES PLAYED: versus Iran
CURRENT OCCUPATION: Director of Rangers' commercial department
OTHER: A couple of theories why he was nicknamed 'Sandy' – (a) hair colouring, (b) very good at training on beaches. He played over 1,000 first-class matches. His record for Rangers was 773 games and 93 goals, but he went on to enjoy an 'Indian summer' at Heart of Midlothian, playing sweeper with characteristic elegance. He was at Hearts as a youth, started career at Rangers as a centre-forward, but moved into defence following the £100,000 signing of striker Colin Stein from Hibernian (the first £100,000 transfer between two Scottish clubs). Captain of the club, he was one of only three players to be twice named Player of the Year by the Scottish Football Writers (the other two being fellow Rangers John Greig and Brian Laudrup). Fittingly, he recorded his 1,000th first-class match versus Rangers in 1986. He retired just short of his 39th birthday to concentrate on co-management with Alex MacDonald. Dismissed in early part of 1988–89 season, he went on to work for Scottish & Newcastle Brewers.

FULL NAME: **Derek Johnstone.**
POSITION: centre-forward/centre-half
BORN: 4 November 1953, Dundee

CLUBS (PLAYER): **St Francis Boys' Club** (n/a), **St Columba's Dundee** (n/a), **Rangers** (July 1970, 369 league appearances, 132 goals), **Chelsea** (£30,000, September 1983, including loan spell at Dundee United during October 1983. At Chelsea, 1+3 league apps, no goals. At Dundee United, 2+2 league apps, no goals), **Rangers** (less than £25,000, January 1985 – July 1986, 19 league apps, one goal); (MANAGER): **Partick Thistle** (July 1986 – February 1987)

CAPS: 14; 1972–73 season versus Wales, Northern Ireland, England, Sweden, Brazil; 1974–75 versus East Germany, Sweden; 1975–76 versus Switzerland, Northern Ireland, England; 1977–78 versus Bulgaria, Northern Ireland, Wales; 1979–80 versus Belgium

SCOTLAND GOALS: 2; versus Northern Ireland, Wales

CLUB HONOURS (PLAYER): Rangers: European Cup Winners' Cup winners' medal, 1972; League Championship medal, 1975, 1976, 1978; Scottish Cup winners' medal, 1973, 1976, 1978, 1979, 1981; Scottish Cup runners-up medal, 1971, 1977, 1980; Scottish League Cup winners' medal, 1971, 1978, 1979, 1982; Scottish League Cup runners-up medal, 1983; OTHER HONOURS: Scotland Schoolboy international; Scotland Youth international; Scotland amateur international; Under-23 international (six appearances), Scottish League (one appearance); SPFA Player of the Year and Scottish Football Writers' Player of the Year, 1978

ARGENTINA QUALIFYING ROUNDS PLAYED: none

ARGENTINA WORLD CUP MATCHES PLAYED: none

CURRENT OCCUPATION: radio journalist

OTHER: A versatile player, who often played centre-half even though he was a successful centre-forward, Johnstone became the youngest player both to appear in and score in a major British cup final – the 1970 Scottish League Cup, aged 16 (for Rangers against Celtic). He holds the distinction of scoring in a Scottish Cup final – against Hearts in 1976 – before the clock had reached the official kick-off time of 3 p.m. With the game starting ahead of schedule, he scored after only 41 seconds, heading home a free-kick which he had won off Hearts' Jim Jefferies.

FULL NAME: **William Johnston**

POSITION: winger

BORN: 19 December 1946, Glasgow

CLUBS (PLAYER): **Lochore Welfare** (n/a), **Rangers** (July 1962, 246 league appearances, 91 goals); **West Bromwich Albion** (£135,000, December 1972, 203+4 league apps, 18 goals); **Vancouver Whitecaps** (£100,000, March 1979, including a loan spell at **Birmingham City** October 1979 – March 1980. At Vancouver, 36 apps, three goals. At Birmingham, 15 league apps, no goals); **Vancouver Whitecaps** (March 1980, 12+2 apps, two goals); **Rangers** (£40,000, August 1980, 27+8 league apps, two goals); **Vancouver Whitecaps** (March 1982, 14+4 apps, no goals); **Heart of Midlothian** (free, as player-coach, September 1982, 30+28 league apps, nine goals); **East Fife** (as player-coach, April 1985 – May 1985, three league apps, no goals, followed by retirement)

CAPS: 22; 1965–66 season versus Wales, England, Poland, Holland; 1967–68 versus Wales, England; 1968–69 versus Northern Ireland; 1969-70 versus Northern Ireland; 1970–71 versus Denmark; 1976–77 versus Sweden, Wales, Northern Ireland, England, Chile, Argentina, Brazil; 1977–78 versus East Germany, Czechoslovakia, Wales (x2), England, Peru

SCOTLAND GOALS: none

CLUB HONOURS (PLAYER): Rangers: European Cup Winners' Cup winners' medal, 1972; European Cup Winners' Cup runners-up medal, 1967; Scottish Cup winners' medal, 1966, 1981; Scottish Cup runners-up medal, 1969, 1971; Scottish League Cup winners' medal, 1965, 1971; Scottish League Cup runners-up medal, 1966, 1967. WBA: Promotion to First Division, 1976. Birmingham: Promotion to First Division, 1980. Vancouver: US Soccer Bowl winners' medal, 1979; OTHER HONOURS: Scotland Youth international; Scotland Under-23 international (two appearances); Scottish League (two appearances including one as substitute)

CURRENT OCCUPATION: Publican in Kirkcaldy, Fife

ARGENTINA QUALIFYING ROUNDS PLAYED: versus Czechoslovakia (home), Wales (away)

ARGENTINA WORLD CUP MATCHES PLAYED: versus Peru

OTHER: Nicknamed 'Bud', Johnston was a colourful, fiery winger with a temperament to match. His infamous disciplinary record consisted of 16 sendings-off, often for retaliation. His tenth red card, for example, was for attempting to kick the referee when playing for West Bromwich Albion against Brighton on 22 September 1976. Remarkably, the Football Association accepted his plea of frustration and let him off relatively lightly. When he moved to WBA from Rangers, aged 25, he had already been red-carded six times, the situation reaching a head when he was suspended for 67 days. He was sent off against Argentina during a tour of South America in 1977, though this time for reasons unknown. He never played for Scotland after being sent home in disgrace from the 1978 World Cup after testing positive for illegal stimulants.

FULL NAME: **Joseph Jordan**

POSITION: Centre-forward

BORN: 15 December 1951, Carluke, Lanarkshire

CLUBS (PLAYER): **Blantyre Victoria** (n/a), **Greenock Morton** (October 1968, 11+1 league appearances, two goals), **Leeds United** (£15,000, October 1970, 139+30 league apps, 35 goals), **Manchester United** (£350,000, January 1978, 109 league apps, 37 goals), **AC Milan** (£325,000, July 1981, 52 league apps, 12 goals), **Verona** (July 1983, 12 league apps, one goal), **Southampton** (£150,000, August 1984, 48 league apps, 12 goals), **Bristol City** (free, February 1987 – September 1990, becoming player-coach in November 1987, then player-manager in March 1988, 38+19 league apps, eight goals); (PLAYER-MANAGER, HAVING PREVIOUSLY BEEN PLAYER-COACH): **Bristol City** (March 1988 – September 1990); (MANAGER): **Heart of Midlothian** (September 1990 – April 1993), **Stoke City** (November 1993 – September 1994), **Bristol City** (again) (November 1994 – March 1997); (ASSISTANT-MANAGER): **Celtic** (July 1993 – October 1993)

CAPS: 52; 1972–73 season versus England, Switzerland, Brazil; 1973–74 versus Czechoslovakia (x2), West Germany, Northern Ireland, Wales, England, Belgium, Norway, Zaire, Brazil, Yugoslavia; 1974–75 versus East Germany, Spain (x2); 1975–76 versus Northern Ireland, Wales, England; 1976–77 versus Czechoslovakia, Wales, Northern Ireland, England; 1977–78 versus East Germany, Czechoslovakia, Wales, Bulgaria, Northern Ireland, England, Peru, Iran, Holland; 1978–79 versus Austria, Portugal, Wales, Northern Ireland, England, Norway; 1979–80 versus Belgium, Northern Ireland, Wales, England, Poland; 80–81 versus Israel, Wales, England; 1981–82 versus Sweden, Holland, Wales, England, USSR

SCOTLAND GOALS: 10; versus Czechoslovakia (x 2), England, Norway (x 2), Zaire, Yugoslavia, Spain, Peru, USSR

CLUB HONOURS (PLAYER): Leeds: European Cup runners-up medal, 1975; European Cup Winners' Cup runners-up medal, 1973; League Championship medal, 1974. Manchester United: FA Cup runners-up medal, 1979. Bristol City: Freight Rover Trophy winners' medal, 1987; (MANAGER): Bristol City: Promotion to the Second Division, 1990; Littlewoods League Cup semi-finalist, 1989. Hearts: Scottish League runners-up, 1992; OTHER HONOURS: Scotland Under-23 international (one appearance)

CURRENT OCCUPATION: Occasional pundit on Channel Four's *Football Italia*

ARGENTINA QUALIFYING ROUNDS PLAYED: versus Czechoslovakia (home and away), Wales (home and away)

ARGENTINA WORLD CUP MATCHES PLAYED: versus Peru, Iran and Holland

OTHER: Jordan joined Manchester United from Leeds on 6 January 1978 for £350,000, the biggest transfer deal between two English clubs (the record lasted just four days, when Liverpool paid Middlesbrough £352,000 for Graeme Souness). When he moved from Leeds, Jordan was quoted saying Machester United were the only British club who could have got him. (At the time, Ajax were also trailing him.) He played in the final stages of three World Cups –1974, 1978 and 1982 – scoring in each of them (versus Zaire and Yugoslavia in 1974, versus Peru in 1978 and versus Russia in 1982). He was reunited with his ex-Leeds team-mate Terry Cooper at Bristol City, soon succeeding him as player-manager.

FULL NAME: **Stuart Robert Kennedy**

POSITION: full-back

BORN: 31 May 1953, Grangemouth

CLUBS (PLAYER): **Falkirk** (July 1971, 107+3 league appearances, one goal), **Aberdeen** (£40,000, July 1976 – April 1983, 223 league apps, three goals)

CAPS: 8; 1977–78 season versus Bulgaria, Wales, England, Peru, Holland; 1978–79 versus Austria, Portugal; 1981–82 versus Portugal

SCOTLAND GOALS: none

CLUB HONOURS (PLAYER): Aberdeen: League Championship medal, 1980; Scottish Cup winners' medal, 1983, 1984; Scottish Cup runners-up medal, 1978; Scottish League Cup winners' medal, 1977; Scottish League Cup runners-up medal, 1979, 1980; OTHER HONOURS: Scotland Under-23 international (three appearances)

ARGENTINA QUALIFYING ROUNDS PLAYED: none

ARGENTINA WORLD CUP MATCHES PLAYED: versus Peru and Holland

CURRENT OCCUPATION: publican in Falkirk

OTHER: Forced to retire from football in 1983 because of injury

FULL NAME: **Lou Macari**

POSITION: midfield/forward

BORN: 7 June 1949, Edinburgh

CLUBS (PLAYER): **Celtic** (July 1966, 58 league appearances, 27 goals), **Manchester United** (£200,000, January 1973, 311+18 league apps, 78 goals), **Swindon Town** (free, as player-manager July 1984, 33+3 league apps, three goals; retired from playing March 1985); (PLAYER-MANAGER THEN MANAGER): **Swindon Town** (July 1984 – July 1989); (MANAGER): **West Ham United** (July 1989 – February 1990), **Birmingham City** (March 1991 – May 1991), **Stoke City** (May 1991 – November 1993), **Celtic** (November 1993 – June 1994),

Stoke City (September 1994 – May 1997)

CAPS: 24; 1971–72 season versus Wales, England, Yugoslavia, Czechoslovakia, Brazil; 1972–73 versus Denmark, England (x2), Wales, Northern Ireland; 1974–75 versus Sweden, Portugal, Wales, England, Romania; 1976–77 versus Northern Ireland, England, Chile, Argentina; 1977–78 versus East Germany, Wales, Bulgaria, Peru, Iran

SCOTLAND GOALS: 5; versus Yugoslavia (x2), Denmark, Chile (x2)

CLUB HONOURS (PLAYER): Celtic: League Championship medal, 1970, 1972; Scottish Cup winners' medal, 1971; Scottish League Cup runners-up medal, 1971, 1972, 1973. Manchester United: Division Two Champions medal, 1975; FA Cup winners' medal, 1977; FA Cup runners-up medal, 1976, 1979; League Cup runners-up medal, 1983; (MANAGER): Swindon Town: Fourth Division Champions, 1986; Promotion to the Second Division, 1987. Birmingham City: Leyland DAF Cup winners, 1991. Stoke City: Autoglass Trophy winners, 1992; Second Division Champions, 1993; OTHER HONOURS: Scotland Schoolboy international; Scotland Youth International; Scotland Under-23 international (two appearances)

ARGENTINA QUALIFYING ROUNDS PLAYED: versus Wales (away)

ARGENTINA WORLD CUP MATCHES PLAYED: versus Peru and Iran

CURRENT OCCUPATION: Voluntarily out of work, pending court case

OTHER: Macari was dismissed from the Swindon management in April 1985 because of a row with his assistant, Harry Gregg, only to be reinstated six days later. He steered Swindon from the Fourth Division to the Second in successive seasons and then reached the play-offs for the First, only to lose to Crystal Palace. He lasted just seven months at West Ham, leaving Upton Park five days after a 0–6 defeat by Oldham Athletic in the League Cup semi-final. When he left Birmingham City for Stoke, he claimed the Midlands club lacked ambition. He left Stoke City in May 1997 to pursue a claim of unfair dismissal against Celtic, seeking £432,000 compensation.

FULL NAME: **Donald Sandison Masson**

POSITION: midfield

BORN: 26 August 1946, Banchory, Kincardineshire

CLUBS (PLAYER): **Middlesbrough** (apprentice July 1961, pro September 1963, 50+3 league appearances, six goals), **Notts County** (£6,000, September 1968, 273 league apps, 81 goals), **Queen's Park Rangers** (£100,000, December 1974, 116 league apps, 18 goals), **Derby County** (in exchange for Leighton James [thus making it, in reality, a transfer fee in excess of £200,000], October 1977, 23 league apps, one goal), **Notts County** (nominal fee, August 1978, 127 league apps, 11 goals), **Minnesota Kicks** (as player-coach, May 1981, 28 apps, two goals), **Notts County** (free, September 1981,16 apps, one goal), **Bulova**, Hong Kong (May 1982 – September 1982), **Kettering Town** (as player-manager, April 1983 – October 1983), **Los Angeles Kickers** (as player-manager, March 1987 – August 1987); (PLAYER-MANAGER): **Kettering Town** (April 1983 – October 1983), **Los Angeles Kickers** (March 1987 – August 1987).

CAPS: 17; 1975–76 season versus Northern Ireland, Wales, England; 1976–77 versus Finland, Czechoslovakia, Wales, Northern Ireland, England, Chile, Argentina, Brazil; 1977–78 versus East Germany, Czechoslovakia, Wales, Northern Ireland, England, Peru

SCOTLAND GOALS: 5; versus Northern Ireland, England, Finland (penalty), Argentina (penalty), Wales (penalty)

CLUB HONOURS (PLAYER): Middlesbrough: Promotion to the Second Division, 1967. Notts

County: Division Four Champions medal, 1971; Promotion to the Second Division, 1973; Promotion to the First Division, 1981. QPR: First Division runners-up, 1976; OTHER HONOURS: Player of the Year awards at both Notts County and QPR

ARGENTINA QUALIFYING ROUNDS PLAYED: versus Czechoslovakia (home and away), Wales (away)

ARGENTINA WORLD CUP MATCHES PLAYED: versus Peru

CURRENT OCCUPATION: hotelier in Nottingham

OTHER: In almost 600 league appearances for various clubs, Masson scored 117 goals, but was not selected for his country until he was nearly 30. He skippered Notts County from the Fourth Division to the Second, then returned to lead them into the First. He joined QPR to replace Terry Venables and was an ever-present at the club when they were First Division runners-up in 1975–76. He starred for QPR as they reached the semi-final of the League Cup and the quarter-final of the UEFA Cup the following season. Masson continues to be an excellent tennis player.

FULL NAME: **Gordon McQueen**

POSITION: central defender

BORN: 26 June 1952; Kilburnie, Ayrshire

CLUBS (PLAYER): **St Mirren** (July 1970, 57 league appearances, five goals), **Leeds United** (£40,000, September 1972, 140 league apps, 15 goals), **Manchester United** (£495,000, February 1978, 184 league apps, 20 goals), **Seiko FC**, Hong Kong (player-coach June 1985 – June 1986); (MANAGER): **Airdrie** (1987–89); (RESERVE-TEAM COACH): **Middlesbrough** (July 1994 – present)

CAPS: 30; 1973–74 season versus Belgium; 1974–75 versus Spain (x2), Portugal, Wales, Northern Ireland, England, Romania; 1975–76 versus Denmark; 1976–77 versus Czechoslovakia, Wales (x2), Northern Ireland, England; 1977–78 versus East Germany, Czechoslovakia, Wales (x2), Bulgaria, Northern Ireland; 1978–79 versus Austria, Norway (x2), Portugal, Northern Ireland, England; 1979–80 versus Peru, Austria, Belgium; 1980–81 versus Wales

SCOTLAND GOALS: 5; versus Romania, Northern Ireland, England, Austria, Norway

CLUB HONOURS (PLAYER): Leeds United: European Cup Winners' Cup runners-up medal, 1973; League Championship medal, 1974. Manchester United: FA Cup winners' medal, 1983; FA Cup runners-up medal, 1979; League Cup runners-up medal, 1983

ARGENTINA QUALIFYING ROUNDS PLAYED: versus Czechoslovakia (home and away), Wales (home and away)

ARGENTINA WORLD CUP MATCHES PLAYED: none

CURRENT OCCUPATION: reserve-team coach, Middlesbrough

OTHER: The son of Tom McQueen, a former Queen of the South and Accrington Stanley goalkeeper, Gordon also played in goal at school. He followed fellow Scots Joe Jordan and Graeme Souness by becoming the subject of a British record transfer fee (£495,000 move from Leeds United to Manchester United) in early 1978. A real threat at set-pieces, one of his best-ever goals was a thunderous header from a free-kick against England in June 1977. After leaving Airdrie, he became a pundit with Scottish Television.

FULL NAME: **Bruce David Rioch**

POSITION: midfield

BORN: 6 September 1947, Aldershot

CLUBS (PLAYER): **Luton Town** (apprentice July 1963, pro September 1964, 148+1 league appearances, 47 goals), **Aston Villa** (£100,000, July 1969, 149+5 league apps, 34 goals), **Derby County** (£200,000, February 1974, 106 league apps, 34 goals), **Everton** (£180,000, December 1976, 30 league apps, three goals), **Derby County** (£150,000, November 1977, including loan spells at **Birmingham City** December 1978 and **Sheffield United** March – May 1979. At Derby, 40+1 league apps, four goals; at Birmingham, three league apps, no goals; at Sheffield United, eight league apps, one goal), **Seattle Sounders**, USA (March 1980, 35 apps, four goals), **Torquay United** (as player-coach then player-manager, October 1980 – January 1984, 64+7 league apps, six goals, including loan spell at **Seattle Sounders** March 1981 – June 1981, 14 apps, one goal); (PLAYER-MANAGER): **Torquay United** (July 1982 – January 1984); (COACH): **Seattle Sounders** (July 1985 – January 1986); (COACH/ CARETAKER/MANAGER): **Middlesbrough** (January 1986 – March 1990, full manager from March 1986); (MANAGER): **Millwall** (April 1990 – March 1992), **Bolton Wanderers** (May 1992 – June 1995), **Arsenal** (June 1995 – August 1996); (ASSISTANT MANAGER): **Queen's Park Rangers** (September 1996 – November 1997)

CAPS: 24; 1974–75 season versus Portugal, Wales, Northern Ireland, England, Romania; 1975–76 versus Denmark (x2), Romania, Northern Ireland, Wales, England; 1976–77 versus Finland, Czechoslovakia, Wales (x2), Northern Ireland, England, Chile, Brazil; 1977–78 versus Czechoslovakia, Northern Ireland, England, Peru, Holland

SCOTLAND GOALS: 6; versus Wales (x 2), England (pen), Denmark, Romania, Finland

CLUB HONOURS (PLAYER): Luton: Division Four Champions medal, 1968. Aston Villa: League Cup runners-up medal, 1971; Division Three Champions medal, 1972. Derby: League Championship medal, 1975; (MANAGER): Middlesbrough: promotion to the Second Division, 1987; promotion to the First Division, 1988. Bolton: promotion to the First Division, 1993; promotion to the Premiership, 1995; Coca-Cola League Cup runners-up, 1995

ARGENTINA QUALIFYING ROUNDS PLAYED: versus Czechoslovakia (home and away), Wales (home)

ARGENTINA WORLD CUP MATCHES PLAYED: versus Peru and Holland

CURRENT OCCUPATION: occasional television work

OTHER: Born of Scottish parents, Bruce's father was an army sergeant-major and also a GB athlete. Rioch possessed a blistering shot. He was captain of Scotland during the finals of the 1978 World Cup. He once scored four goals in a single match, for Derby County against Tottenham Hotspur in October 1976. His brother Neil was also a footballer – they were at Luton Town and Aston Villa together, and his nephew, Matt Holmes, plays for Charlton Athletic. Rioch was manager at Middlesbrough when the club was on the brink of liquidation, but he took them from the Third to the First Division. Relegation the following season led to his sacking. He was manager at Millwall when the club was floated on the stock exchange, took them to the Second Division play-offs in 1991, and resigned in March 1992. After taking Bolton to League and Cup success, he left to succeed George Graham as manager of Arsenal. After being relieved of his post at Highbury, he became assistant to his own former assistant at Arsenal, Stewart Houston.

FULL NAME: **John Neilson Robertson**

POSITION: left-winger

BORN: 20 January 1953, Uddingston, Lanarkshire

CLUBS (PLAYER): **Drumchapel Amateurs** (n/a), **Nottingham Forest** (apprentice July 1968, pro May 1970, 374+13 league appearances, 61 goals), **Derby County** (£135,000, June 1983, 72 league apps, three goals), **Nottingham Forest** (free, August 1985, 10+1 league apps, no goals), **Corby Town** (August 1986), **Stamford** (July 1987), **Grantham** (as player-coach, August 1987), **Shepshed** (July 1989); (PLAYER-ASSISTANT MANAGER): **Charterhouse** (June 1989 – September 1989); (PLAYER-MANAGER): **Grantham** (February 1990 – March 1992); (ASSISTANT-MANAGER): **Wycombe Wanderers** (March 1992), **Norwich City** (June 1995), **Leicester City** (December 1995 – present)

CAPS: 28; 1977–78 season versus Northern Ireland, Wales, Iran; 1978–1979 versus Portugal, Norway; 1979–80 versus Peru, Austria, Belgium (x2), Portugal; 1980–81 versus Sweden, Portugal, Israel, Northern Ireland (x2), England; 1981–82 versus Sweden, Northern Ireland (x2), England, New Zealand, Brazil, USSR; 1982–83 versus East Germany, Switzerland; 1983–84 versus Uruguay, Belgium

SCOTLAND GOALS: 8; versus Norway, Belgium, Israel (x 2 [2 penalties]), England (penalty), Sweden (penalty), New Zealand, Uruguay (penalty)

CLUB HONOURS (PLAYER): Nottingham Forest (first spell): European Cup winners' medal, 1979, 1980; League Championship medal, 1978; League Cup winners' medal, 1978, 1979; League Cup runners-up medal, 1980; promotion to First Division, 1977; (ASSISTANT MANAGER): Leicester City: Promotion to the Premiership, 1996; Coca-Cola League Cup winners, 1997; OTHER HONOURS: Scotland Schoolboy international; Scotland Youth international

ARGENTINA QUALIFYING ROUNDS PLAYED: none

ARGENTINA WORLD CUP MATCHES PLAYED: versus Iran

CURRENT OCCUPATION: assistant manager at Leicester City

OTHER: At the time of writing, John Robertson is the last Scot to have scored the winner against the 'auld enemy', England, at Wembley. That was in May 1981, from the penalty spot, after Steve Archibald was adjudged to have been tripped by Bryan Robson, caught on his blind side as Archibald went for a marvellous through ball by Davie Provan.

Before his current responsibilities with Leicester, Robertson had been scouting for them and playing non-league football for Wollaton Hemlockstone FC.

Brian Clough, his boss at Forest, said of him: 'When I felt off-colour I'd sit next to Robbo because then I'd look like Errol Flynn. Yet if you gave him a ball and a yard of grass, he became an artist.' Touched greatness during Forest's successes under Clough and Peter Taylor, he followed Taylor to Derby County but had cartilage problems and was not the player to turn a struggling team. Arthur Cox, who succeeded Taylor at Derby, allowed him to return to Forest on a free transfer. He has been working with Martin O'Neill, a team-mate at Forest, at Grantham, Wycombe Wanderers, Norwich and Leicester.

FULL NAME: **Allan Roderick Rough**

POSITION: goalkeeper

BORN: 25 November 1951, Glasgow

CLUBS (PLAYER): **Partick Thistle** (November 1969, 410 league appearances); **Hibernian** (£60,000, November 1982, 175 league apps), **Orlando Lions**, USA (March 1988, n/a),

Celtic (free, July 1988 – May 1989, five league apps); (MANAGER): **Glenafton** (July 1991 – present)

CAPS: 53; 1975–76 season versus Switzerland, Northern Ireland, Wales, England; 1976–77 versus Finland, Czechoslovakia, Wales (x2), Sweden, Northern Ireland, England, Chile, Argentina, Brazil; 1977–78 versus Czechoslovakia, Wales, Northern Ireland, England, Peru, Iran, Holland; 1978–79 versus Austria, Portugal, Wales, Argentina, Norway; 1979–80 versus Peru, Austria, Belgium (x2), Portugal, Wales, England, Poland, Hungary; 1980–81 versus Sweden, Portugal, Israel (x2), Northern Ireland, Wales, England; 1981–82 versus Sweden, Northern Ireland, Spain, Holland, Wales, England, New Zealand, Brazil, USSR; 1985–86 versus Wales, England

SCOTLAND CLEAN SHEETS: 16; versus Switzerland, Northern Ireland (x 3), Finland, England, Wales (x 5), Norway, Sweden (x 2), Portugal, Israel

CLUB HONOURS (PLAYER): Partick Thistle: Scottish League Cup winners' medal, 1972; Scottish First Division Champions medal, 1976. Hibernian: Scottish League Cup runners-up medal, 1986; (MANAGER): Glenafton: Scottish Junior Cup winners – 1993; Scottish Junior Cup runners-up, 1992, 1994; OTHER HONOURS: Scotland Youth international; Scotland Under-23 international (nine appearances); Scottish League (one appearance); Scottish Football Writers' Player of the Year, 1981

ARGENTINA QUALIFYING ROUNDS PLAYED: versus Czechoslovakia (home and away), Wales (home and away)

ARGENTINA WORLD CUP MATCHES PLAYED: versus Peru, Iran and Holland

CURRENT OCCUPATION: events promotor

OTHER: Infamous for his perm in the late '70s–early '80s. Holder of the league appearance record for Partick Thistle.

FULL NAME: **Graeme James Souness**
POSITION: midfield
BORN: 6 May 1953, Edinburgh
CLUBS (PLAYER): **Tottenham Hotspur** (apprentice April 1969, pro May 1970, no first-team league apps), **Middlesbrough** (£30,000, January 1973, 174+2 league appearances, 22 goals), **Liverpool** (£352,000, January 1978, 246+1 league apps, 38 goals), **Sampdoria** (£650,000, July 1984), **Rangers** (£300,000, as player-manager May 1986 – April 1991, playing last game in May 1990, 38+12 league apps, three goals); (PLAYER-MANAGER): **Rangers** (May 1986 – April 1991); (MANAGER): **Liverpool** (April 1991 – January 1994), **Galatasaray** (May 1995 – May 1996), **Southampton** (July 1996 – May 1997), **Torino** (June 1997 – October 1997), **Benfica** (October 1997 to present)
CAPS: 54; 1974–75 season versus East Germany, Spain, Sweden, 1977–78 versus Bulgaria, Wales, England, Holland; 1978–79 versus Austria, Norway, Wales, Northern Ireland, England; 1979–80 versus Peru, Austria, Belgium, Portugal, Northern Ireland; 1980–81 versus Portugal, Israel (x 2); 1981–82 versus Northern Ireland, Portugal, Spain, Wales, England, New Zealand, Brazil, USSR; 1982–83 versus East Germany, Switzerland (x2), Belgium, Wales, England, Canada (x3); 1983–84 versus Uruguay, Northern Ireland, Wales; 1984–85 versus Yugoslavia, Iceland (x2), Spain (x2), Wales, England; 1985–86 versus East Germany, Australia (x2), Romania, England, Denmark, West Germany
SCOTLAND GOALS: 3; versus USSR, Yugoslavia, England
CLUB HONOURS (PLAYER): Tottenham Hotspur: FA Youth Cup winners' medal, 1970.
Middlesbrough: Division Two Champions medal, 1974. Liverpool: European Cup winners'

medal, 1978, 1981, 1984; League Championship medal, 1979, 1980, 1982, 1983, 1984; League Cup winners' medal, 1981, 1982, 1983, 1984; (PLAYER-MANAGER): Rangers: League Champions, 1987, 1989, 1990; League Cup winners, 1987, 1988, 1989, 1991; Scottish Cup runners-up, 1989; (MANAGER): Liverpool: FA Cup winners, 1992; OTHER HONOURS: Scotland Schoolboy international; Scotland Youth international; Scotland Under-23 international (two appearances)

ARGENTINA QUALIFYING ROUNDS PLAYED: none

ARGENTINA WORLD CUP MATCHES PLAYED: versus Holland

CURRENT OCCUPATION: manager of Benfica

OTHER: Was briefly holder of the record transfer fee between two British clubs when Liverpool paid Middlesbrough £352,000 for him on 10 January 1978. Four days earlier, Joe Jordan had moved from Leeds to Manchester United for a record £350,000. In February Gordon McQueen became the new record-holder when he moved from Leeds to Manchester United for £495,000. While manager of Liverpool, he underwent triple bypass heart operation in April 1992 but still managed to attend his side's win in the FA Cup final that year. He went to the same Edinburgh school as Dave Mackay. He left Spurs because he was homesick. He resurrected Rangers – 'The Souness Revolution' – signing several England internationals. He was infamously sent off in his first game for Rangers, against Hibernian at Easter Road. He also had a famous spat with Aggie, the tea lady at St Johnstone. At Liverpool he succeeded Kenny Dalglish, survived a boardroom bid to oust him in May 1993, but resigned in January 1994. He kept Southampton in the Premiership in 1996–97. He left, typically, in controversial circumstances.

Select Bibliography

The Absolute Game, fanzine, March-April 1993

Dalglish, Kenny – My Autobiography, publ Hodder & Stoughton, 290pp, 1996

The Flowers of Scotland – The Official Book of Scotland's World Cup Squad, edited by Ken Gallacher, publ The Daily Record, 104pp, 1978

Football Against the Enemy, by Simon Kuper, publ Orion, 223pp, 1994

Football is a Funny Game, by Ian St John and Jimmy Greaves, publ Stanley Paul, 104pp, 1986

Football is Still a Funny Game, by Ian St John and Jimmy Greaves, publ Stanley Paul, 128pp, 1988

Guinness Book of World Soccer (2nd edition), by Guy Oliver, publ Guinness, 914pp, 1995

Guinness Record of the World Cup 1930-1994, by Jack Rollin, publ Guinness, 192pp, 1994

Hand of God, by Jimmy Burns, publ Bloomsbury, 224pp, 1997 (adapted extract publ in *FourFour Two*, September 1997

The Hollow Drum, by Arnold Kemp, publ Mainstream, 239pp, 1993

Journeys of the Magi, by William McIlvanney, part of a collection of short stories, *Surviving the Shipwreck*, publ Mainstream, 253pp, 1991

McIlvanney on Football by Hugh McIlvanney, publ Mainstream, 328pp, 1996

MacLeod, Ally, The Story – An Autobiography, publ Stanley Paul, 159pp, 1979

Macpherson, Archie – Action Replays, publ Chapmans, 276pp, 1991

Passion of the people? Football in South America, by Tony Mason, publ Verso, 174pp, 1995

The Radio Rentals Book of the World Cup 1978 by John Morgan and David Emery, publ Woodhead-Faulkner, 128pp, 1978

Rangers My Team by Derek Johnstone, publ Souvenir Press, 188pp, 1979

The Referendum Experience, ed by John Bochel, David Denver, Allan Macartney, publ Aberdeen University Press, 210pp, 1981

Rothmans Football Yearbook – Football Annual, publ Headline

Rough at the Top by Alan Rough, publ John Donald, 130pp, 1988

Score and More by Sandy Jardine, publ Mainstream, 160pp, 1987

Scotland the Brave – World Cup Souvenir, publ Selwood Press Ltd, 64pp, 1978

Scotland, Escosia, Schottland – Information leaflet, publ Scottish Football Association, 20pp, 1978

Scotland The Team by Andrew Ward, publ Breedon Books, 159pp, 1987

Scotland's Quest for the World Cup – A Complete Record 1950-1986 by Clive Leatherdale, publ John Donald, 247pp, 1986

Scotland, Yes! World Cup Football Poems by Alan Bold, publ Paul Harris, 1978

Scottish Football Association Annual Reports 1977-78 and 1978-79

Scottish Football Association Minutes 1977-78 and 1978-79

Scottish Football League Review – Football Annual publ Scottish Football League

Scottish Football Quotations by Kenny MacDonald, publ Mainstream Publishing, 244pp, 1994

Scottish Soccer Internationalists' Who's Who 1872-1986 by Douglas Lamming, publ Hutton Press, 271pp, 1987

Scottish Sport in the Making of a Nation, edited by Grant Jarvie and Graham Walker, publ Leicester University Press, 200pp, 1994.

Souness, Graeme – No Half Measures, publ Grafton Books, 272pp, 1987

Wee Red Book – Football Annual, publ The Evening Times newspaper

When Will We See Tour Like Again? – The Changing Face of Scottish Football, collection of football essays edited by Mike Aitken, publ EUSPB, 78pp, 1977

Willie Johnston On the Wing!, Willie Johnston with Alex Hosie, publ Arthur Baker, 148pp, no date given

World Cup Argentina, by Colin Malam, publ Collins, 128pp, 1978

World Cup – The Argentina Story, by David Miller, publ Frederick Warne, 192pp, 1978

The World Cup 1930-1990, by John Robinson, publ Soccer Book Publishing Limited, 187pp, 1990

World Cup Soccer – The Encyclopedia of, by Orlando Duarte, publ McGraw-Hill, 435pp, 1994